ΣR

By Dr. Robinson

The Principles of Reasoning
The Principles of Conduct
Crucial Issues in Philosophy

Editor of

Josiah Royce's Logical Essays
The Story of Scottish Philosophy

Sir William Hamilton	Dugald Stewart	Thomas Brown
Adam Smith	DAVID HUME	Thomas Reid
James Frederick Ferrier	Francis Hutcheson	James McCosh

The Story of Scottish Philosophy

A Compendium of Selections From the Writings of Nine Pre-eminent Scottish Philosophers, With Biobibliographical Essays

Compiled and Edited, and With an Introduction and a Supplementary Essay

by Daniel Sommer Robinson, Ph.D., Litt.D.

Director Emeritus,
School of Philosophy, University of Southern California

FOREWORD *by* PERRY E. GRESHAM, LL.D., LITT.D.

The King's Library

An Exposition–University Book

EXPOSITION PRESS   NEW YORK

This book is dedicated to the memory of
all those sages
whose writings it contains,
"of whom the world was not worthy,"
"who, being dead, yet speaketh."

EXPOSITION PRESS INC., 386 Park Avenue South, New York 16, N.Y.

FIRST EDITION

Foreword

THERE IS nothing local about philosophy. Wisdom transcends the barriers of nations, periods, tongues, and civilizations. Yet the history of thought defines some interesting configurations of ideas which are readily identified with times and places as well as with persons. Greek philosophy is a basic concept in intellectual history, and German philosophy has illustrated the interaction of language, locality, temper, and point of view along with various other cultural factors which give meaning to the term. Scotland provides a less-striking identity of thought and culture, since it is not unique in language, nor has it enjoyed the isolation characterized by certain other communities. Nevertheless, there is a definite and identifiable set of ideas, attitudes, and insights which are as Scottish as reformed theology, oatmeal, and certain potables. This Scottish Philosophy deserves a wider consideration in the intellectual market place, inasmuch as it bears on every phase of Western culture and exercises a substantial influence on contemporary affairs. It is most fortunate, therefore, that Professor Robinson has found time to bring the stalwart thinkers of that little island together in a single volume with selected writings from each. This is a distinct contribution to the great conversation.

It is still more fortunate that a seasoned scholar has undertaken the selection. Criticism is the art of the mature and disciplined mind rather than the prerogative of an aspiring bright young pilgrim. Only the man who has long surveyed the clusters of thought which mark the intellectual adventures of mankind is able to see Scottish Philosophy in a world perspective of space and time. D. S. Robinson has a long and honorable career in study, teaching, and writing to draw from as he presents the best of Old Scotia. The best minds of more than half a century have been his intellectual companions for conversation, criticism, and debate. His penetrating analyses of major philosophical fields and ideas have become a part of the literature of the discipline. His hundreds of students will find reward in this systematic presentation of Scottish Philosophy, which has been suggested in classwork and lecture but not fully developed.

I first met Dr. Robinson when I was a young teacher at Texas Christian University. I was so charmed by his genial manner and sensible philosophy that I made inquiry about some graduate study with him at Indiana University. Twenty-five years later it was my privilege to welcome him to the Bethany College faculty as Distinguished Professor of Philosophy. He created so much interest in his courses that enrollments had to be limited. The fact that Bethany College is deliberately related to the University of Glasgow, where Alexander Campbell studied, gave additional interest to the Robinson lectures in Scottish Philosophy. The added fact that Professor Robinson is a long-time member of the religious body known variously as the Christian Churches (Disciples of Christ), or Churches of Christ, of which Campbell was a pioneering founder, created additional interest among the various people associated with Bethany College. The college was founded by Campbell in 1840.

The Christian Churches would do well to study the Scottish sources of the rational philosophy which Campbell brought with him from Glasgow. There is a strong measure of Adam Smith in the political ethics of the communion. Thomas Reid exercised a substantial influence over the thought of the pioneers who set the norms whereby the congregations have developed. The reasonable approach to worship and Bible study came from the moon of common sense which dominated the University of Glasgow at the turn of the century when Thomas and Alexander Campbell were students. The economic and social philosophy which underlies A. Campbell's argument against Robert Owen on the occasion of the famous debate in 1829 is an interesting blend of Scottish thought adapted to the frontier in America.

Americans who cherish the intellectual heritage prevalent in the nascent period of this Republic would do well to take a new and deliberate look at the Scottish ideas which have been somewhat neglected on account of a preoccupation with the French Enlightenment as a challenge to and modification of Puritan thought. The real and practical approach to early American affairs has a striking similarity to the principles expounded by the nine philosophers who have found a place in Professor Robinson's hall of fame. I refer to business leaders such as Andrew Carnegie, along with statesmen such as the Adams family and Alexander Hamilton. The affinity of early American letters for the Scottish ways of thinking is very well illustrated in Emerson's esteem and affection for Thomas Carlyle.

The present tendencies in American life toward centralized government with the consequent loss of individual liberty and the disposition toward an irrational approach to life illustrated by the new interest in Kirkegaard in religion and Freud in psychology, as well as a fascination with Marx in social and economic thought, might very well send thoughtful people to the Scottish wellsprings of liberty for a reasonable corrective which is long overdue. All of us would do well to have a fresh look at Hume and McCosh, Hutcheson and Stewart, and the perennial Adam Smith as we attempt to think afresh the goals and principles of the American way of life.

PERRY E. GRESHAM, *President*
Bethany College
Bethany, West Virginia

Preface

THE NINE pre-eminent Scottish philosophers, excerpts from whose writings constitute the major part of this book, are all original thinkers who have made rich contributions to the development of Western philosophy. The Introduction indicates what some of the legacies they have left us are, and the excerpts clearly state the positions of each author on philosophical issues that are as important to readers of the middle of the twentieth century as they were to students of philosophy living when these men wrote.

My interest in the Story of Scottish Philosophy was especially stimulated by studies I made in the Library of Bethany College while I was serving as Visiting Professor of Philosophy on the John Hay Whitney Foundation, and I am deeply indebted to President Perry Epler Gresham and the Foundation for the opportunity to serve in that honorable position.

Here I desire also to acknowledge my indebtedness to my wife, Oma Glasburn Robinson, for typing the material and for assisting me in numberless ways in preparing it for publication. I am also indebted to my friend Mr. Wallace R. Nethery, Librarian of the Hoose Library of Philosophy at the University of Southern California, for assembling the pictures that are reproduced as the frontispiece.

The picture of Professor Ferrier is here reproduced by courtesy of St. Andrews University and that of President McCosh by courtesy of Princeton University. The other pictures are from various volumes of the authors' writings in the Hoose Library of Philosophy.

D. S. R.

Contents

CHAPTER IV
Thomas Reid
(1710–1796)

CHAPTER V
Dugald Stewart
(1753–1828)

CHAPTER VI
Thomas Brown
(1778–1820)

Introduction

THE STORY OF SCOTTISH PHILOSOPHY is an integral and a significant, although an overly neglected, fragment of the complete
story of philosophy. This compendium of biographies, bibliog-
raphies, and typical selections from the best writings of nine
pre-eminent Scottish philosophers of the eighteenth and nineteenth centuries aims to help bring about a correction of this
neglect. It makes available in a single reader's-digest volume not
only authoritative summaries of their writings by competent
scholars but a sufficient number of selections from the extant
philosophical literature penned by these distinguished thinkers
to give readers a clear understanding of the unique contributions which they have made to the history of philosophical ideas,
opinions, theories, and especially criticisms.

Professors and students in universities, colleges, junior colleges, and other institutions of higher learning, as well as all
serious readers with scholarly and intellectual interests, will
surely welcome the appearance of such a compendium. It should
be useful as source material for courses in religion, theology,
and philosophy. It will also be highly informative to anyone
desirous of obtaining a firsthand knowledge of this distinctively
Scottish philosophical literature. Librarians will find this compendium suitable for use as a reference book on Scottish
philosophy.

It is rather a unique paradox that David Hume, who is everywhere and by every competent authority recognized as the greatest Scottish philosopher, is himself not really a member of the
so-called Scottish School of Philosophy. Nevertheless, the writings of the chief members of this School abound with quotations
from his works, and with interpretations, criticisms, and comments on his skeptical doctrines and theories. As a matter of
fact, one of the most instructive aspects of this literature, an
example of which will be discussed presently, is the way in
which one representative of the Scottish School will correct and

try to set right another with respect to some particular interpretation of Hume. Consequently, although he is not really a member of the Scottish School of Philosophy, Chapter II contains a biographical account and selections from his writings. Recently there has been a pronounced revival of interest in Hume's philosophy. Certainly no student of Hume can afford to ignore what the members of the Scottish School have written about him. Readers wishing to make a deeper study of this movement of thought will find T. E. Jessop's *Bibliography of David Hume and of Scottish Philosophy* comprehensive and reliable. S. A. Garvie's excellent critical study *The Scottish Philosophy of Common Sense* (Oxford, at the Clarendon Press, 1960) is also recommended.

In the chapter on Thomas Reid I have included a selection entitled "Of Mr. Hume's Opinion of the Idea of Power," which is a fair sample of the way in which the founder of the School criticized Hume. Reid's attack has been answered in behalf of Hume by Thomas Brown in Section VI of his now classic treatise entitled *An Inquiry into the Relation of Cause and Effect*. Brown gives there an interesting argument which is here briefly summarized, since it is an informative illustration of how the founder of the Scottish School differs from one of his later ablest disciples with regard to one of Hume's most important theories. Reid claimed that Hume denied that we have any idea of power in the cause to produce its effects, on the ground that we can find no sense impression in our experience which we can trace to this supposed power. To clarify the issue Brown constructs a pair of syllogisms to prove that Reid's interpretation of Hume is erroneous.

Reid's Syllogism	Hume's Syllogism
Major Premise: We have no idea which is not a copy of some impression.	We have no idea which is not a copy of some impression.
Minor Premise: We have no impression of power.	We have an idea of power.
Conclusion: Therefore, we have no idea of power.	Therefore, we have an impression of power.

Brown points out that according to Hume we do have a sense impression, from which the idea of power may be said to be copied "in the feeling of a customary connection of ideas, by which, after the experience of the sequence of two events, the mind passes readily from the idea of one to the idea of the other." This is a so-called law of association of ideas by cause and effect, and Brown agrees with Hume in reducing causality to the temporal sequence which the law embodies. Nevertheless, Brown agrees fundamentally with Reid against Hume in rejecting the major premise that is common to both of the above syllogisms, and in treating cause and effect as an intuitive and self-evident belief that is implanted in original human nature by the Creator. Contemporary students of Hume would agree with Brown that Reid misinterpreted Hume's theory of causality, but many of them accept the dogma of empirical verifiability and reject the theory that causality is an intuitive belief, whereas this is a basic theory that is shared by practically all the representatives of the Scottish School of Philosophy. On this point see especially the selection from Dugald Stewart entitled "The Fundamental Laws of Human Belief."

Thomas Reid has been severely criticized for his attitude toward Hume by another great Scottish philosopher, the late Professor Norman Kemp Smith. In his *The Philosophy of David Hume* (London: Macmillan & Co., Ltd., 1949) this distinguished Kantian scholar points out what he calls the Reid-Beattie error in the interpretation of the origin of Hume's skeptical philosophy, which consisted in their charging him with an "unconsidered acceptance of the hypothesis commonly entitled the 'theory of ideas'" (p. 4). Kemp Smith designates his own theory the Hutchesonian. He argues persuasively that Francis Hutcheson's basic idea that reason, understanding, and intellect are subordinate to sentiment, desire, and volition was the real source of Hume's philosophy, and that he was originally inspired by Hutcheson's moral philosophy in the writing of his *Treatise of Human Nature*. Kemp Smith says that Hume followed Hutcheson in reversing "the roles hitherto ascribed to Reason and Feeling respectively" (p. 8). Consequently it is a mistake to

treat Hume's ethical theories as secondary, and his development
of the Locke-Berkeley theory of ideas as primary, in making an
over-all evaluation of his philosophy, as Reid and the other
members of the Scottish School did. Smith gives special attention to Reid's letter to Hume, claiming that it is naïve and
shows a complete lack of understanding of Hume's deeper
thought, as do also his comments on Hume's *Inquiry Concerning Human Understanding*. Reid was born one year before
Hume, but he lived twenty years after Hume's death in 1776,
during which period he wrote his most systematic treatise, *The
Essay on the Intellectual Powers of Man* (1785).

Kemp Smith's use of Reid's letter in support of his Hutchesonian theory of the origin of Hume's philosophy is a justification of the inclusion in this compendium of the two letters
exchanged by Hume and Reid (see Chapter IV). It also justifies
beginning the book with selections from two contemporaries of
Hume, Francis Hutcheson and Adam Smith. Both of these writers, however, as well as Hume, should be called precursors
rather than founders of the Scottish School of Philosophy. Adam
Smith was a close friend of David Hume, and they shared the
impartial-spectator theory of ethics, which is well expounded
in the selections from Adam Smith in Chapter III. Hume also
corresponded with Francis Hutcheson concerning the ethical
part of the *Treatise*.[1] Nevertheless, the founders of the Scottish
School are Thomas Reid and Dugald Stewart.

The well-known and oft-quoted statement of Immanuel Kant
that Hume awoke him from his dogmatic slumbers raises the
question of the relation of the Scottish School of Philosophy
to Kantianism. Here we find Dugald Stewart in sharp opposition
to Sir William Hamilton. Admitting that he found it impossible
to understand Kant's writings and that, not knowing German, he
could only read his Latin treatise and a Latin translation of his
German works and that his knowledge of Kant was largely

---

[1] All of these letters have been published in J.V.T. Grieg's *The Letters
of David Hume*, 2 volumes, Oxford at the Clarendon Press, 1932.

gleaned from secondary sources, Stewart did not hesitate to pronounce a severe judgment on the Kantian philosophy, to dwell on its obscurity, and to predict its speedy downfall. On the other hand, Sir William Hamilton, who was one of the most learned philosophers of the nineteenth century and editor of the *Works* of both Reid and Stewart, studied the works of Kant assiduously and made a serious but not altogether successful attempt to incorporate Kantian doctrines into his own system of ideas. As Professor N. K. Smith points out, "the parallel between Reid and Kant is . . . only partial and may prove misleading . . ." (p. 7).

A third controversy raged within the School over the nature of consciousness, sensation, and perception. What Reid affirmed, Stewart modified and Brown rejected, while Sir William Hamilton strongly objected to Brown's ideas. Sir William added voluminous notes to his editions of the *Collected Works* of both Reid and Stewart to elucidate their positions and purge their expositions of what he took to be errors in their conceptions of perception, sensation, and consciousness. Here is an example of how he dealt with consciousness. In Lecture IX of his *Lectures on Metaphysics,* he discusses the terms *self* and *ego* and says "they are absolutely convertible." He then inserts his own translation of a notable passage from the *First Alcibiades* of Plato, the genuineness of which is questionable, to clarify this statement. Following is a very brief portion of the dialogue:

Socrates.   Now, then, does not a man use his whole body?
Alcibiades.   Unquestionably.
Socrates.   But we are agreed that he who uses and that which is used are different?
Alcibiades.   Yes.
Socrates.   A man is, therefore, different from his body?
Alcibiades.   So I think.
Socrates.   What is the man?
Alcibiades.   I cannot say.
Socrates.   You can at least say that the man is that which uses the body?

Alcibiades.   True.
Socrates.   Now, does anything use the body but the mind?
Alcibiades.   Nothing.
Socrates.   The mind is, therefore, the man?
Alcibiades.   The mind alone.

And Sir William adds: "To the same effect Aristotle asserts that
the mind contains the man, not the man the mind," and he goes
on to quote Cicero, Hierocles, Macrobius, and others to the
same effect.

In evaluating this argument, one cannot help wondering
why Sir William Hamilton did not refer to Aristotle's famous
saying in Book IX, Chapter 9, of the *Nicomachean Ethics,* the
genuineness of which is not questionable, to prove his major
thesis, since this is the passage that was used by St. Thomas
Aquinas in support of essentially the same theory. For this saying is strikingly similar to Sir William's own statement—indeed,
even more so than the above dialogue from the *First Alcibiades.*
Aristotle wrote: "And with respect to all the other functions,
in like manner there is something which perceives that we are
exercising them, so that we can perceive that we perceive and
think that we think. But this [perceiving] that we perceive or
think, is perceiving that we exist; for existing, as we said [Chap-
ter 7], consists in perceiving or thinking." (Grant's translation.)
In the lecture on "The Nature of Consciousness" reprinted below, Sir William Hamilton writes: ". . . this knowledge, which
I, the subject, have of these modifications of my being, and
through which knowledge alone these modifications are possible,
is what we call *consciousness.* The expressions *I know that I
know, I know that I feel, I know that I desire,* are thus translated by *I am conscious that I know, I am conscious that I feel,
I am conscious that I desire.*" Of course Aristotle did not say
that perceiving that we perceive is consciousness, since, as Sir
William Hamilton says, Descartes was the first philosopher to
use the term *consciousness,* but we can see clearly that Aristotle
meant just what Sir William asserts. And so did St. Thomas and
Descartes and many other philosophers. I have discussed this
whole issue at some length in my essay "Precursors of Descartes'

Cogito Argument." (See Chapter xxvi of my *Crucial Issues in Philosophy* [Boston: Christopher Publishing House].)

In spite of all of these and other differences among the leading representatives of the Scottish School there are enough doctrines on which they are in substantial agreement to justify treating this century-and-a-half-long movement of thought as a single school of philosophy.

The selection from Sir William Hamilton in Chapter VII on the general characteristics of "The Scottish Philosophy" gives a good idea of what these doctrines are, as does also the selection with a similar title by James McCosh in Chapter IX. Sir William indicates how influential the School was in France and even in Italy. The writings of Dugald Stewart and Sir William Hamilton and their numerous disciples also had a far-reaching influence in Canada and the United States. From about 1750 to 1900 this School arose and flourished. It has left a rich deposit of philosophical material in English literature by some of the most gifted and best-informed philosophers of modern times. Surely this literature is worthy of the attention of all who are interested in serious discussions of the deeper problems of human existence.

It is well known among leaders of the Church of Christ, or Disciples of Christ, which is the largest Protestant group founded in the United States, that the founders, Thomas Campbell and his illustrious son, Alexander Campbell, who was also founder and the first President of Bethany College in West Virginia, were both strongly influenced by the Scottish philosophers. This is rightly emphasized by Professor Lester G. McAllister in his authoritative biography *Thomas Campbell: Man of the Book* (St. Louis: Bethany Press, 1954). Dr. McAllister writes: "Reid's philosophy undoubtedly had a profound influence on the later development of Thomas Campbell's deepest convictions" (p. 27). President Perry Epler Gresham, of Bethany College, who formerly taught philosophy at Texas Christian University and is currently President of the International Convention of the Disciples of Christ, properly emphasized the indebtedness of the Campbell founding fathers to the Scottish philosophers in his scholarly address, entitled "Proud Heritage From Scotland," delivered at the World Convention of Christian Churches at Edinburgh, Scotland, August 3, 1960. He referred to "the common sense tradition of Locke and Reid which Campbell brought to religion."[2] A careful examination of Alexander Campbell's contributions to the *Millenial Harbinger*, as well as his other writings, especially his famous debates, will reveal many evidences that his underlying philosophical ideas were communicated to him by his reading of John Locke and the Scottish philosophers. Of course, what the Campbells and their followers, as well as many other religionists, liked about the Scottish philosophers was their basing all valid religious knowledge on divine revelation, well expressed in the motto of the Disciples of Christ: "Where the Scriptures speak, we speak; where the Scriptures are silent, we are silent."

Professor O. W. Wight prepared a one-volume collection of the writings of Sir William Hamilton which was widely used as a textbook. It was copyrighted in 1853 and the sixth edition appeared in 1860. The title page bears the inscription "For the use of Schools and Colleges." Another evidence of the importance of Sir William Hamilton's philosophy in the United States is the fact that Henry James, Sr., published a critical review entitled "The Works of Sir William Hamilton" in *Putnam's Magazine* in November, 1853 (Vol. II, pp. 470–81). Later textbooks by James McCosh and by other representatives of the Scottish School were in wide use. Throughout most of the nineteenth century Protestant ministerial students in the colleges and seminaries of this country were schooled in this philosophy.

In making the selections for this compendium from the extensive literature in which this philosophy is expounded and defended, I have aimed to include selections that would indicate how one representative differs from another but that at the same time would emphasize the threads of connection that are more or less common to all the representatives of the School.

---

[2] A printed copy of this important address can be obtained by addressing a request to President Gresham, Bethany College, Bethany, West Virginia.

To assist the reader in understanding the selections and the importance of their respective authors, I have put at the beginning of each chapter a biographical sketch and summary of each representative's philosophy by a competent authority. The summary of James McCosh is taken from the late Professor Harvey Gates Townsend's *Philosophical Ideas in the United States* (American Book Co., 1934), a widely used textbook prepared for courses in American Philosophy. In the case of Hume, I have used the biographical sketch by H. A. Mikkelsen from Warner's *Library of the World's Best Literature*. The other summaries are taken, with a few omissions, from the excellent account entitled *Philosophy in Great Britain and America* by Noah Porter (1811–92). This essay was especially prepared to serve as a supplement to the English translation by George S. Morris of Friedrich Ueberweg's monumental *History of Philosophy*. (See *History of Modern Philosophy* [Scribner, Armstrong & Co., 1877], Vol. II, Appendix I, pp. 349–460. Chapters V, VI, and VII deal with the Scottish School.) Because this important essay appeared as an appendix to supplement Ueberweg's *History of Philosophy*, it has been unduly neglected, although Noah Porter is recognized as having a prominent place in the history of American Philosophy. Professor Herbert W. Schneider writes: "Noah Porter was in many ways the greatest and most erudite of the professors of philosophy" (*History of American Philosophy* [New York: Columbia University Press, 1946], p. 245). Noah Porter was Professor of Metaphysics and Moral Philosophy at Yale University from 1846 to 1871, when he was elected President of the University, in which position he served with distinction until his retirement in 1886. His summaries of seven of the representative Scottish philosophers, from whose writings I have made selections for this compendium, are especially valuable for four reasons: (i) They give the essential biographical data concerning each man. (ii) They list each author's writings, and contain other useful biographical addenda. (iii) Porter gives adequate and scholarly summaries of the major writings of each philosopher. (iv) They contain pertinent critical comments and evaluations by Porter that are objective, sympathetic, fair, and dependable and which are all the more valuable because it is obvious that he is not a follower of the Scottish School. I have been guided by Porter's comments in making some of the selections.

The supplementary essay to Chapter V entitled "Dugald Stewart on Hindu Philosophy" was written during the winter of 1959. It brings together a number of quotations from Sir William Jones on Hindu Philosophy and comments of Stewart on them. It also quotes a long and curious letter written to Stewart by his friend Sir James Macintosh, who was an important member of the Scottish School, expressing the author's opinion as to the origin of the Vedanta Philosophy. The reader's attention is also called to Thomas Brown's reference to Sir William Jones and his comment on the Hindu Philosophy at the end of the first selection from his writings in Chapter VI. In view of the recent emphasis on East-West Philosophy, and because they come down to us from the first quarter of the nineteenth century, these comments of Sir William Jones, Dugald Stewart, Sir James Macintosh, and Thomas Brown on Hindu Philosophy should be of special interest today.

I regret that there was not enough space available to include selections from all Scottish philosophers who have contributed to the extant literature of this school of philosophy. Especially important are writings of the two editors of *Sir William Hamilton's Lectures*, H. L. Mansel and John Veitch. The former wrote *The Limits of Religious Thought* (1858) and *The Philosophy of the Conditioned* (1866); and the latter wrote *Hamilton* (1882), *Knowing and Being* (1889), and *Dualism and Monism* (1895). Less important are the two representatives of the Scottish School referred to by Immanuel Kant, James Beattie and James Oswald. Beattie wrote a popular and vulgar book entitled *Essay on the Nature and Immutability of Truth in Opposition to Sophistry and Skepticism* (1770), which was translated into German. In one of his letters, Hume writes: ". . . that bigotted and silly fellow, Beattie." James Oswald wrote *An Appeal to Common Sense in Behalf of Religion* (Vol. I, 1766, and Vol. II, 1772). Neither Beattie nor Oswald added anything substantial to the common-sense theory of Reid. There were several other Scottish philosophers of minor importance. Henry Laurie's informative *The Scottish Philosophy in Its National Development* (Glasgow: James Macelhouse & Sons, 1902) contains chapters on Andrew Baxter, Lord Kames, George Campbell, Lord Monbodo, Adam Ferguson, and Thomas Chambers. Consult the Index for references to some of these writers quoted in the selections in this compendium.

Another omission needs explanation. Nearly a decade after the death of Sir William Hamilton, John Stuart Mill spent three years working on a refutation of his philosophy because he considered it dangerous. In 1865 he published in two volumes the result of these labors, *Examination of the Philosophy of Sir William Hamilton*. The following year he was answered by James McCosh in *An Examination of John Stuart Mill's Philosophy, Being a Defense of Fundamental Truths*. More than twenty years later McCosh wrote: "Hamilton, in his famous *Note A*, appended to his edition of Reid's *Collected Works*, has shown that all thinkers, including even sceptics, have been obliged to assume something without proof, and to justify themselves in doing so. In my *Examination of Mr. J. S. Mill's Philosophy*, I have shown that, in his *Examination of Hamilton's Philosophy* he has assumed between twenty and thirty such principles." (*Realistic Philosophy* [London: Macmillan & Co., 1887], Vol. II, p. 164.) The consensus among competent scholars is that Mill considerably modified his empirical philosophy by concessions he made in his attempted refutation of Sir William Hamilton's philosophy. In this compendium there are no selections dealing with this controversy, but readers are advised to examine the treatises of Mill and McCosh in following up their studies of Scottish Philosophy.

By the end of the nineteenth century the Scottish Philosophy had been supplanted in England and America by the Kantian-based idealistic philosophies of such thinkers as T. H. Green, F. H. Bradley, Bernard Bosanquet, Pringle Pattison, N. K. Smith, J. H. Muirhead, and others in England, and by B. P. Bowne, W. T. Harris, G. H. Howison, J. E. Creighton, John Watson,

Josiah Royce, and others in the United States and Canada. Coleridge and Carlyle pioneered this development in English literature, and Emerson's transcendentalism represented it in American literature.

It is interesting to note that in his article entitled "Idealism," published in the fourteenth edition of the *Encyclopaedia Britannica*, J. H. Muirhead names J. F. Ferrier as a precursor of Anglo-American absolute idealism. And his definition of idealism in this article shows that he himself was considerably influenced by Ferrier's epistemology. This means that the dialectical wheel came full circle in the philosophy of Ferrier. Reid's common-sense realism arose as a replacement of the incomplete idealism of Berkeley and the radical skepticism of Hume. But if he had used his own criteria to judge common-sense realism, Ferrier would have pronounced it improperly reasoned and essentially untrue. However, he would not have returned to the subjective idealism of Berkeley and Hume, for he was more of a precursor of Anglo-American objective idealism than he was a slavish follower of the so-called "fundamental beliefs" of his predecessors among the Scottish philosophers.

Ferrier's appreciative evaluation of Berkeley in his essay "Berkeley and Idealism" supports this interpretation of his role in the development of the Scottish philosophy. He writes:[3]

But the history of philosophy repairs any injustice which may be done to philosophy itself; and the doctrines of Berkeley, incomplete as they appear when viewed as the isolated tenets of an individual, and short as they no doubt fell, in his hands, of their proper and ultimate expression, acquire a fuller and a profounder significance when studied in connection with the speculations which have since followed in their train. The great problems of humanity have no room to work themselves out within the limits of an individual mind. Time alone weaves a canvas wide enough to do justice to their true proportions; and a few broad strokes is all that the genius of any one man, however gifted, is permitted to add to the mighty and illimitable

---

[3] *Professor Ferrier's Works*, Vol. III, *Philosophical Remains* (New Edition, Edinburgh, 1883), pp. 292 f.

work. It is therefore no reproach to Berkeley to say that he left his labours incomplete; that he was frequently misunderstood, that his reasonings fell short of their aim, and that he perhaps failed to carry with him the unreserved and permanent convictions of any one of his contemporaries. The subsequent progress of philosophy shows how much the science of man is indebted to his researches. He certainly was the first to stamp the indelible impress of his powerful understanding on those principles of our nature, which, since his time, have brightened into imperishable truths in the light of genuine speculation. His genius was the first to swell the current of that mighty stream of tendency towards which all modern meditation flows, the great gulf-stream of Absolute Idealism.

Today the dialectical wheel has been given a new whirl, and those who are in the operator's seat are even more confident than were their predecessors that they have found the true method of philosophizing, if not the true philosophy. Logical positivists and philosophical analysts are clamoring for and claiming the ascendance in the domain of philosophy, and neo-orthodox and utopian theologians in that of Protestant theology. The confident leaders of these contemporary philosophical and theological movements will find much to support their contentions in the writings of the Scottish philosophers. It is the Editor's hope that this compendium may contribute to the awakening of their interest, as well as that of their adherents and many others, in this vast storehouse of philosophical, psychological, and theological doctrines and theories.

D. S. R.

CHAPTER I

Francis Hutcheson
(1694–1746)

The Man and His Work

By Noah Porter

The Scottish School of Metaphysics began, in the judgment of
Sir William Hamilton,[1] with Gerschom Carmichael, Professor
of Moral Philosophy in Glasgow, immediately before Hutcheson.
He published about 1720 an edition of Puffendorf, *De Officio
Hominis et Civis*, with comments. The first well-known writer
of this school is Francis Hutcheson, 1694–1747, born in the north
of Ireland and educated at the University of Glasgow, a licen-
tiate of divinity, and many years a popular teacher in Dublin.
In 1729 he was elected Professor of Moral Philosophy in the
University of Glasgow. His works are: *An Inquiry into the
Original of Our Ideas of Beauty*, Lond., 1725. *An Essay on the
Passions and Affections*, Lond., 1728. *Metaphysicae Synopsis*,
etc., 1742. *System of Moral Philosophy with Life*, etc., Glasgow,
1755. *Letters on Virtue*, 1772.

Hutcheson is best known by his assertion of the doctrine
that moral distinctions are apprehended directly by means or
as the consequence of a special capacity of the soul, designated
as the moral sense. "Moral goodness denotes an idea of some
quality apprehended in actions which procures approbation and
love toward the actor from those who receive no advantage by
the action." "Moral evil, our idea of a contrary quality, which
excites aversion and dislike towards the actor, even from persons
unconcerned in its natural tendency."

---
[1] Hamilton's *Life of T. Reid*, p. 30.

As the bodily senses give us their appropriate "sensitive perceptions," and furnish the mind with the simple ideas proper to each, so there is a capacity for that idea called Beauty, and another for the idea called Harmony. These are properly called internal senses, and also reflex and secondary senses, because they presuppose objects furnished by the external senses. These superior powers of perception are also called senses, because the pleasure does not arise from any knowledge of principles, proportions, causes, or the usefulness of the object, but is directly imparted. In addition to the Sense of Society, we have a moral sense to direct our actions and to give us nobler pleasures. This moral sense does not suppose any innate ideas, knowledge, or practical propositions, but is only a "determination of our minds to receive amiable or disagreeable ideas of actions, antecedent to any opinion of advantage or loss to redound to ourselves from them." The universal quality or characteristic of the actions which are agreeable to the moral sense is benevolent intention; i.e., all the actions which are approved by the moral sense as virtuous are disinterestedly benevolent actions.

The metaphysical doctrines which connect Hutcheson with the so-called Scottish School and which justify his being considered the precursor of Reid, are the circumstance that he anticipated Reid in his dissent from Locke, and used the term *suggestion* in the same import in which Reid employs it in his *Inquiry.* Vide *Met. Syn.* P.I,c.l, *quae omnia perspecta suggerunt, rationis aut habitudinis quae inter res intercedit, notionem.* His dissent from Locke's account of the origin of our ideas is as decided as is that of Reid. *Essay on the Origin,* etc., II, c. 12. "Every sensation is *accompanied* with the idea of duration, and yet duration is not a sensible idea, since it also accompanies ideas of internal consciousness or reflection." "Extension, figure, motion or rest seems therefore to be more properly called ideas *accompanying* the sensations of sight and touch, than the sensations of either of these senses." *Vide* also *Essay on the Passions,* Sec. I., note. Mor. Phil., B.I.c.i.s3. "These latter for distinction we may call *concomitant* ideas of sensation" etc. "But none therefore imagines that it is reason, and not sense,

which discovers these *concomitant ideas,* or *primary qualities."*
Illus. of Moral Sense, Sec. 4. The merit and relative originality
of Hutcheson are acknowledged by Dr. Price. Review, ch. p.
56, ed. 1. *Phil. Essays* I. ch. III. Cf. also Sir W. Hamilton, *Works
of Reid,* p. 124, *n.* Royer Collard, *Oeuvres de Reid,* Tom. iii. p.
430.

Hutcheson also shows his independence of Locke in his doctrine of axioms. *Met.* P. I. c.iii. of Consciousness; *Met.* P. II, c.i.,
as well as in his doctrine of the secondary or reflex senses of
Beauty and Moral qualities. He contends that in a proper sense
of the term, though not in that rejected by Locke, certain ideas
are innate, and holds that we accept them not on grounds of
experience, but by an independent power which is *menti con-
genita intelligendi vis.*

Concerning the Finer Powers of Perception

By FRANCIS HUTCHESON

This selection gives a clear account of the author's doctrine of the
finer powers of perception of human beings, including the moral
sense. It is taken from *A System of Moral Philosophy* by Francis
Hutcheson, LL.D., published from the original manuscript by his
son, Francis Hutcheson, M.D. (Glasgow, MDCCLV), Vol. I, Chapter II, pp. 15–29. The spelling of a number of words has been mod-
ernized. Some footnotes have been omitted, and therefore the footnotes in this essay are not consecutively numbered.

I. AFTER THE GENERAL ACCOUNT of the perceptive powers, and of
the will, we proceed to consider some finer powers of perception, and some other natural determinations of will, and general
laws of the human constitution.

To the senses of seeing and hearing, are superadded in most
men, though in very different degrees, certain powers of perception of a finer kind than what we have reason to imagine

are in most of the lower animals, who yet perceive the several colours and figures, and hear the several sounds. These we may call the senses of beauty and harmony, or, with Mr. Addison, the *imagination*. Whatever name we give them, 'tis manifest that, the several following qualities in objects, are sources of pleasure constituted by nature; or, men have natural powers or determinations to perceive pleasure from them.

1. Certain forms are more grateful to the eye than others, even abstracting from all pleasure of any lively colours, such complex ones, especially, where, uniformity, or equality of proportion among the parts, is observable; nor can we, by command of our will, cause all forms indifferently to appear pleasant, more than we can make all objects grateful to the taste.

2. As a disposition to imitate is natural to mankind from their infancy, so they universally receive pleasure from imitation. Where the original is beautiful, we may have a double pleasure; but an exact imitation, whether of beauty or deformity, whether by colours, figures, speech, voice, motion or action, gives of itself a natural pleasure.

3. Certain compositions of notes are immediately pleasant to the generality of men, which the artists can easily inform us of. The simpler pleasures arise from the concords; but an higher pleasure arises from such compositions as, in sound and time, imitate those modulations of the human voice, which indicate the several affections of the soul in important affairs. Hence PLATO and LYCURGUS observed a moral character in music, and looked upon it as of some consequence in influencing the manners of a people.

4. As we are endued with reason to discern the fitness of means for an end, and the several relations and connections of things; so, there is an immediate pleasure in knowledge, distinct from the Judgment itself, though naturally joined with it. We have a pleasure also in beholding the effects of art and design, in any ingenious machinery adapted to valuable purposes, in any utensil well fitted for its end; whether we hope to have the use of it or not. We have delight in exercising our own rational, inventive, and active powers; we are pleased to behold

the like exercises of others, and the artful effects of them. In such works of art we are pleased to see intermixed the beauty of form, and imitation, as far as it consists with the design; but the superior pleasure from the execution of the design makes us omit the inferior when it is inconsistent.

II. Granting all these dispositions to be natural, we may account for all that diversity of fancies and tastes which we observe, since so many qualities are naturally pleasing, some of which may be chiefly regarded by one, and others by others. The necessitous, the busy, or the slothful, may neglect that beauty in dress, architecture, and furniture, which they might obtain, and yet not be insensible to it. One may pursue only the simpler kind in the uniformity of parts; others may also intersperse imitation of the beautiful works of nature; and, of these, some may choose one set of natural objects, and others may choose other objects of greater beauty or dignity: the manner too of imitation may be more or less perfect. Again, some in their works may chiefly regard the pleasure from appearance of design, and usefulness, admitting only the pleasures of beauty and imitation as far as they consist with it. In the most fantastic dresses there is uniformity of parts, and some aptitude to the human shape, and frequently imitation. But our modern dresses are less fitted for easy motion, and the displaying of the human shape, than the ancient. Spectators who regard these ends may prefer the ancient dresses; those who do not think of them, or regard them, may prefer the modern.

In like manner as to architecture; they who discern the imitation of the proportions of the human body in certain parts, may relish one manner on that account. Others, who know the uses of which certain parts present the appearance, may relish this design; others, without these views, may be pleased with the uniformity of the parts: others may like or dislike through some[5] associations of ideas; of which hereafter.

One who would reduce all sense of beauty in forms to some

---

[5] See the *Inquiry into Beauty*. b.i.c.7, par. 4.

real or apparent usefulness discerned, will never be able to explain how the spectator relishes those useful forms from which he gets no benefit, nor expects any beyond the pleasure of beholding them; nor how we are pleased with the forms of flowers, of birds, and wild beasts, when we know not any real or apparent uses indicated by them; nor how any spectator, quite a stranger to the views of the architect, shall be pleased with the first appearance of the work; nor whence it is that we are all pleased with imitations of objects, which, were they really placed where their images are, would be of no advantage; one may as well assert that, before we can be pleased with a favour, we must know the figures of the minute particles, and see their inoffensive nature to our nerves.

The pleasures of these[6] finer senses are of no small importance in life. How much soever they seem neglected by the votaries of wealth and power, they are generally much in their view for themselves, in some future period of life, or for their posterity: as for others who have a more elegant taste, they are the end of a great part of their labours: and the greatest part of men, when they are tolerably provided against the uneasy cravings of appetite, show a relish for these pleasures: no sooner are nations settled in peace than they begin to cultivate the arts subservient to them, as all histories will inform us.

To these pleasures of the imagination may be added two other grateful perceptions arising from novelty and grandeur. The former ever causes a grateful commotion when we are at leisure; which perhaps arises from that curiosity or desire of knowledge which is deeply rooted in the soul; of which hereafter. Grandeur also is generally a very grateful circumstance in any object of contemplation distinct from its beauty or proportion. Nay, where none of these are observed, the mind is agreeably moved with what is large, spacious, high, or deep, even when no advantage arising from these circumstances is

---

[6] One who would make all these to be perceptions of the external senses, and deny that we have any distinct powers of perception, may as well assert that the pleasures of geometry, or perspective, are sensual, because 'tis by the senses we receive the ideas of figure.

regarded. The final causes of these natural determinations or senses of pleasure may be seen in some[7] late authors.

III. Another important determination or sense of the soul we may call the *sympathetic*, different from all the external senses; by which, when we apprehend the state of others, our hearts naturally have a fellow-feeling with them. When we see or know the pain, distress, or misery of any kind which another suffers, and turn our thoughts to it, we feel a strong sense of pity, and a great proneness to relieve, where no contrary passion withholds us. And this[8] without any artful views of advantage to accrue to us from giving relief, or of loss we shall sustain by these sufferings. We see this principle strongly working in children, where there are the fewest distant views of interest; so strongly sometimes, even in some not of the softest mould, at cruel executions, as to occasion fainting and sickness. This principle continues generally during all our lives.

We have a like natural disposition to Congratulation with others in their joys; where no prior emulation, imagined opposition of interest, or prejudice, prevents it. We have this sympathy even with the brute animals; and hence poets so successfully please us with descriptions of their joys. But as our own selfish passions which repel evil, such as fear, anger, resentment, are generally stronger commotions of soul than the passions pursuing private good; so pity is a stronger benevolent passion than congratulation. And all this is wisely contrived, since immunity from pain seems previously necessary to the enjoyment of good. Thus the stronger motions of the mind are directed toward that which is most necessary. This sympathy seems to extend to all our affections and passions. They all seem naturally contagious. We not only sorrow with the distressed, and rejoice with the prosperous; but admiration, or surprise, discovered in one, raises a correspondent commotion of mind in all who behold him. Fear observed raises fear in the *observer* before he knows the cause, laughter moves to laugh, love begets love, and the devout affections displayed dispose

---

[7] See *Spectator* N. 412, and the *Inquiry into Beauty*, last section.

[8] See *Inquiry into Virtue*, sect. 2.

others to devotion. One easily sees how directly subservient this sympathy is to that grand determination of the soul toward universal happiness.

IV. Before we mention some other finer senses, which have actions of men for their objects, we must observe one general determination of the soul to exercise all its active powers. We may see in our species, from the very cradle, a constant propensity to action and motion; children grasping, handling, viewing, tasting everything. As they advance they exert other powers, making all trials possible; observing all changes, and inquiring into their causes; and this from an impulse to action and an implanted instinct toward knowledge, even where they are not allured by any prospects of advantage. Nay we see almost all other animals, as soon as they come to light, exercising their several powers by like instincts, in the way that the Author of Nature intended; and by this exercise, though often laborious and fatiguing, made happier than any state of slothful sensuality could make them. Serpents try their reptile motions; beasts raise themselves and walk or run; birds attempt to raise themselves with their wings and soar on high; waterfowl take to the water as soon as they see it. The colt is practising for the race,[9] the bull is butting with his horns, and the hound exercising himself for the chase.

Children are ever in motion while they are awake, nor do they decline weariness and toil; they show an aversion to sleep till it over-powers them against their wills; they observe whatever occurs, they remember and inquire about it; they learn the names of things, inquire into their natures, structures, uses, and causes; nor will their curiosity yield to rebukes and affronts. Kind affections soon break out toward those who are kind to them; strong gratitude, and an ardor to excel in any thing that is praised; in vying with their fellows they are transported with success and victory, and exceedingly dejected when they are outdone by others. They are soon provoked to anger upon any

---

[9] *Dente lupus,* &c. Hor. lib. i. fat. i. l. 52.

imagined injury or hurt; are afraid of experienced pain, and provoked at the cause of it; but soon appeased by finding it undesigned, or by professions of repentance. Nothing do they more resent than false accusation or reproach. They are prone to sincerity, and truth, and openness of mind, until they have experienced some evils following upon it. They are impatient to relate to others any thing new or strange, or apt to move admiration or laughter; ready to gratify any one with what they have no use for themselves; fond of pleasing, and void of suspicion, till they have had experience of injuries.

This impulse to action continues during life, while we retain the use of our powers. The men who are most worthless and slothful yet are not wholly idle; they have their games, their cabals and conversation to employ them, or some mean ingenuity about sensual pleasures. We see in general that mankind can be happy only by action of one kind or other; and the exercise of the intellectual powers is one source of natural delight from the cradle to the grave. Children are transported with discoveries of any thing new or artificial, and impatient to show them to others. Public shows, rarities, magnificence, give them high entertainment; but above all, the important actions of great characters; the fortunes of such men, and of the states where they lived, whether related, read, or represented by action, are the delight of all ages. Here the pleasure is heightened by our social feelings of joy, and the keenness of inquiry increased by our impulse to compassion, and our concern about the persons we admire.

When men have the proper genius, and access to more laborious knowledge, what ardour of mind do some show for geometry, numbers, astronomy, and natural history? All toils and watchings are born with joy. Need we mention even fabulous history, mythology, philology? 'Tis manifest there is an high natural pleasure in knowledge without any allurements of other advantage. There is a like pleasure in practical knowledge about the business of life, and the effects of actions upon the happiness of individuals, or that of societies. How contrary are all these appearances of Nature to that Philosophy which makes the sole impulse or determination of the soul to be a desire of such pleasures as arise from the body and are referred to it, or of immunity from bodily pain!

V. Action is constituted to mankind the grand source of their happiness by an higher power of perception than any yet mentioned; namely, that by which they receive the moral notions of actions and characters. Never was there any of the human species, except idiots, to whom all actions appeared indifferent. Moral differences of action are discerned by all, even when they consider no advantage or disadvantage to redound to themselves from them. As this moral sense is of high importance, it shall be more fully considered in a subsequent chapter. It may suffice at present to observe what we all feel, that a certain temper, a set of affections, and actions consequent on them, when we are conscious of them in ourselves, raise the most joyful sensations of approbation and inward satisfaction; and when the like are observed in others, we have a warm feeling of approbation, a sense of their excellence, and, in consequence of it, great goodwill and zeal for their happiness. If we are conscious of contrary affections and actions, we feel an inward remorse, and dislike to ourselves; when we observe the like in others, we dislike and condemn their dispositions, reputing them base and odious.

The affections which excite this moral approbation are all either directly benevolent, or naturally connected with such dispositions; those which are disapproved and condemned, are either ill-natured, by which one is inclined to occasion misery to others; or such selfish dispositions as argue some unkind affection, or the want of that degree of the benevolent affections which is requisite for the public good, and commonly expected in our species.

This moral discernment is not peculiar to persons of a fine education and much reflection. The rudest of mankind show such notions; and young minds, who think least of the distant influences of actions upon themselves or others, and have small precaution about their own future interests, are rather more moved with *moral forms* than others. Hence that strong inclination in children, as soon as they understand the names of the several affections and tempers, to hear such stories as present the moral characters of agents and their fortunes. Hence that joy in the prosperity of the kind, the faithful, and the just; and that indignation and sorrow upon the successes of the cruel and treacherous. Of this power we shall treat more fully hereafter.

VI. As by the former determination we are led to approve or condemn ourselves or others according to the temper displayed, so by another natural determination, which we may call a sense of honour and shame, an high pleasure is felt upon our gaining the approbation and esteem of others for our good actions, and upon their expressing their sentiments of gratitude; and on the other hand, we are cut to the heart by censure, condemnation, and reproach. All this appears in the countenance. The fear of infamy, or censure, or contempt, displays itself by blushing.

'Tis true, we may observe from our infancy, that men are prone to do good offices to those they approve and honour. But we appeal to the hearts of men, whether they have not an immediate pleasure in being honoured and esteemed, without thinking of any future advantages, and even when they previously know that they can receive none. Are not we generally solicitous about our characters after our death? And whence is it that blushing accompanies this sort of fear, and not the fears of other disadvantages, if this is not an immediate principle?

Aristotle's[10] account of this pleasure, though more elegant, is not just "that we relish honour as it is a testimony to our virtue, which we are previously conscious is the greatest good." This consideration may sometimes make honour very grateful to men who are doubtful and diffident of their own conduct. But have not also the men of greatest abilities, who are perfectly assured of the goodness of their conduct, a like natural joy in being praised, distinct from their inward self-approbation?

---

[10] *Nichomachean Ethics*, Book 1, Chap. 5.

The kind intention of God in implanting this principle is obvious. 'Tis a strong incitement to every thing excellent and amiable: it gives a grateful reward to virtue: it often surmounts the obstacles to it from low worldly interests: and even men of little virtue are excited by it to such useful services as they would have otherways declined. The selfish are thus, beyond their inclinations, made subservient to a public interest; and such are punished who counteract it.

What may further prove that this sense of honour is an original principle, is this; we value the praise of others, not in proportion to their abilities to serve us, but in proportion to their capacity of judging in such matters. We feel the difference, between the interested desire of pleasing the man in power who can promote us: and the inward joy from the approbation of the judicious or ingenious, who cannot do us any other good offices. The desire of praise is acknowledged to be one of the most universal passions of the soul.

VII. Though it is by the moral sense that actions become of the greatest consequence to our happiness or misery; yet 'tis plain the mind naturally perceives some other sorts of excellence in many powers of body and mind; must admire them, whether in ourselves or others; and must be pleased with certain exercises of them, without conceiving them as moral virtues. We often use words too promiscuously, and do not express distinctly the different feelings or sensations of the soul. Let us keep *moral approbation* for our sentiments of such dispositions, affections, and consequent actions, as we repute virtuous. We find this warm approbation a very different perception from the admiration or liking which we have for several other powers and dispositions; which are also relished by a sense of *decency* or *dignity*. This sense also is natural to us, but the perceptions very different from moral approbation. We not only know the use of such valuable powers, and of their exercise, to the person possessed of them; but have agreeable commotions of admiration and liking, and these in several degrees. Thus beauty, strength, swiftness, agility of body, are more decent and esteemable than a strong voracious stomach, or a delicate palate. The manly diversions of riding, or hunting, are beheld with more pleasure and admiration than eating and drinking even in a moderate degree. A taste for these manly exercises is often valued; whereas pursuits of mere sensuality appear despicable even when they do not run into excess, and at best are only innocent. Nay there is something graceful, in the very shape gesture and motion, and something indecent and uncomely; abstracting from any indications of advantage discerned by the spectators.

But this is still more obvious about the powers of the mind and their exercise. A penetrating genius, capacity for business, patience of application and labour, a tenacious memory, a quick wit, are naturally admirable, and relished by all observers; but with a quite different feeling from moral approbation. To every natural power there seems to be a corresponding sense or taste, recommending one sort of exercise, and disliking the contrary. Thus we relish the exercise of all the ingenious arts, machinery of every kind, imitation in painting, sculpture, statuary, poetry, gardening, architecture, music. We not only behold the works with pleasure, but have a natural admiration of the persons in whom we discern a taste and genius for these arts. Whereas the exercise of our lower powers, merely subservient to sensual gratification, are at best beheld with indifference, are often matter of shame, and the cause of contempt.

Thus according to the just observation of Aristotle, "The chief happiness of active beings must arise from action; and that not from action of every sort, but from that sort to which their nature is adapted, and which is recommended by nature." When we gratify the bodily appetites, there is an immediate sense of pleasure, such as the brutes enjoy, but no further satisfaction; no sense of dignity upon reflection, no good-liking of others for their being thus employed. There is an exercise of some other bodily powers which seem more manly and graceful. There is a manifest gradation; some fine tastes in the ingenious arts are still more agreeable; the exercise is delightful; the works are pleasant to the spectator, and reputable to the artist. The exercise of the higher powers of the understanding, in discovery of truth, and just reasoning, is more esteemable, when the subjects are important. But the noblest of all are the virtuous affections and actions, the objects of the moral sense.

Concerning the Moral Sense, or Faculty of Perceiving Moral Excellence, and Its Supreme Objects

By Francis Hutcheson

This selection gives a fuller account of the ways in which the moral sense functions. It is from Volume I, Chapter IV, pp. 62–78, of *A System of Moral Philosophy.*

VII. LET US NEXT CONSIDER the several powers or dispositions approved or disapproved by this faculty. And here 'tis plain that the primary objects of this faculty are the affections of the will, and that the several affections which are approved, though in very different degrees, yet all agree in one general character, of tendency to the happiness of others, and to the moral perfection of the mind possessing them. No actions, however in fact beneficial to society, are approved as virtuous if they are imagined to flow from no inward good-will to any person, or from such dispositions as do not naturally suppose good-will in the agent, or at least exclude the highest selfishness. The desires of glory, or even of rewards in a future state, were they supposed the sole affections moving an agent in the most beneficial services, without any love to God, esteem of his moral excellencies, gratitude to him, or good-will to men, would not obtain our approbation as morally good dispositions: and yet a firm belief of future happiness to be obtained by Divine appointment, upon our doing beneficent actions, might be as steady and effectual a cause of or motive to such actions as any other.

But mere desire of one's own happiness, without any love to God, or man, is never the object of approbation. This itself may show us how distinct moral approbation is from a persuasion of the tendency of actions to the interest of the approver, since he might hope equally great advantages from such a steady interested disposition to actions in fact beneficent, as from any kind affection.

That some sort of benevolent affections, or some dispositions imagined to be connected with them, are the natural objects of approbation; and the opposite affections, or the want of the kind ones, the objects of condemnation, will be plain from almost all our reasonings in praising or censuring, applauding or condemning the characters and actions of mankind. We point out some kind or beneficent intention, or some beneficent purposes proposed by the agent in what we praise, or would vindicate from censure. We show some detriment ensuing to others, either intended or known, or what easily might have been known by one who had any tender regard for the interests of others, as the evidence either of ill-nature in the agent, or such selfishness, or such selfish passions as over-power all kindness and humanity.

VIII. There is a plain gradation in the objects of our approbation and condemnation, from the indifferent set of actions ascending to the highest virtue, or descending to the lowest vice. It is not easy to settle exactly the several intermediate steps in due order, but the highest and lowest are manifest. The indifferent affections and actions are such as pursue the innocent advantages of the agent without any detriment to society, and yet without any reference made by the agent to any good of others. Such are the necessary and moderate gratifications of appetite, and many trifling actions. To explain the different degrees, we must observe what was hinted at formerly, that beside the moral approbation of virtue, there is also another relish or sense of a certain dignity or decency in many dispositions and actions not conceived as virtuous. Thus we value the pursuits of the ingenious arts, and of knowledge, nay even some

bodily perfections, such as strength and agility, more than mere
brutal sensuality. We in like manner value more in another
activity, patience of labour, sagacity, and spirit in business, provided they are not injurious, though we conceive them solely
exercised for his own promotion to wealth and honour, than a
lazy inactive indolence.

The calm desire of private good, though it is not approved
as virtue, yet it is far from being condemned as vice. And none
of the truly natural and selfish appetites and passions are of
themselves condemned as evil, when they are within certain
bounds, even though they are not referred by the agent to any
public interest. It was necessary for the general good that all
such affections should be implanted in our species; and therefore it would have been utterly unnatural to have made them
matter of disapprobation even while they were not hurtful. Nay,
as these selfish affections are aiming at an end necessary to the
general good, to wit the good of each individual, and as the
abilities of gratifying them are powers which may be very use-
fully employed in subserviency to the most generous affections,
it was highly proper and benign in the Author of Nature to
invite us to the culture of these powers by an immediate relish
for them wherever we observe them, in ourselves or in others;
though this relish is plainly different from moral approbation.

We all have by consciousness and experience a notion of the
human constitution, and of a certain proportion of affections
requisite to an innocent character. The selfish affections are then
only disapproved when we imagine them beyond that innocent
proportion, so as to exclude or over-power the amiable affections, and engross the mind wholly to the purposes of selfishness, or even to obstruct the proper degree of the generous
affections in the station and circumstances of the agent.

IX. But there is another set of dispositions and abilities still
of a finer nature, though distinct from both the calm universal
benevolence and the particular kind affections; which however
are naturally connected with such affections, natural evidences
of them, and plainly inconsistent with the highest sorts of selfish-

ness and sensuality; and these seem immediate objects of the *moral sense*, though perhaps not the highest. They seem to be approved immediately, even before we think of this connexion with disinterested affections, or imagine directly that the agent is referring them to beneficent purposes. Of these moral dispositions there are several sorts, all immediately approved, unless the mind directly discerns that they are employed in vicious purposes. Thus is fortitude approved, as it imports that something moral is more valued than life, and as plainly inconsistent with the highest selfishness: if indeed it be seen employed in rapine, and merely selfish purposes, such as those of lust or avarice, it becomes the object of horror. Candour and openness of mind, and sincerity, can scarce ever be unattended with a kind honest heart; as 'tis virtue and innocence alone which need no disguise. And these dispositions too are immediately approved, perhaps before we think of this connexion; so is also a steadfast principle of veracity whenever we speak.

I know not if Cicero's account of this be exact; "that we naturally desire knowledge, and are averse to ignorance, and error, and being deceived; and thence relish these dispositions which are the natural means of knowledge, and the preservatives against deceptions." Veracity seems to be immediately and strongly approved, and that from our infancy; as we see the first natural impulse of the young mind is to speak truth, till by experiencing some inconveniences it is taught to counteract the natural impulse. One needs not mention here courtesy and good manners: they are the very dress of virtue, the direct profession of kind affections, and are thus approved. As all these abilities and dispositions are of great importance in life, highly beneficial to mankind when exerted in consequence of kind affections, and are naturally connected with them, or exclude the opposite extreme, 'tis with the highest goodness and wisdom that they are immediately recommended to our approbation by the constitution of our *moral faculty*.

But of all such dispositions of our nature, different from all our kind affections, none is so nearly connected with them, none so natural an evidence of them, none so immediately and necessarily subservient to them, as an acute moral sense itself, a strong desire of moral excellence, with an high relish of it wherever it is observed. We do not call the power or sense itself virtuous; but the having this sense in an high degree naturally raises a strong desire of having all generous affections; it surmounts all the little obstacles to them, and determines the mind to use all the natural means of raising them. Now, as the mind can make any of its own powers the object of its reflex contemplation, this high sense of moral excellence is approved above all other abilities. And the consequent desire of moral excellence, the consequent strong love, esteem, and good-will to the persons where it is found, are immediately approved, as most amiable affections, and the highest virtues.

X. Having premised these considerations, we may observe the following degrees of approbation, as they arise above what is merely indifferent.

1. One may rank in the first step, as the object of some sort of esteem or good liking, the exercise even of those more manly powers, which have no necessary or natural connexion with virtue, but show a taste above sensuality and the lower selfishness: such as the pursuits of the ingenious arts, of the elegance of life, and speculative sciences. Every one sees a dignity in these pleasures, and must relish the desires of them; and indeed they are far less opposite to virtue, or the public interest, than keen tastes or appetites of a lower kind.

2. 'Tis plain however, that our moral sense puts a much higher value upon abilities and dispositions immediately connected with virtuous affections, and which exclude the worst sorts of selfishness. Thus candour, veracity, fortitude, and a strong sense of honour, have a moral estimation above other abilities.

3. But to come to the more immediate objects of moral approbation, the kind affections themselves; 'tis certain that, among affections of equal extent, we more approve the calm stable resolute purposes of heart, than the turbulent and passionate. And that of affections in this respect alike, we more approve

those which are more extensive, and less approve those which are more confined. Thus, the stable conjugal and parental love, or the resolute calm purpose of promoting the true happiness of persons thus related to us, is preferable to the turbulent passionate dispositions of tenderness. And the love of a society, a country, is more excellent than domestic affections. We see plainly the superior dignity in these cases from this, that, notwithstanding the struggle felt in our breasts, and the opposition made by the passionate or more limited affections, yet, when we resolutely follow the calm and extensive notwithstanding of this opposition, the soul in its calmest hours and most deliberate reflections approves of its own conduct; and scarce ever fails to approve the like conduct in others at once; as in the case of others its passions are not raised to give opposition. On the contrary, when we have yielded to the passions or the limited affection, in opposition to the calm or more extensive principle, the soul upon reflection is dissatisfied with itself, and at first view it condemns the like conduct in others.

That disposition therefore which is most excellent, and naturally gains the highest moral approbation, is the calm, stable, universal good-will to all, or the most extensive benevolence. And this seems the most distinct notion we can form of the moral excellency of the Deity.

Another disposition inseparable from this in men, and probably in all beings who are capable of such extensive affection, is the relish or approbation of this affection, and a naturally consequent desire of this moral excellence, and an esteem and good-will of an higher kind to all in whom it is found. This love of moral excellence is also an high object of approbation, when we find it in ourselves by reflection, or observe it in another. It is a pretty different affection from benevolence or the desire of communicating happiness; and is as it were in another order of affections; so that one cannot well determine whether it can be compared with the other. It seems co-ordinate, and the highest possible of that kind; never in opposition to benevolence, nay always conspiring with and assisting it. This desire of moral excellence, and love to the mind where it resides,

with the consequent acts of esteem, veneration, trust, and resig-
nation, are the essence of true piety toward God.

We never speak of benevolence toward God; as that word
carries with it some supposal of indigence, or want of some
good, in the object. And yet, as we have benevolence toward
a friend when he may need our assistance; so, the same emotion of soul, or the same disposition toward him, shall remain
when he is raised to the best state we can wish; and it then
exerts itself in congratulation, or rejoicing in his happiness. In
this manner may our souls be affected toward the Deity, without any supposition of his indigence, by the highest joy and
complacence in his absolute happiness.

XI. 'Tis easy to observe the like gradation from the indifferent state of the soul through the several degrees of moral
turpitude. The first may be the want of these more reputable
abilities; which indeed implies no evil affection, and yet plainly
makes a character despicable, though not immoral. Thus we
dislike the imprudent conduct of any man with respect to his
own interest, without thinking of any detriment to arise to
society from it. Thus negligence, rashness, sloth, indolence, are
naturally disliked, abstracting from their effects upon society.
So is a mind insensible to the more manly pleasures of arts and
genius. When indeed imprudent conduct, in point of private
interest, is considered also as affecting a public, or some other
persons than the agent, whose interests he ought to have regarded, as it generally does; then it may be matter of high
moral condemnation and remorse; so may the meanness of our
talents or abilities, when occasioned by our immoderate sloth
and sensuality, and a defect of generous affections.

1. The objects of the gentlest moral disapprobation or censure are those cases "where one in gratifying some lovely narrower affection has inadvertently omitted what would have most
tended to the public good." Such is the promoting a good friend
or benefactor in opposition to a competitor of superior merit
and abilities. The preferring, in such cases, a less worthy friend

to one's self, may be censured indeed as a want of due proportion among these lovely affections, when a more extensive one yields to the more limited; but the moral beauty of some limited affections is so great that we readily overlook some defects in the more extensive. The same is the case if one has served a friend at a trouble or expense to himself much above the value of the good he has done his friend; perhaps too incapacitating himself for some wiser services hereafter. Where indeed one preferred to himself a friend of equal merit, the public interest is as well promoted this way, and a beautiful affection of friendship is displayed. And yet the contrary conduct, when there are no special circumstances pleading for a friend, could not be censured as immoral.

2. Other objects of lighter censure are those actions detrimental to the public which a person is forced to do to avoid death torture or slavery; when yet the public detriment is still greater than those evils he avoids. Here the agent may have no ill-will; nay may have many generous affections though not of that heroic strength which the moral sense would recommend. The guilt is exceedingly extenuated by the greatness of the temptation, which few have sufficient strength of soul to resist. In order to retain the character of innocence, we expect, not only the absence of all malicious dispositions, but many good affections, and those too of an extensive nature; with much caution about the interests of others. The precise degree cannot well be determined; nor is it necessary. But the stronger and the more extensive the generous affections are, so much the better is the temper; the lower they are and the more that any opposite or narrower ones prevail against them, so much the temper is the worse. 'Tis our business to aim at the highest moral excellence, and not content ourselves with merely avoiding infamy and censure.

3. Another degree of vice are the sudden passionate motions of anger, resentment, and ill-will, upon provocation either falsely apprehended, or aggravated beyond any real ground. Such passions when they lead to injury are vicious, though not in the

highest degree. When indeed by indulgence they turn into habitual rancour and settled malice or revenge, they form a most
odious character.

4. A more deformed sort of vice is when the selfish passions
and sensual appetites lead men into like injuries. These are
worse excuses and weaker extenuations of guilt than the angry
passions.

5. A degree more deformed is when calm selfishness raises
deliberate purposes of injury known to be such. In these cases
the moral faculty must be quite over-powered, and deprived of
all its natural force in the soul, and so must all humanity. The
like is the case when men from mere selfishness, without any
grievous temptation, or without any motives of public interest,
counteract their moral sentiments by falsehood, treachery, in-
gratitude, a neglect of honour, or low cowardice dreading to lose
some positive advantages, even while there is no such evil im-
pending as could much affect a brave and good man.

6. In this class, or rather in a worse one, we must rank
impiety, or the want of all due affections to the Deity, when
he is known and conceived to be good. Our moral faculty must
be strangely asleep where the desire of knowing the Supreme
Excellence is a-wanting, or love to it when it is known: or where
there is no care to cultivate devout affections of gratitude where
there have been the greatest benefits received, and where they
are repeated every moment.

There is a disposition still worse, conceivable in the abstract,
but scarce incident to mankind, or the creatures of a good Deity;
a fixed unprovoked original malice, or a desire of the misery of
others for itself, without any motives of interest.

XII. Without a distinct consideration of this moral faculty,
a species endued with such a variety of senses, and of desires
frequently interfering, must appear a complex confused fabric,
without any order or regular consistent design. By means of it,
all is capable of harmony, and all its powers may conspire in
one direction, and be consistent with each other. 'Tis already
proved that we are capable of many generous affections ulti-

mately terminating on the good of others, neither arising from any selfish view, nor terminating on private good. This moral faculty plainly shows that we are also capable of a calm settled universal benevolence, and that this is destined, as the supreme determination of the generous kind, to govern and control our particular generous as well as selfish affections; as the heart must entirely approve its doing thus in its calmest reflections: even as in the order of selfish affections, our self-love, or our calm regard to the greatest private interest controls our particular selfish passions; and the heart is satisfied in its doing so.

To acknowledge the several generous ultimate affections of a limited kind to be natural, and yet maintain that we have no general controlling principle but self-love, which indulges or checks the generous affections as they conduce to, or oppose, our own noblest interest; sometimes allowing these kind affections their full exercise, because of that high enjoyment we expect to ourselves in gratifying them; at other times checking them, when their gratification does not over-balance the loss we may sustain by it; is a scheme which brings indeed all the powers of the mind into one direction by means of the reference made of them all to the calm desire of our own happiness, in our previous deliberations about our conduct: and it may be justly alleged that the Author of Nature has made a connexion in the event at last between our gratifying our generous affections, and our own highest interest. But the feelings of our heart, reason, and history, revolt against this account: which seems however to have been maintained by excellent authors and strenuous defenders of the cause of virtue.

This connexion of our own highest interests with the gratifying our generous affections, in many cases is imperceptible to the mind; and the kind heart acts from its generous impulse, not thinking of its own interest. Nay all its own interests have sometimes appeared to it as opposite to, and inconsistent with, the generous part in which it persisted. Now were there no other calm original determination of soul but that toward one's own interest, that man must be approved entirely who steadily pursues his own happiness, in opposition to all kind affections and all public interest. That which is the sole calm determination, must justify every action in consequence of it, however opposite to particular kind affections. If it be said "that 'tis a mistake to imagine our interest opposite to them while there is a good providence": grant it to be a mistake; this is only a defect of reasoning: but that disposition of mind must upon this scheme be approved which coolly sacrifices the interest of the universe to its own interest. This is plainly contrary to the feelings of our hearts.

Can that be deemed the sole ultimate determination, the sole ultimate end which the mind in the exercise of its noblest powers can calmly resolve, with inward approbation, deliberately to counteract? are there not instances of men who have voluntarily sacrificed their lives, without thinking of any other state of existence, for the sake of their friends or their country? does not every heart approve this temper and conduct, and admire it the more, the less presumption there is of the love of glory and posthumous fame, or of any sublimer private interest mixing itself with the generous affection? does not the admiration rise higher, the more deliberately such resolutions are formed and executed? All this is unquestionably true, and yet would be absurd and impossible if self-interest of any kind is the sole ultimate determination of all calm desire. There is therefore another ultimate determination which our souls are capable of, destined to be also an original spring of the calmest and most deliberate purposes of action; a desire of communicating happiness, an ultimate good-will, not referred to any private interest, and often operating without such reference.

In those cases where some inconsistency appears between these two determinations, the moral faculty at once points out and recommends the glorious, the amiable part; not by suggesting prospects of future interests of a sublime sort by pleasures of self-approbation, or of praise. It recommends the generous part by an immediate undefinable perception; it approves the kind ardour of the heart in the sacrificing even life itself, and that even in those who have no hopes of surviving, or no attention to a future life in another world. And thus, where the moral sense is in its full vigour, it makes the generous determination to public happiness the supreme one in the soul, with that commanding power which it is naturally destined to exercise.

It must be obvious we are not speaking here of the ordinary condition of mankind, as if these calm determinations were generally exercised, and habitually controlled the particular passions; but of the condition our nature can be raised to by due culture; and of the principles which may and ought to operate, when by attention we present to our minds the objects or representations fit to excite them. Doubtless some good men have exercised in life only the particular kind affections, and found a constant approbation of them, without either the most extensive views of the whole system, or the most universal benevolence. Scarce any of the vicious have ever considered wherein it is that their highest private happiness consists, and in consequence of it exerted the calm rational self-love; but merely follow inconsiderately the selfish appetites and affections. Much less have all good men made actual references of all private or generous affections to the extensive benevolence, though the mind can make them; or bad men made references of all their affections to calm self-love.

CHAPTER II

David Hume
(1711–1776)

The Man and His Work

By M. A. Mikkelsen

This biographical sketch is taken from the *Library of the World's Best Literature,* edited by Charles Dudley Warner (New York: R. S. Peale & J. K. Hill, 1897), Vol. XIII, pp. 7777–81. Some paragraphs of the author's comments have been omitted.

DAVID HUME not only founded the literary school of English history, and originated some of the more important doctrines of modern political economy, but also exercised a paramount influence on the philosophic thought of the eighteenth century.

He was the younger son of Joseph Hume, laird of Ninewells in Berwickshire; and was born at Edinburgh April 26th (O.S.), 1711. He appears to have entered the University of Edinburgh at the age of twelve, and to have left at fourteen or fifteen without taking a degree. He began the study of law, but abandoned it in order to devote himself to the "pursuits of philosophy and learning." His first work, the *Treatise of Human Nature,* was published partly in 1739 and partly in 1740; the books entitled "Of the Understanding" and "Of the Passions" appearing in the former, and that entitled "Of Morals" in the latter year. The *Treatise of Human Nature* is the final and most complete exposition of the fundamental principles of the old school of empirical philosophy—the school to which belonged Bacon, Locke, and Berkeley. According to Hume, the contents of the mind are embraced in the term "perceptions." Perceptions con-

sist of sensuous impressions and ideas. Ideas are merely images
of sensuous impressions. Knowledge is the cognition of the relation between two perceptions. There is no necessary connection between cause and effect. The idea of cause depends on
the habit of the mind which expects the event that usually follows another. Mind is but a series or succession of isolated
impressions and ideas. As knowledge is dependent on experience derived through the senses, and as the senses frequently
deceive, one can have no absolute knowledge of things, but
only of one's impressions of them. . . .

In 1763 Hume accepted the post of secretary to Lord Hert-
ford, then ambassador to France. In France Hume's reputation
stood even higher than in Britain, and he immediately became
a social lion in the Parisian world of fashion. Great nobles
feted him, and gatherings at noted salons were incomplete without his presence. He left France in 1766, and after a short term
as Under-Secretary of State (1767–1769) returned to Edinburgh,
where he died August 25th, 1776.

Among his works of importance not hitherto mentioned are
Philosophical Essays concerning Human Understanding, 1748;
An Enquiry concerning the Principles of Morals, 1751; and *Dia-
logues concerning Natural Religion,* 1779.

Hume's personal character was thus described by himself
in his *Autobiography,* written four months before his death:
"I am . . . a man of mild disposition, of command of temper, of
an open, social, and cheerful humor, capable of attachment but
little susceptible of enmity, and of great moderation in all my
passions." The accuracy of this description is confirmed by the
testimony of his contemporaries and the tone of his private
correspondence. It was not until he had reached middle age that
he was able to gratify his taste for intellectual society by remov-
from the country to the town, "the true scene for a man of
letters.". . .

Hume befriended Rousseau, when the latter sought refuge
in England from persecution. On this occasion, however, his kind
offices plunged him into a disagreeable literary quarrel with the
morbid and perhaps mentally irresponsible beneficiary.

Absence of jealousy was a notable trait in Hume's character. He gave assistance and encouragement to several of the younger generation of Scottish writers; and his magnanimity is further illustrated by the helpful letter to his chief adversary, Thomas Reid, which he wrote on returning the manuscript of the *Inquiry into the Human Mind,* submitted by the younger philosopher for the elder's criticism.

In 1741 appeared the first volume of the *Essays Moral and Political,* the second volume coming out in the following year. These essays, with some additions and omissions, were republished in 1748 under the expanded title *Essays Moral, Political, and Literary,* which has been retained in the many subsequent editions. Hume's essays are models of their kind, full of sparkle, interest, and animation. As an essayist he has not been surpassed in purity of diction, and no English writer except Addison equals him in the sense of harmony. His essays are characterized by intellectual impartiality, and by a philosophical breadth of view coupled with critical acuteness in matters of detail. His *Political Discourses,* which were written in the same vein as the Essays, appeared in 1752. . . .

Till the age of forty, Hume's life was spent chiefly in the seclusion of Ninewells, the family estate; interrupted by a sojourn of three years in France from 1734 to 1737, by a few months' absence as companion to the Marquis of Annandale in 1745 and 1746, and by a short period of service as secretary to General St. Clair, whom he accompanied on the expedition against Port L'Orient in 1746 and on a military embassy to Vienna and Turin. In 1751 he removed to Edinburgh, where in the following year he was appointed keeper of the library of the Faculty of Advocates, a post which he occupied until 1757. The library of the Faculty was the largest in Scotland, and afforded him an opportunity, long desired, of turning his attention to historical studies. In 1754 he published a volume on the reigns of James I and Charles I; followed in 1756 by a volume on the period from the execution of Charles to the Revolution of 1688, in 1759 by two volumes on the house of Tudor, and in 1761 by two more on the period from Julius Caesar to Henry VII. Thus in the short space of ten years he wrote and published his famous *History of Great Britain*, covering the entire period from the Roman conquest to the Revolution of 1688. . . .

Of the Origin of the Natural Virtues and Vices

By DAVID HUME

This selection is taken from A *Treatise of Human Nature*, Book III, Part III, Section I, as printed in *The Philosophical Works of David Hume* (in four volumes; Boston: Little, Brown & Co., 1854), Vol. II, pp. 355–60. A footnote is here omitted.

To DISCOVER the true origin of morals, and of that love or hatred which arises from mental qualities, we must take the matter pretty deep, and compare some principles which have been already examined and explained.

We may begin with considering anew the nature and force of *sympathy*. The minds of all men are similar in their feelings and operations; nor can anyone be actuated by any affection of which all others are not in some degree susceptible. As in strings equally wound up, the motion of one communicates itself to the rest, so all the affections readily pass from one person to another, and beget correspondent movements in every human creature. When I see the *effects* of passion in the voice and gesture of any person, my mind immediately passes from these effects to their causes, and forms such a lively idea of the passion as is presently converted into the passion itself. In like manner, when I perceive the *causes* of any emotion, my mind is conveyed to the effects, and is actuated with a like emotion. Were I present at any of the more terrible operations of surgery, it is certain that, even before it begun, the preparation of the instruments, the laying of the bandages in order, the heating of the irons, with all the signs of anxiety and concern in the patient and assistants, would have great effect upon my mind, and excite the strongest sentiments of pity and terror. No passion of another discovers itself immediately to the mind. We are only sensible of its causes or effects. From *these* we infer the passion; and consequently *these* give rise to our sympathy.

Our sense of beauty depends very much on this principle; and where any object has a tendency to produce pleasure in its possessor, it is always regarded as beautiful; as every object that has a tendency to produce pain is disagreeable and deformed. Thus, the conveniency of a house, the fertility of a field, the strength of a horse, the capacity, security, and swift-sailing of a vessel, form the principal beauty of these several objects. Here the object, which is denominated beautiful, pleases only by its tendency to produce a certain effect. That effect is the pleasure or advantage of some other person. Now, the pleasure of a stranger for whom we have no friendship, pleases us only by sympathy. To this principle, therefore, is owing the beauty which we find in everything that is useful. How considerable part this is of beauty will easily appear upon reflection. Wherever an object has a tendency to produce pleasure in the possessor, or, in other words, is the proper *cause* of pleasure, it is sure to please the spectator by a delicate sympathy with the possessor. Most of the works of art are esteemed beautiful, in proportion to their fitness for the use of man; and even many of the productions of nature derive their beauty from that source. Handsome and beautiful, on most occasions, is not an absolute, but a relative quality, and pleases us by nothing but its tendency to produce an end that is agreeable.

The same principle produces, in many instances, our sentiments of morals, as well as those of beauty. No virtue is more esteemed than justice, and no vice more detested than injustice; nor are there any qualities which go further to the fixing the character, either as amiable or odious. Now justice is a moral virtue, merely because it has that tendency to the good of mankind, and indeed is nothing but an artificial invention to that purpose. The same may be said of allegiance, of the laws of nations, of modesty, and of good manners. All of these are mere human contrivances for the interest of society. And since there is a very strong sentiment of morals, which in all nations and all ages has attended them, we must allow that the reflecting on the tendencies of characters and mental qualities is sufficient to give us the sentiments of approbation and blame. Now, as the means to an end can only be agreeable where the end is agreeable, and as the good of society, where our own interest is not concerned, or that of our friends, pleases only by sympathy, it follows, that sympathy is the source of the esteem which we pay to all the artificial virtues.

Thus it appears, *that* sympathy is a very powerful principle in human nature, *that* it has a great influence on our taste of beauty, and *that* it produces our sentiment of morals in all the artificial virtues. From thence we may presume, that it also gives rise to many of the other virtues, and that qualities acquire our approbation because of their tendency to the good of mankind. This presumption must become a certainty, when we find that most of those qualities which we *naturally* approve of, have actually that tendency, and render a man a proper member of society; while the qualities which we *naturally* disapprove of have a contrary tendency, and render any intercourse with the person dangerous or disagreeable. For having found, that such tendencies have force enough to produce the strongest sentiment of morals, we can never reasonably, in these cases, look for any other cause of approbation or blame; it being an inviolable maxim in philosophy, that where any particular cause is sufficient for an effect, we ought to rest satisfied with it, and ought not to multiply causes without necessity. We have happily attained experiments in the artificial virtues, where the tendency of qualities to the good of society is the *sole* cause of our approbation, without any suspicion of the concurrence of another principle. From thence we learn the force of that principle. And where that principle may take place, and the quality approved of is really beneficial to society, a true philosopher will never require any other principle to account for the strongest approbation and esteem.

That many of the natural virtues have this tendency to the good of society, no one can doubt of. Meekness, beneficence, charity, generosity, clemency, moderation, equity, bear the greatest figure among the moral qualities, and are commonly denominated the *social* virtues, to mark their tendency to the good of society. This goes so far, that some philosophers have represented all moral distinctions as the effect of artifice and education, when skilful politicians endeavored to restrain the turbulent passions of men, and make them operate to the public good, by the notions of honor and shame. This system, however, is not consistent with experience. For, first, There are other virtues and vices beside those which have this tendency to the public advantage and loss. Secondly, Had not men a natural sentiment of approbation and blame, it could never be excited by politicians; nor would the words *laudable* and *praiseworthy, blamable,* and *odious,* be any more intelligible than if they were a language perfectly unknown to us, as we have already observed. But though this system be erroneous, it may teach us that moral distinctions arise in a great measure from the tendency of qualities and characters to the interests of society, and that it is our concern for that interest which makes us approve or disapprove of them. Now, we have no such extensive concern for society, but from sympathy; and consequently it is that principle which takes us so far out of ourselves as to give us the same pleasure or uneasiness in the characters of others, as if they had a tendency to our own advantage or loss.

The only difference betwixt the natural virtues and justice lies in this, that the good which results from the former arises from every single act, and is the object of some natural passion; whereas a single act of justice, considered in itself, may often be contrary to the public good; and it is only the concurrence of mankind in a general scheme or system of action, which is advantageous. When I relieve persons in distress, my natural humanity is my motive; and so far as my succor extends, so far have I promoted the happiness of my fellow-creatures. But if we examine all the questions that come before any tribunal of justice, we shall find that, considering each case apart, it would as often be an instance of humanity to decide contrary to the laws of justice as conformable to them. Judges take from a poor man to give to a rich; they bestow on the dissolute the labor of the industrious; and put into the hands of the vicious the means of harming both themselves and others. The whole scheme, however, of law and justice is advantageous to the society; and it was with a view to this advantage that men, by their voluntary conventions, established it. After it is once established by these conventions, it is *naturally* attended with a strong sentiment of morals, which can proceed from nothing but our sympathy with the interests of society. We need no one explication of that esteem which attends such of the natural virtues as have a tendency to the public good.[1]

The Origin of Our Ideas

By DAVID HUME

This selection is taken from *A Treatise of Human Nature,* Vol. I, Book I, Section I, *loco citato,* Vol. I, pp. 15–18.

ALL THE PERCEPTIONS of the human mind resolve themselves into two distinct kinds, which I shall call *impressions* and *ideas.* The difference betwixt these consists in the degrees of force and liveliness, with which they strike upon the mind, and make their

---

[1] In the postscript to his letter to Francis Hutcheson, dated Sept. 17, 1739, Hume wrote: "I cannot forbear recommending another thing to your consideration. Actions are not virtuous nor vicious; but only so far as there are proofs of certain qualities or durable principles in the mind. This is a point I should have established more expressly than I have done. Now I desire you to consider, if there be any quality, that is virtuous, without having a tendency either to the public good or to the good of the person who possesses it. If there be none without these tendencies, we may conclude, that their merit is derived from sympathy. I desire you would only consider the tendencies of qualities, not their actual operation, which depends on chance." From *Letters of David Hume,* edited by J. Y. T. Grieg. Oxford at the Clarendon Press, 1932, Vol. I, Letter 13, p. 34. *(Editor's note.)*

way into our thought or consciousness. Those perceptions which enter with most force and violence, we may name *impressions;* and, under this name, I comprehend all our sensations, passions, and emotions, as they make their first appearance in the soul. By *ideas* I mean the faint images of these in thinking and reasoning; such as, for instance, all the perceptions excited by the present discourse, excepting only those which arise from the sight and touch, and excepting the immediate pleasure or uneasiness it may occasion. I believe it will not be very necessary to employ many words in explaining this distinction. Everyone of himself will readily perceive the difference betwixt feeling and thinking. The common degrees of these are easily distinguished; though it is not impossible but, in particular instances, they may very nearly approach to each other. Thus, in sleep, in a fever, in madness, or in any very violent emotions of soul, our ideas may approach to our impressions: as, on the other hand, it sometimes happens, that our impressions are so faint and low, that we cannot distinguish them from our ideas. But, notwithstanding this near resemblance in a few instances, they are in general so very different that no one can make a scruple to rank them under distinct heads, and assign to each a peculiar name to mark the difference.[1]

There is another division of our perceptions, which it will be convenient to observe, and which extends itself both to our impressions and ideas. This division is into *simple* and *complex.* Simple perceptions, or impressions and ideas, are such as admit of no distinction nor separation. The complex are the contrary to these, and may be distinguished into parts. Though a particular color, taste, and smell, are qualities all united together in

---

[1] I here make use of these terms, *impression* and *idea,* in a sense different from what is usual, and I hope this liberty will be allowed me. Perhaps I rather restore the word idea to its original sense, from which Mr. Locke had perverted it, in making it stand for all our perceptions. By the term of impression, I would not be understood to express the manner in which our lively perceptions are produced in the soul, but merely the perceptions themselves; for which there is no particular name, either in English or any other language that I know of.

this apple, it is easy to perceive they are not the same, but are at least distinguishable from each other.

Having, by these divisions, given an order and arrangement to our objects, we may now apply ourselves to consider, with the more accuracy, their qualities and relations. The first circumstance that strikes my eye, is the great resemblance betwixt our impressions and ideas in every other particular, except their degree of force and vivacity. The one seems to be, in a manner, the reflection of the other; so that all the perceptions of the mind are double, and appear both as impressions and ideas. When I shut my eyes, and think of my chamber, the ideas I form are exact representations of the impressions I felt; nor is there any circumstance of the one which is not to be found in the other. In running over my other perceptions, I find still the same resemblance and representation. Ideas and impressions appear always to correspond to each other. This circumstance seems to me remarkable, and engages my attention for a moment.

Upon a more accurate survey I find I have been carried away too far by the first appearance, and that I must make use of the distinction of perceptions into *simple* and *complex*, to limit this general decision, *that all our ideas and impressions are resembling*. I observe that many of our complex ideas never had impressions that corresponded to them, and that many of our complex impressions never are exactly copied in ideas. I can imagine to myself such a city as the New Jerusalem, whose pavement is gold, and walls are rubies, though I never saw any such. I have seen Paris; but shall I affirm I can form such an idea of that city, as will perfectly represent all its streets and houses in their real and just proportions?

I perceive, therefore, that though there is, in general, a great resemblance betwixt our *complex* impressions and ideas, yet the rule is not universally true, that they are exact copies of each other. We may next consider, how the case stands with our *simple* perceptions. After the most accurate examination of which I am capable, I venture to affirm, that the rule here holds without any exception, and that every simple idea has a simple impression, which resembles it, and every simple impression a correspondent idea. The idea of red, which we form in the dark, and that impression which strikes our eyes in sunshine, differ only in degree, not in nature. That the case is the same with all our simple impressions and ideas it is impossible to prove by a particular enumeration of them. Every one may satisfy himself in this point by running over as many as he pleases. But if any one should deny this universal resemblance, I know no way of convincing him, but by desiring him to show a simple impression that has not a correspondent idea, or a simple idea that has not a correspondent impression. If he does not answer this challenge, as it is certain he cannot, we may, from his silence and our observation, establish our conclusion.

Thus we find that all simple ideas and impressions resemble each other; and, as the complex are formed from them, that these two species of perception are exactly correspondent. . . . Therefore, we shall here content ourselves with establishing one general proposition: *That all our simple ideas in their first appearance, are derived from simple impressions, which are correspondent to them, and which they exactly represent.*

The Ideas of Cause and Effect and Necessary Connection

By DAVID HUME

This selection is taken from *A Treatise of Human Nature,* Book I, Part III, Section II, *loco citato,* Vol. I, pp. 101–05, 199–200, 212–13.

WE MUST CONSIDER the idea of causation, and see from what origin it is derived. It is impossible to reason justly, without understanding perfectly the idea concerning which we reason; and it is impossible perfectly to understand any idea, without tracing it up to its origin, and examining that primary impression, from which it arises. The examination of the impression bestows a clearness on the idea; and the examination of the idea bestows a like clearness on all our reasoning.

Let us therefore cast our eye on any two objects, which we will call cause and effect, and turn them on all sides, in order to find that impression, which produces an idea of such prodigious consequence. At first sight I perceive, that I must not search for it in any of the particular *qualities* of the objects; since, whichever of these qualities I pitch on, I find some object that is not possessed of it, and yet falls under the denomination of cause or effect. And indeed there is nothing existent, either externally or internally, which is not to be considered either as a cause or an effect; though it is plain there is no one quality which universally belongs to all beings, and gives them a title to that denomination.

The idea then of causation must be derived from some *relation* among objects; and that relation we must now endeavor to discover. I find in the first place, that whatever objects are considered as causes or effects, are *contiguous;* and that nothing can operate in a time or place, which is ever so little removed from those of its existence. Though distant objects may sometimes seem productive of each other, they are commonly found upon examination to be linked by a chain of causes, which are contiguous among themselves, and to the distant objects; and when in any particular instance we cannot discover this connection we still presume it to exist. We may therefore consider the relation of *contiguity* as essential to that of causation. . . .

The second relation I shall observe as essential to causes and effects, is not so universally acknowledged, but is liable to some controversy. It is that of *priority* of time in the cause before the effect. Some pretend that it is not absolutely necessary a cause should precede its effect; but that any object or action, in the very first moment of its existence, may exert its productive quality, and give rise to another object or action, perfectly contemporary with itself. But beside that experience in most instances seems to contradict this opinion, we may establish the relation of priority by a kind of inference or reasoning. It is an established maxim, both in natural and moral philosophy, that an object, which exists for any time in its full perfection without producing another, is not its sole cause; but is assisted by some other principle which pushes it from its state of inactivity, and makes it exert that energy, of which it was secretly possessed. Now if any cause may be perfectly contemporary with its effect, it is certain, according to this maxim, that they must all of them be so; since any one of them, which retards its operation for a single moment, exerts not itself at that very individual time, in which it might have operated; and therefore is no proper cause. The consequence of this would be no less than the destruction of that succession of cause, which we observe in the world; and indeed the utter annihilation of time. For if one cause were contemporary with *its* effect, and so on, it is plain there would be no such thing as succession, and all objects must be coexistent.

If this argument appear satisfactory, it is well. If not, I beg the reader to allow me the same liberty, which I have used in the preceding case, of supposing it such. For he shall find, that the affair is of no great importance.

Having thus discovered or supposed the two relations of *contiguity* and *succession* to be essential to causes and effects, I find I am stopped short, and can proceed no further in considering any single instance of cause and effect. Motion in one body is regarded upon impulse as the cause of motion in another. When we consider these objects with the utmost attention, we find only that the one body approaches the other; and that the motion of it precedes that of the other, but without any sensible interval. It is in vain to rack ourselves with *further* thought and reflection upon this subject. We can go no *further* in considering this particular instance.

Should anyone leave this instance, and pretend to define a cause, by saying it is something productive of another, it is evident he would say nothing. For what does he mean by *production?* Can he give any definition of it, that will not be the same with that of causation? If he can, I desire it may be produced. If he cannot, he here runs in a circle, and gives a synonymous term instead of a definition.

Shall we then rest content with these two relations of contiguity and succession, as affording a complete idea of causation? By no means. An object may be contiguous and prior to another, without being considered as its cause. There is a *necessary connection* to be taken into consideration; and that relation is of much greater importance, than any of the other two above mentioned. . . .

What is our idea of necessity, when we say that two objects are necessarily connected together? Upon this head I repeat, what I have often had occasion to observe, that as we have no idea that is not derived from an impression, we must find some impression that gives rise to this idea of necessity, if we assert we have really such an idea. In order to do this, I consider in what objects necessity is commonly supposed to lie: and, finding that it is always ascribed to causes and effects, I turn my eye to two objects supposed to be placed in that relation, and examine them in all the situations of which they are susceptible. I immediately perceive that they are *contiguous* in time and place, and that the object we call cause *precedes* the other we call effect. In no one instance can I go any further, nor is it possible for me to discover any third relation betwixt these objects. I therefore enlarge my view to comprehend several instances, where I find like objects always existing in like relations of contiguity and succession. At first sight this seems to serve but little to my purpose. The reflection on several instances only repeats the same objects; and therefore can never give rise to a new idea. But upon further inquiry I find, that the repetition is not in every particular the same, but produces a new impression, and by that means the idea which I at present examine. For after a frequent repetition I find, that upon the appearance of one of the objects, the mind is *determined* by custom to consider its usual attendant, and to consider it in a stronger light upon account of its relation to the first object. It is this impression, then, or *determination,* which affords me the idea of necessity. . . .

The necessary connection betwixt causes and effects is the foundation of our inference from one to the other. The foundation of our inference is the transition arising from the accustomed union. They are, therefore, the same.

The idea of necessity arises from some impression. There is no impression conveyed by our senses, which can give rise to that idea. It must, therefore, be derived from some internal impression, or impression of reflection. There is no internal impression which has any relation to the present business, but that propensity, which custom produces, to pass from an object to the idea of its usual attendant. This, therefore, is the essence of necessity. Upon the whole, necessity is something that exists in the mind, not in objects; nor is it possible for us ever to form the most distant idea of it, considered as a quality in bodies. Either we have no idea of necessity, or necessity is nothing but that determination of the thought to pass from causes to effects, and from effects to causes, according to their experienced union.

Thus, as the necessity, which makes two times two equal to four, or three angles of a triangle equal to two right ones, lies only in the act of the understanding, by which we consider and compare these ideas; in like manner, the necessity of power, which unites causes and effects, lies in the determination of the mind to pass from the one to the other. The efficacy or energy of causes is neither placed in the causes themselves, nor in the Deity, nor in the concurrence of these two principles; but belongs entirely to the soul, which considers the union of two or more objects in all past instances. It is here that the real power of cause is placed, along with their connection and necessity.

Scepticism

By David Hume

This selection is from *A Treatise of Human Nature*, Book I, Sections I & VI, *loco citato*, Vol. I, pp. 229–34, 238–40, 310–15, 331–32.

IN ALL demonstrative sciences the rules are certain and infallible; but when we apply them, our fallible and uncertain faculties are very apt to depart from them, and fall into error. We must, therefore, in every reasoning form a new judgment, as a check or control on our first judgment or belief; and must enlarge our view to comprehend a kind of history of all the instances, wherein our understanding has deceived us, compared with those wherein its testimony was just and true. Our reason must be considered as a kind of cause, of which truth is the natural effect; but such a one as, by the irruption of other causes, and by the inconstancy of our mental powers, may frequently be prevented. By this means all knowledge degenerates into probability; and this probability is greater or less, according to our experience of the veracity or deceitfulness of our understanding, and according to the simplicity or intricacy of the question.

There is no algebraist nor mathematician so expert in his science, as to place entire confidence in any truth immediately upon his discovery of it, or regard it as any thing but a mere probability. Every time he runs over his proofs, his confidence increases; but still more by the approbation of his friends; and is raised to its utmost perfection by the universal assent and applauses of the learned world. Now, it is evident that this gradual increase of assurance is nothing but the addition of new probabilities, and is derived from the constant union of causes and effects, according to past experience and observation.

In accounts of any length or importance, merchants seldom trust to the infallible certainty of numbers for their security, but by the artificial structure of the accounts, produce a probability beyond what is derived from the skill and experience of the accountant. For that is plainly of itself some degree of probability; though uncertain and variable, according to the degrees of his experience and length of account. Now as none will maintain, that our assurance in a long numeration exceeds probability, I may safely affirm, that there scarce is any proposition concerning numbers, of which we can have a fuller security. For it is easily possible, by gradually diminishing the numbers, to reduce the longest series of addition to the most simple question which can be formed, to an addition of two single numbers; and upon this supposition we shall find it impracticable to show the precise limits of knowledge and of probability, or discover that particular number at which the one ends and the other begins. But knowledge and probability are of such contrary and disagreeing natures, that they cannot well run insensibly into each other, and that because they will not divide, but must be either entirely present or entirely absent. Besides, if any single addition were certain, every one would be so, and consequently the whole or total sum; unless the whole can be different from all its parts. I had almost said, that this was certain; but I reflect that it must reduce *itself*, as well as every other reasoning, and from knowledge degenerate into probability.

Since, therefore, all knowledge resolves itself into probability, and becomes at last of the same nature with that evidence which we employ in common life, we must now examine this latter species of reasoning, and see on what foundation it stands.

In every judgment which we can form concerning probability, as well concerning knowledge, we ought always to correct the first judgment, derived from the nature of the object, by another judgment, derived from the nature of the understanding. It is certain a man of solid sense and long experience ought to have, and usually has, a greater assurance in his opinions, than one that is foolish and ignorant, and that our sentiments have different degrees of authority, even with ourselves, in proportion to the degrees of our reason and experience. In the man of the best sense and longest experience, this authority is never entire, since even such a one must be conscious of many errors in the past, and must still dread the like for the future. Here then arises a new species of probability to correct and regulate the first, and fix its just standard and proportion. As demonstration is subject to the control of probability, so is probability liable to a new correction by a reflex act of the mind, wherein the nature of our understanding, and our reasoning from the first probability, become our objects.

Having thus found in every probability, beside the original uncertainty inherent in the subject, a new uncertainty, derived from the weakness of that faculty which judges, and having adjusted these two together, we are obliged by our reason to add a new doubt, derived from the possibility of error in the estimation we make of the truth and fidelity of our faculties. This is a doubt which immediately occurs to us, and of which, if we would closely pursue our reason, we cannot avoid giving a decision. But this decision, though it should be favorable to our preceding judgment, being founded only on probability, must weaken still further our first evidence, and must itself be weakened by a fourth doubt of the same kind, and so on *in infinitum;* till at last there remain nothing of the original probability, however great we may suppose it to have been, and however small the diminution by every new uncertainty. No finite object can subsist under a decrease repeated *in infinitum;* and even the vastest quantity, which can enter into human imagination, must in this manner be reduced to nothing. Let our first belief be never so strong, it must infallibly perish, by passing through so many new examinations of which each diminishes somewhat of its force and vigor. When I reflect on the natural fallibility of my judgment, I have less confidence in my opinions, than when I only consider the objects concerning which I reason; and when I proceed still further, to turn the scrutiny against every successive estimation I make of my faculties, all the rules of logic require a continual diminution, and at last a total extinction of belief and evidence.

Should it here be asked me, whether I sincerely assent to this argument, which I seem to take such pains to inculcate, and whether I be really one of those sceptics, who hold that all is uncertain, and that our judgment is not in *any* thing possessed of *any* measures of truth and falsehood: I should reply, that this question is entirely superfluous, and that neither I, nor any other person, was ever sincerely and constantly of that opinion. Nature, by an absolute and uncontrollable necessity, has determined us to judge as well as to breathe and feel: nor can we any more forbear viewing certain objects in a stronger and fuller light, on account of their customary connection with a present impression, than we can hinder ourselves from thinking, as long as we are awake, or seeing the surrounding bodies, when we turn our eyes towards them in broad sunshine. Whoever has taken the pains to refute the cavils of this *total* scepticism, has really disputed without an antagonist, and endeavoured by arguments to establish a faculty, which nature has antecedently implanted in the mind, and rendered unavoidable.

My intention then in displaying so carefully the arguments of that fantastic sect, is only to make the reader sensible of the truth of my hypothesis, *that all our reasonings concerning causes and effects, are derived from nothing but custom; and that belief is more properly an act of the sensitive, than of the cogitative part of our natures. . . .*

We may well ask, *What causes induce us to believe in the existence of body?* but it is in vain to ask, *Whether there be body or not?* The subject, then, of our present inquiry, is concerning the *causes* which induce us to believe in the existence of body; and my reasonings on this head I shall begin with a distinction, which at first sight may seem superfluous, but which will contribute very much to the perfect understanding of what follows. We ought to examine apart these two questions, which are commonly confounded together, viz. Why we attribute a *continued* existence to objects, even when they are not present to the senses; and why we suppose them to have an existence *distinct* from the mind and perception? Under this last head I comprehend their situation as well as relations, their *external* position as well as the *independence* of their existence and operation. These two questions concerning the continued and distinct existence of body are intimately connected together. For if the objects of our senses continue to exist, even when they are not perceived, their existence is of course independent of and distinct from the perception; and *vice versa*, if their existence be independent of the perception, and distinct from it, they must continue to exist, even though they be not perceived. But though the decision of the one question decides the other; yet that we may the more easily discover the principles of human nature, from whence the decision arises, we shall carry along with us this distinction, and shall consider, whether it be the *senses*, *reason*, or the *imagination* that produces the opinion of a *continued* or of a *distinct* existence. These are the only questions that are intelligible on the present subject. For as to the notion of external existence, when taken for something specifically different from our perceptions, we have already shown its absurdity. (See Part II, Sect. 6.)

To begin with the *senses*, it is evident these faculties are incapable of giving rise to the notion of the *continued* existence of their objects, after they no longer appear to the senses. For that is a contradiction in terms, and supposes that the senses continue to operate, even after they have ceased all manner of operation. These faculties, therefore, if they have any influence in the present case, must produce the opinion of a distinct, not of a continued existence; and in order to do that, must present their impressions either as images and representations, or as these very distinct and external existences.

That our senses offer not their impressions as the images of something *distinct*, or *independent*, and *external*, is evident; because they convey to us nothing but a single perception, and never give us the least intimation of any thing beyond. A single perception can never produce the idea of a double existence, but by some inference either of reason or imagination. When the mind looks further than what immediately appears to it, its conclusions can never be put to the account of the senses; and it certainly looks further, when from a single perception it infers a double existence, and supposes the relations of resemblance and causation betwixt them.

If our senses, therefore, suggest any idea of distinct existences, they must convey the impressions as those very existences,
by a kind of fallacy and illusion. Upon this head we may
observe, that all sensations are felt by the mind, such as they
really are, and that, when we doubt whether they present themselves as distinct objects, or as mere impressions, the difficulty
is not concerning their nature, but concerning their relations
and situation. Now, if the senses presented our impressions as
external to, and independent of ourselves, both the objects and
ourselves must be obvious to our senses, otherwise they could
not be compared by these faculties. The difficulty then, is, how
far we are *ourselves* the objects of our senses. . . .

There are some philosophers, who imagine we are every
moment intimately conscious of what we call our *self;* that we
feel its existence and its continuance in existence; and are certain, beyond the evidence of a demonstration, both of its perfect
identity and simplicity. The strongest sensation, the most violent
passion, say they, instead of distracting us from this view, only
fix it the more intensely, and make us consider their influence
on *self* either by their pain or pleasure. To attempt a further
proof of this were to weaken its evidence; since no proof can
be derived from any fact of which we are so intimately conscious; nor is there any thing, of which we can be certain, if we
doubt of this.

Unluckily all these positive assertions are contrary to that
very experience which is pleaded for them; nor have we any
idea of *self,* after the manner it is here explained. For, from
what impression could this idea be derived. This question it is
impossible to answer without a manifest contradiction and
absurdity; and yet it is a question which must necessarily be
answered, if we would have the idea of self pass for clear and
intelligible. It must be some one impression that gives rise to
every real idea. But self or person is not any one impression, but
that to which our several impressions and ideas are supposed
to have a reference. If any impression gives rise to the idea of
self, that impression must continue invariably the same, through
the whole course of our lives, since self is supposed to exist

after that manner. But there is no impression constant and invariable. Pain and pleasure, grief and joy, passions and sensations succeed each other, and never all exist at the same time. It cannot therefore be from any of these impressions, or from any other, that the idea of self is derived; and consequently there is no such idea.

But further, what must become of all our particular perceptions upon this hypothesis? All these are different, and distinguishable, and separable from each other, and may be separately considered, and may exist separately, and have no need of anything to support their existence. After what manner therefore do they belong to self, and how are they connected with it? For my part, when I enter most intimately into what I call *myself*, I always stumble on some particular perception or other, of heat or cold, light or shade, love or hatred, pain or pleasure. I never can catch *myself* at any time without a perception, and never can observe any thing but the perception. When my perceptions are removed for any time, as by sound sleep, so long am I insensible of *myself*, and may truly be said not to exist. And were all my perceptions removed by death, and could I neither think, nor feel, nor see, nor love, nor hate, after the dissolution of my body, I should be entirely annihilated, nor do I conceive what is further requisite to make me a perfect nonentity. If any one, upon serious and unprejudiced reflection, thinks he has a different notion of *himself*, I must confess I can reason no longer with him. All I can allow him is, that he may be in the right as well as I, and that we are essentially different in this particular. He may, perhaps, perceive something simple and continued, which he calls *himself;* though I am certain there is no such principle in me.

But setting aside some metaphysicians of this kind, I may venture to affirm of the rest of mankind, that they are nothing but a bundle or collection of different perceptions, which succeed each other with an inconceivable rapidity, and are in a perpetual flux and movement. Our eyes cannot turn in their sockets without varying our perceptions. Our thought is still more variable than our sight; and all our other senses and faculties contribute to this change; nor is there any single power of the soul, which remains unalterably the same, perhaps for one moment. The mind is a kind of theatre, where several perceptions successively make their appearance; pass, repass, glide away, and mingle in an infinite variety of postures and situations. There is properly no *simplicity* in it at one time, nor *identity* in different, whatever natural propension we may have to imagine that simplicity and identity. The comparison of the theatre must not mislead us. They are the successive perceptions only, that constitute the mind; nor have we the most distant notion of the place where these scenes are represented, or of the materials of which it is composed.

What then gives us so great a propension to ascribe an identity to these successive perceptions, and to suppose ourselves possessed of an invariable and uninterrupted existence through the whole course of our lives? In order to answer this question, we must distinguish betwixt personal identity, as it regards our thought or imagination, and as it regards our passions or the concern we take in ourselves. The first is our present subject; and to explain it perfectly we must take the matter pretty deep, and account for that identity, which we attribute to plants and animals; there being a great analogy betwixt it and the identity of a self or person.

We have a distinct idea of an object that remains invariable and uninterrupted through a supposed variation of time; and this idea we call that of *identity* or *sameness.* We have also a distinct idea of several different objects existing in succession, and connected together by a close relation; and this to an accurate view affords as perfect a notion of *diversity*, as if there were no manner of relation among the objects. But though these two ideas of identity and a succession of related objects, be in themselves perfectly distinct, and even contrary, yet it is certain that, in our common way of thinking, they are generally confounded with each other. That action of the imagination by which we consider the uninterrupted and invariable object, and that by which we reflect on the succession of related objects, are almost the same to the feeling; nor is there much more effort of thought required in the latter case than in the former. The relation facilitates the transition of the mind from one object to another, and renders its passage as smooth as if it contemplated one continued object. The resemblance is the cause of the confusion and mistake, and makes us substitute the notion of identity, instead of that of related objects. However at one instant we may consider the related succession as variable or interrupted, we are sure the next to ascribe to it a perfect identity, and regard it as invariable and uninterrupted. Our propensity to this mistake is so great from the resemblance above mentioned, that we fall into it before we are aware; and though we incessantly correct ourselves by reflection, and return to a more accurate method of thinking, yet we cannot long sustain our philosophy, or take off this bias from the imagination. Our last resort is to yield to it, and boldly assert that these different related objects are in effect the same, however interrupted and variable. In order to justify to ourselves this absurdity, we often feign some new and unintelligible principle, that connects the objects together, and prevents their interruption or variation. Thus we feign the continued existence of the perceptions of our senses, to remove the interruption; and run into the notion of a *soul*, and *self*, and *substance*, to disguise the variation. . . .

The *intense* view of these manifold contradictions and imperfections in human reason has so wrought upon me, and heated my brain, that I am ready to reject all belief and reasoning, and can look upon no opinion even as more probable or likely than another. Where am I, or what? From what causes do I derive my existence, and to what condition shall I return? Whose favor shall I court, and whose anger must I dread? What beings surround me? and on whom have I any influence, or who have any influence on me? I am confounded with all these questions, and begin to fancy myself in the most deplorable condition imaginable, environed with the deepest darkness, and utterly deprived of the use of every member and faculty.

Most fortunately it happens, that since reason is incapable of dispelling these clouds, Nature herself suffices to that purpose, and cures me of this philosophical melancholy and delirium, either by relaxing this bent of mind, or by some avocation, and lively impression of my senses, which obliterate all these chimeras. I dine, I play a game of backgammon, I converse, and am merry with my friends; and when, after three or four hours' amusement, I would return to these speculations, they appear so cold, and strained, and ridiculous, that I cannot find in my heart to enter into them any further.

Here, then, I find myself absolutely and necessarily determined to live, and talk, and act like other people in the common affairs of life. But notwithstanding that my natural propensity, and the course of my animal spirits and passions reduce me to this indolent belief in the general maxims of the world, I still feel such remains of my former disposition, that I am ready to throw all my books and papers into the fire, and resolve never more to renounce the pleasures of life for the sake of reasoning and philosophy.[1]

---

[1] See Sir William Hamilton's evaluation of Hume's skepticism, pp. 220 ff., below. (Editor's note.)

CHAPTER III

Adam Smith

(1723–1790)

The Man and His Work

By Noah Porter

Adam Smith, 1723–1790, was born at Kirkaldy, Scotland; studied at the University of Glasgow, 1737–40, and at Balliol College, Oxford, 1740–1747. Lecturer at Edinburgh, 1748–57. Professor of Logic in the University of Glasgow, 1751–2, and Professor of Moral Philosophy, 1752–1763. Travelled on the continent, 1764–1766. Composed his *Wealth of Nations* at Kirkaldy, 1766–78. Resided at London, 1776–78. Commissioner of Customs at Edinburgh, 1776–1790. In 1787, Rector of the University of Glasgow.

Adam Smith is best known by his *Wealth of Nations,* London, 1776. Additions and corrections to first and second editions, 1784. Third edition, with additions and corrections, 1784, and many subsequent editions in England and America. *The Theory of Moral Sentiments,* 1759, was his most important contribution to Ethical Philosophy, and is characterized by consummate ingenuity in its analyses of ethical phenomena, and by the affluence of its interesting illustrations, and the elegance of its somewhat elaborate diction. The theory of Smith is an offshoot of the theory of Hume.

David Hume, in his *Enquiry concerning the Principles of Morals,* had agreed with Hutcheson—in this differing from Hobbes, with whom he affiliates in so many particulars—in holding that man is capable of a disinterested regard for others. He had also discriminated in ethical experiences between the functions of *reason* and *sentiment*—in this making an important advance upon Hutcheson, who did not assign to reason a distinct and special office. He emphasized with great earnestness the doctrine that utility is the fundamental characteristic of virtuous actions. Hume had also insisted, almost in the spirit of paradox, that virtue and vice, merit and demerit, are as properly affirmed of the operations of the understanding, and even of any pleasing or displeasing corporeal or personal qualities, as of the sentiments or acts in which there is a voluntary element. That which leads us to approve or disapprove moral excellences and defects he calls Benevolence in the *Enquiry,* and Sympathy in the *Treatise of Human Nature.*

The doctrine of sympathy, which Hume had suggested, was accepted by Smith, then was established as a fundamental and all-comprehensive principle, and expanded into an elaborate theory. *The Theory of Moral Sentiments* is devoted especially to the analyses of those ethical experiences which are subjective, rather than to the definition of the objective conceptions which are the material of moral science. The sense of Propriety, of Merit and Demerit, and the sense of Approbation and Disapprobation, are the prominent topics of discussion in the first three parts of the *Essay.* All these are resolved into an original capacity in man to sympathize with the real or supposed sentiments of his fellow men. To sympathize with the feelings of another, in the view of Adam Smith, is to approve them. All those actions with which we entirely sympathize we judge to be morally proper. As we must alternately lower or elevate our feelings to the tone of those which we suppose to be entertained by our fellow-men, we have the feeling of the morally beautiful and the morally sublime. This sympathy is sometimes divided between two classes of actions which conflict. In the benevolent affections there is a double motive, in our sympathy with those who feel these affections and with those who are the objectives of these affections.

Merit and demerit arise from our sympathy with the supposed gratitude of those who are benefited, and the resentment of those who are injured. The sentiment is compound, being made up of a direct sympathy with the sentiments of the agent, and an indirect sympathy with the gratitude of the recipient. Our sentiments of moral approbation and disapprobation depend on our sympathy with the supposed approbation of our fellow-men in general. "We suppose ourselves the spectators of our own behavior, and endeavor to imagine what effect it would in this light produce in us." Man could no more originate nor apply the conception of the law of duty, except in society, than he could judge of his own face without the aid of a mirror. The rules of morality are all derived from, and constituted by, these supposed opinions of society. They coincide with what Locke calls the philosophical law of right and wrong, or the law of opinion or reputation. (*Essay*, B. II., c. xxviii, section 10.)

Other elements which are secondary come in subsequently to modify and enforce the sentiments which originate in sympathy. "When we approve of any character or action, our sentiments are derived from four sources: *first*, we sympathize with the motives of the agent; *secondly*, we enter into the gratitude of those who have been benefited by his actions; *thirdly*, we observe that his conduct has been agreeable to the general rules by which these two sympathies generally act; and last of all, when we consider such actions as forming parts of a system of behavior which tends to promote happiness of the individual or of society, they appear to derive a beauty from this utility not unlike that which we ascribe to any well-contrived machine."

It hardly need be added that Smith agrees with Hume in attaching great importance to custom, *i.e.*, in impliedly recognizing the operation of association as supreme. His theory in its fundamental assumptions in a certain sense brings him back to this as the principle which is formative of the entire structure of our moral judgments and emotions.

Adam Smith's Theory of Moral Sentiment

By DUGALD STEWART

This selection is from Dugald Stewart's memoir of Adam Smith entitled *Account of the Life and Writings of Adam Smith*. It is taken from *The Collected Works of Dugald Stewart*, edited by Sir William Hamilton (Edinburgh: Thomas Constable and Co., 1858), Vol. X, pp. 16–30. However, on the death of Hamilton in May, 1856, John Veitch became editor, and he did part of the editorial work on Volume X. See the Preface to that volume. This memoir is reprinted as the Introduction to the Bohn's Libraries edition of Adam Smith's *The Theory of Moral Sentiments*. It was also published in the third volume of the *Transactions of the Royal Society of Edinburgh,* and was read by Stewart at different periods in 1793 at meetings of the Royal Society.

IT WAS THE OPINION of Dr. Cudworth, and also of Dr. Clarke, that moral distinctions are perceived by that power of the mind, which distinguishes truth from falsehood. This system it was one great object of Dr. Hutcheson's philosophy to refute, and in opposition to it, to show that the words Right and Wrong express certain agreeable and disagreeable qualities in actions, which it is not the province of reason but of feeling to perceive; and to that power of perception which renders us susceptible of pleasure or of pain from the view of virtue or of vice, he gave the name of the *Moral Sense*. His reasonings upon the subject are in the main acquiesced in, both by Mr. Hume and Mr. Smith; but they differ from him in one important particular—Dr. Hutcheson plainly supposing, that the Moral Sense is a simple principle of our constitution, of which no account can be given; whereas the other two philosophers have both attempted to analyze it into other principles more general. Their systems, however, with respect to it are very different from each other. According to Mr. Hume, all the qualities which are denominated virtuous are useful either to ourselves or to others, and the pleasure which we derive from the view of them is the pleasure of *utility*. Mr. Smith, without rejecting entirely Mr. Hume's doctrine, proposes another of his own far more comprehensive, a doctrine with which he thinks all the most celebrated theories of morality invented by his predecessors coincide in part, and from some partial view of which he apprehends that they have all proceeded. . . .

The fundamental principle of Mr. Smith's theory is, that the primary objects of our moral perceptions are the actions of other men; and that our moral judgments with respect to our own conduct are only applications to ourselves of decisions which we have already passed on the conduct of our neighbour. His work accordingly includes *two* distinct inquiries, which, although sometimes blended together in the execution of his general design, it is necessary for the reader to discriminate carefully from each other, in order to comprehend all the different bearings of the author's argument. The aim of the former inquiry is, to explain in what manner we learn to judge of the conduct of our neighbour; that of the latter, to show how, by applying these judgments to ourselves, we acquire *a sense of duty,* and a feeling of its paramount authority over all our other principles of action.

Our moral judgments, both with respect to our own conduct and that of others, include *two* distinct perceptions: *first,* A perception of conduct as right or wrong; and, *secondly,* A perception of the merit or demerit of the agent. To that quality of conduct which moralists, in general, express by the word Rectitude, Mr. Smith gives the name of Propriety; and he begins his theory with inquiring in what it consists, and how we are led to form the idea of it. The leading principles of his doctrine on this subject are comprehended in the following propositions:

1. It is from our own experience alone, that we can form any idea of what passes in the mind of another person on any particular occasion; and the only way in which we can form this idea is by supposing ourselves in the same circumstances with him, and conceiving how we should be affected if we were so situated. It is impossible for us, however, to conceive our-

selves placed in any situation, whether agreeable or otherwise, without feeling an effect of the same kind with what would be produced by the situation itself; and of consequence the attention we give at any time to the circumstances of our neighbour, must affect us somewhat in the same manner, although by no means in the same degree, as if these circumstances were our own.

That this imaginary change of place with other men, is the real source of the interest we take in their fortunes, Mr. Smith attempts to prove by various instances. "When we see a stroke aimed, and just ready to fall upon the leg or arm of another person, we naturally shrink and draw back our own leg or our own arm; and when it does fall, we feel it in some measure, and are hurt by it as well as the sufferer. The mob, when they are gazing at a dancer on the slack-rope, naturally writhe and twist and balance their own bodies, as they see him do, and as they feel that they themselves must do if in his situation." [1] The same thing takes place, according to Mr. Smith, in every case in which our attention is turned to the condition of our neighbour. "Whatever is the passion which arises from any object in the person principally concerned, an analogous emotion springs up, at the thought of his situation, in the breast of every attentive spectator. . . . In every passion of which the mind of man is susceptible, the emotions of the bystander always correspond to what, by bringing the case home to himself, he imagines should be the sentiments of the sufferer." [2]

To this principle of our nature which leads us to enter into the situation of other men, and to partake with them in the passions which these situations have a tendency to excite, Mr. Smith gives the name of *Sympathy* or *Fellow-feeling*, which two words he employs as synonymous. Upon some occasions he acknowledges, that sympathy arises merely from the view of a certain emotion in another person; but in general it arises, not so much from the view of the emotion, as from that of the situation which excites it.

---

[1] *Moral Sentiments,* Part I, sect. i, chap. 1; sixth and later editions.
[2] *Ibid.*

2. A sympathy or fellow-feeling between different persons is always agreeable to both. When I am in a situation which excites any passion, it is pleasant to me to know, that the spectators of my situation enter with me into all its various circumstances, and are affected with them in the same manner as I am myself. On the other hand, it is pleasant to the spectator to observe this correspondence of his emotions with mine.

3. When the spectator of another man's situation, upon bringing home to himself all its various circumstances, feels himself affected in the same manner with the person principally concerned, he approves of the affection or passion of this person as just and proper, and suitable to its object. The exceptions which occur to this observation are, according to Mr. Smith, only apparent.

> A stranger passes by us in the street with all the marks of the deepest affliction; and we are immediately told that he has just received the news of the death of his father. It is impossible that, in this case, we should not approve of his grief. Yet it may often happen, without any defect of humanity on our part, that, so far from entering into the violence of his sorrow, we should scarce conceive the first movements of concern upon his account. . . . We have learned, however, from experience, that such a misfortune naturally excites such a degree of sorrow, and we know that if we took time to examine his situation fully and in all its parts, we should, without doubt, most sincerely sympathize with him. It is upon the consciousness of this conditional sympathy, that our approbation of his sorrow is founded, even in those cases in which that sympathy does not actually take place; and the general rules derived from our preceding experience of what . . . our sentiments would commonly correspond with, correct the impropriety of our present emotions.[3]

By the *Propriety* therefore of any affection or passion exhibited by another person, is to be understood its suitableness to the object which excites it. Of this suitableness I can judge only from the coincidence of the affection with that which I feel, when I conceive myself in the same circumstances; and the per-

---

[3] *Ibid.,* Part I, sect. i, chap. 3; sixth and later editions.

ception of this coincidence is the foundation of the sentiment of *Moral Approbation*.

4. Although, when we attend to the situation of another person, and conceive ourselves to be placed in his circumstances, an emotion of the same kind with that which he feels naturally arises in our own mind, yet this sympathetic emotion bears but a very small proportion, in point of degree, to what is felt by the person principally concerned. In order, therefore, to obtain the pleasure of mutual sympathy, nature teaches the spectator to strive, as much as he can, to *raise his emotion* to a level with that which the object would really produce: and, on the other hand, she teaches the person whose passion this object has excited, to *bring it down,* as much as he can, to a level with that of the spectator.

5. Upon these two different efforts are founded *two* different sets of virtues. Upon the effort of the spectator to enter into the situation of the person principally concerned, and to raise his sympathetic emotions to a level with the emotions of the actor, are founded the gentle, the amiable virtues; the virtues of candid condescension and indulgent humanity. Upon the effort of the person principally concerned to lower his own emotions, so as to correspond as nearly as possible with those of the spectator, are founded the great, the awful, and respectable virtues; the virtues of self-denial, of self-government, of that command of the passions, which subjects all the movements of our nature to what our own dignity and honour, and the propriety of our own conduct, require.

As a farther illustration of the foregoing doctrine, Mr. Smith considers particularly the degree of the different passions which are consistent with propriety, and endeavours to show, that, in every case, it is decent or indecent to express a passion strongly, according as mankind are disposed, or not disposed, to sympathize with it. It is unbecoming, for example, to express strongly any of those passions which arise from a certain condition of the body; because other men, who are not in the same condition, cannot be expected to sympathize with them. It is unbecoming to cry out with bodily pain; because the sympathy felt by the spectator bears no proportion to the acuteness of what is felt by the sufferer. The case is somewhat similar with those passions which take their origin from a particular turn or habit of the imagination.

In the case of the unsocial passions of hatred and resentment, the sympathy of the spectator is divided between the person who feels the passion, and the person who is the object of it. "We are concerned for both, and our fear for what the one may suffer damps our resentment for what the other has suffered." [4] Hence the imperfect degree in which we sympathize with such passions; and the propriety, when we are under their influence, of moderating their expression to a much greater degree than is required in the case of any other emotions.

The reverse of this takes place with respect to all the social and benevolent affections. The sympathy of the spectator with the person who feels them, coincides with his concern for the person who is the object of them. It is this redoubled sympathy which renders these affections so peculiarly becoming and agreeable.

The selfish emotions of grief and joy, when they are conceived on account of our own private good or bad fortune, hold a sort of middle place between our social and our unsocial passions. They are never so graceful as the one set, nor so odious as the other. Even when excessive, they are never so disagreeable as excessive resentment; because no opposite sympathy can ever interest us against them: and when most suitable to their objects, they are never so agreeable as impartial humanity and just benevolence; because no double sympathy can ever interest us for them.

After these general speculations concerning the propriety of actions, Mr. Smith examines how far the judgments of mankind concerning it are liable to be influenced, in particular cases, by the prosperous or the adverse circumstances of the agent. The scope of his reasoning on this subject is directed to show (in opposition to the common opinion,) that when there is no

---

[4] *Ibid.*, Part I, sect. ii, chap. 3; sixth and later editions.

envy in the case, our propensity to sympathize with joy is much stronger than our propensity to sympathize with sorrow: and, of consequence, that it is more easy to obtain the approbation of mankind in prosperity than in adversity. From the same principle he traces the origin of ambition, or of the desire of rank and pre-eminence; the great object of which passion is, to attain that situation which sets a man most in the view of general sympathy and attention, and gives him an easy empire over the affections of others.

Having finished the analysis of our sense of Propriety and of Impropriety, Mr. Smith proceeds to consider our sense of Merit and Demerit; which he thinks has also a reference, in the first instance, not to our own characters, but to the characters of our neighbours. In explaining the origin of this part of our moral constitution, he avails himself of the same principle of sympathy, into which he resolves the sentiment of moral approbation.

The words *propriety* and *impropriety*, which applied to an affection of the mind, are used in this theory (as has been already observed) to express the suitableness or unsuitableness of the affection to its exciting *cause*. The words *merit* and *demerit* have always a reference (according to Mr. Smith) to the *effect* which the affection tends to produce. When the tendency of an affection is beneficial, the agent appears to us a proper object of reward; when it is hurtful, he appears the proper object of punishment.

The principles of our nature which most directly prompt us to reward and to punish are gratitude and resentment. To say of a person, therefore, that he is deserving of reward or of punishment, is to say, in other words, that he is a proper object of gratitude or of resentment; or, which amounts to the same thing, that he is to some person or persons the object of a gratitude or of a resentment, which every reasonable man is ready to adopt and sympathize with.

It is, however, very necessary to observe, that we do not thoroughly sympathize with the gratitude of one man towards another, merely because this other has been the cause of his good fortune, unless he has been the cause of it from motives which we entirely go along with. Our sense, therefore, of the good desert of an action, is a compounded sentiment, made up of an indirect sympathy with the person to whom the action is beneficial, and of a direct sympathy with the affections and motives of the agent. The same remark applies, *mutatis mutandis,* to our sense of demerit, or of ill-desert.

From these principles, it is inferred, that the only actions which appear to us deserving of reward, are actions of a beneficial tendency, proceeding from proper motives; the only actions which seem to deserve punishment, are actions of a hurtful tendency, proceeding from improper motives. A mere want of beneficence exposes to no punishment; because the mere want of beneficence tends to do no real positive evil. A man, on the other hand, who is barely innocent, and contents himself with observing strictly the laws of justice with respect to others, can merit only, that his neighbours, in their turn, should observe religiously the same laws with respect to him.

These observations lead Mr. Smith to anticipate a little the subject of the second great division of his work, by a short inquiry into the origin of our sense of justice, *as applicable to our own conduct;* and also of our sentiments of remorse, and of good desert.

The origin of our sense of justice, as well as of all our other moral sentiments, he accounts for by means of the principle of sympathy. When I attend only to the feelings of my own breast, my own happiness appears to me of far greater consequence than of all the world besides. But I am conscious that, in this excessive preference, other men cannot possibly sympathize with me, and that to them I appear only one of the crowd, in whom they are no more interested than in any other individual. If I wish, therefore, to secure their sympathy and approbation (which, according to Mr. Smith, are the objects of the strongest desire of my nature), it is necessary for me to regard my happiness, not in that light in which it appears to myself, but in that light in which it appears to mankind in general. If an unprovoked injury is offered to me, I know that society will sympathize with my resentment; but if I injure the interests of another, who never injured me, merely because they stand in the way of my own, I perceive evidently, that society will sympathize with *his* resentment, and that I shall become the object of general indignation.

When upon any occasion I am led by the violence of passion to overlook these considerations, and, in the case of a competition of interests, to act according to my own feelings, and not according to those of impartial spectators, I never fail to incur the punishment of remorse. When my passion is gratified, and I begin to reflect coolly on my conduct I can no longer enter into the motives from which it proceeded; it appears as improper to me as to the rest of the world; I lament the effects it has produced; I pity the unhappy sufferer whom I have injured; and I feel myself a just object of indignation to mankind. "Such," says Mr. Smith, "is the nature of that sentiment which is properly called remorse. It is made up of shame from the sense of the impropriety of past conduct; of grief for the effects of it; of pity for those who suffer by it; and of the dread and terror of punishment from the consciousness of the justly provoked resentment of all rational creatures." [5]

The opposite behaviour of him who, from proper motives, has performed a generous action, inspires, in a similar manner, the opposite sentiment of conscious merit, or of deserved reward.

The foregoing observations contain a general summary of Mr. Smith's principles with respect to the origin of our moral sentiments, in so far at least as they relate to the conduct of others. He acknowledges, at the same time, that the sentiments of which we are conscious, on particular occasions, do not always coincide with these principles; and that they are frequently modified by other considerations, very different from the propriety or impropriety of the affections of the agent, and also from the beneficial or hurtful tendency of these affections. The good or the bad consequences which accidentally follow from an

---

[5] *Ibid.,* Part II, sect. ii, chap. 2; sixth and later editions.

action, and which, as they do not depend on the agent, ought undoubtedly, in point of justice, to have no influence on our opinion, either of the propriety or the merit of his conduct, scarcely ever fail to influence considerably our judgment with respect to both; by leading us to form a good or a bad opinion of the prudence with which the action was performed, and by animating our sense of the merit or demerit of his design. These facts, however, do not furnish any objections which are peculiarly applicable to Mr. Smith's theory; for whatever hypothesis we may adopt with respect to the origin of our moral perceptions, all men must acknowledge, that, in so far as the prosperous or the unprosperous event of an action depends on fortune or on accident, it ought neither to increase nor to diminish our moral approbation or disapprobation of the agent. And accordingly it has, in all ages of the world, been the complaint of moralists, that the actual sentiments of mankind should so often be in opposition to this equitable and indisputable maxim. In examining, therefore, this irregularity of our moral sentiments, Mr. Smith is to be considered, not as obviating an objection peculiar to his own system, but as removing a difficulty which is equally connected with every theory on the subject which has ever been proposed. So far as I know, he is the first philosopher who has been fully aware of the importance of the difficulty, and he has indeed treated it with great ability and success. The explanation which he gives of it is not warped in the least by any peculiarity in his own scheme; and, I must own, it appears to me to be the most solid and valuable improvement he has made in this branch of science. It is impossible to give any abstract of it in a sketch of this kind; and, therefore, I must content myself with remarking, that is consists of three parts. The first explains the causes of this irregularity of sentiment; the second, the extent of its influence; and the third, the important purposes in which it is subservient. His remarks on the last of these heads are more particularly ingenious and pleasing; as their object is to show, in opposition to what we should be disposed at first to apprehend, that when nature implanted the seeds of this irregularity in the human breast, her leading intention was, to promote the happiness and perfection of the species.

The remaining part of Mr. Smith's theory is employed in showing, in what manner *our sense of duty* comes to be formed, in consequence of an application to ourselves of the judgments we have previously passed on the conduct of others.

In entering upon this inquiry, which is undoubtedly the most important in the work, and for which the foregoing speculations are, according to Mr. Smith's theory, a necessary preparation, he begins with stating *the fact* concerning our consciousness of merited praise or blame; and it must be owned, that the first aspect of the fact, as he himself states it, appears not very favourable to his principles. That the great object of a wise and virtuous man, is not to act in such a manner as to obtain the actual approbation of those around him, but to act so as to render himself the *just* and *proper* object of their approbation, and that his satisfaction with his own conduct depends much more on the consciousness of *deserving* this approbation, than from that of really enjoying it, he candidly acknowledges; but still he insists, that although this may seem, at first view, to intimate the existence of some moral faculty which is not borrowed from without, our moral sentiments have always some secret reference, either to what are, or to what upon a certain condition would be, or to what we imagine ought to be, the sentiments of others; and that if it were possible, that a human creature could grow up to manhood without any communication with his own species, he could no more think of his own character, or of the propriety or demerit of his own sentiments and conduct, than of the beauty or deformity of his own face. There is indeed a tribunal within the breast, which is the supreme arbiter of all our actions, and which often mortifies us amidst the applause, and supports us under the censure of the world; yet still, he contends, that if we inquire into the origin of its institution, we shall find that its jurisdiction is, in a great measure, derived from the authority of that very tribunal whose decisions it so often and so justly **reverses.**

When we first come into the world, we, for some time, fondly pursue the impossible project of gaining the good-will and approbation of everybody. We soon, however, find, that this universal approbation is unattainable; that the most equitable conduct must frequently thwart the interests or the inclinations of particular persons, who will seldom have candour enough to enter into the propriety of our motives, or to see that this conduct, how disagreeable soever to them, is perfectly suitable to our situation. In order to defend ourselves from such partial judgments, we soon learn to set up in our own minds, a judge between ourselves and those we live with. We conceive ourselves as acting in the presence of a person, who has no particular relation, either to ourselves, or to those whose interests are affected by our conduct; and we study to act in such a manner as to obtain the approbation of this supposed impartial spectator. It is only by consulting him that we can see whatever relates to ourselves in its proper shape and dimensions.

There are *two* different occasions, on which we examine our own conduct, and endeavour to view it in the light in which the impartial spectator would view it. First, when we are about to act; and, secondly, after we have acted. In both cases, our views are very apt to be partial.

When we are about to act, the eagerness of passion seldom allows us to consider what we are doing with the candour of an indifferent person. When the action is over, and the passions which prompted it have subsided, although we can undoubtedly enter into the sentiments of the indifferent spectator much more coolly than before, yet it is so disagreeable to us to think ill of ourselves, that we often purposely turn away our view from those circumstances which might render our judgment unfavorable. Hence that self-deceit which is the source of half the disorders of human life.

In order to guard ourselves against its delusions, nature leads us to form insensibly, by our continual observations upon the conduct of others, certain general rules concerning what is fit and proper either to be done or avoided. Some of their actions shock all our natural sentiments; and when we observe other people affected in the same manner with ourselves, we are confirmed in the belief, that our disapprobation was just. We naturally, therefore, lay it down as a general rule, that all such actions are to be avoided, as tending to render us odious, contemptible, or punishable; and we endeavour, by habitual reflection, to fix this general rule in our minds, in order to correct the misrepresentations of self-love, if we should ever be called on to act in similar circumstances. The man of furious resentment, if he were to listen to the dictates of that passion, would regard the death of his enemy as but a small compensation for a trifling wrong. But his observations on the conduct of others have taught him how horrible such sanguinary revenges are; and he has impressed it on his mind as an invariable rule, to abstain from them upon all occasions. This rule preserves its authority with him, checks the impetuosity of his passion, and corrects the partial views which self-love suggests; although, if this had been the first time in which he considered such an action, he would undoubtedly have determined it to be just and proper, and what every impartial spectator would approve of. A regard to such general rules of morality, constitutes, according to Mr. Smith, what is properly called *the sense of duty.*

I before hinted, that Mr. Smith does not reject entirely from his system that principle of *utility,* of which the perception in any action or character constitutes, according to Mr. Hume, the sentiment of moral approbation. That no qualities of the mind are approved of as virtues, but such as are useful or agreeable, either to the person himself or to others, he admits to be a proposition that holds universally; and he also admits, that the sentiment of approbation with which we regard virtue, is enlivened by the perception of this utility, or, as he explains the fact, it is enlivened by our sympathy with the happiness of those to whom the utility extends: but still he insists, that it is not the view of this utility which is either the first or principal source of moral approbation.

To sum up the whole of his doctrine in a few words: "When we approve of any character or action, the sentiments which we feel are derived from *four* different sources. First, we sympathize with the motives of the agent; secondly, we enter into the gratitude of those who receive the benefit of his actions; thirdly, we observe that his conduct has been agreeable to the general rules by which those two sympathies generally act; and, lastly, when we consider such actions as making a part of a system of behaviour which tends to promote the happiness either of the individual or of society, they appear to derive a beauty from this utility, not unlike that which we ascribe to any well-contrived machine." These different sentiments, he thinks, exhaust completely, in every instance that can be supposed, the compounded sentiment of moral approbation. "After deducting," says he, "in any one particular case, all that must be acknowledged to proceed from some one or other of these four principles, I should be glad to know what remains; and I shall freely allow this overplus to be ascribed to a moral sense, or to any other peculiar faculty, provided anybody will ascertain precisely what this overplus is." [6]

Mr. Smith's opinion concerning the nature of Virtue is involved in his theory concerning the principle of Moral Approbation. The idea of virtue, he thinks, always implies the idea of propriety, or of the suitableness of the affection to the object which excites it; which suitableness, according to him, can be determined in no other way than by the sympathy of impartial spectators with the motives of the agent. But still he apprehends, that this description of virtue is incomplete; for although in every virtuous action propriety is an essential ingredient, it is not always the sole ingredient. Beneficent actions have in them another quality, by which they appear, not only to deserve approbation, but recompense, and excite a superior degree of esteem, arising from a double sympathy with the motives of the agent, and the gratitude of those who are the objects of his affection. In this respect, beneficence appears to him to be distinguished from the inferior virtues of prudence, vigilance, circumspection, temperance, constancy, firmness, which are always regarded with approbation, but which confer no merit. This

---

[6] *Ibid.*, Part VII, sect. iii, chap. 3; sixth and later editions.

distinction, he apprehends, has not been sufficiently attended to by moralists; the principles of some affording no explanation of the approbation we bestow on the inferior virtues; and those of others accounting as imperfectly for the peculiar excellency which the supreme virtue of beneficence is acknowledged to possess.

Of the Manner in Which We Judge of the Propriety or Impropriety of the Affections of Other Men, by Their Concord or Dissonance With Our Own

By ADAM SMITH

This selection is from Part I, Section II, Chapters 2 and 3, of the first edition of Adam Smith's *The Theory of Moral Sentiments* (London: A. Millar, MDCCLIX), pp. 22–40. It expounds Smith's theory of mutual sympathy and the impartial spectator.

WHEN THE ORIGINAL PASSIONS of the person principally concerned are in perfect concord with the sympathetic emotions of the spectator, they necessarily appear to this last just and proper, and suitable to their objects; and, on the contrary, when, upon bringing the case home to himself, he finds that they do not coincide with what he feels, they necessarily appear to him unjust and improper, and unsuitable to the causes which excite them. To approve of the passions of another, therefore, as suitable to their objects, is the same thing, as to observe that we entirely sympathize with them; and not to approve of them as such, is the same thing as to observe that we do not entirely sympathize with them. The man who resents the injuries that have been done to me, and observes that I resent them precisely as he does, necessarily approves of my resentment. The man whose sympathy keeps time to my grief, cannot but admit the reasonableness of my sorrow. He who admires the same poem, or the same picture, and admires them exactly as I do, must surely allow the justness of my admiration. He who laughs at the same joke, and laughs along with me, cannot well deny the propriety of my laughter. On the contrary, the person who, upon these different occasions, either feels no such emotion as that which I feel, or feels none that bears any proportion to mine, cannot avoid disapproving my sentiments on account of their dissonance with his own. If my animosity goes beyond what the indignation of my friend can correspond to; if my grief exceeds what his most tender compassion can go along with; if my admiration is either too high or too low to tally with his own; if I laugh loud and heartily at what he only smiles, or, on the contrary, only smile when he laughs loud and heartily; in all these cases, as soon as he comes from considering the object, to observe how I am affected by it, according as there is more or less disproportion between his sentiments and mine, I must incur a greater or less degree of his disapprobation: and upon all occasions his own sentiments are the standards and measures by which he judges of mine.

To approve of another man's opinions is to adopt those opinions, and to adopt them is to approve of them. If the same arguments which convince you convince me likewise, I necessarily approve of your conviction; and if they do not, I necessarily disapprove of it: neither can I possibly conceive that I should do the one without the other. To approve or disapprove, therefore, of the opinions of others is acknowledged, by everybody, to mean no more than to observe their agreement or disagreement with our own. But this is equally the case with regard to our approbation or disapprobation of the sentiments or passions of others.

There are, indeed, some cases in which we seem to approve without any sympathy or correspondence of sentiments, and in which, consequently, the sentiment of approbation would seem to be different from the perception of this coincidence. A little attention, however, will convince us that even in these cases our

approbation is ultimately founded upon a sympathy or correspondence of this kind. I shall give an instance in things of a
very frivolous nature, because in them the judgments of mankind
are less apt to be perverted by wrong systems. We may often
approve of a jest, and think the laughter of the company quite
just and proper, though we ourselves do not laugh, because,
perhaps, we are in a grave humour, or happen to have our
attention engaged with other objects. We have learned, however, from experience, what sort of pleasantry is upon most occasions capable of making us laugh, and we observe that this
is one of that kind. We approve, therefore, of the laughter of
the company, and feel that it is natural and suitable to its object; because, though in our present mood we cannot easily
enter into it, we are sensible that upon most occasions we should
very heartily join in it.

The same thing often happens with regard to all the other
passions. A stranger passes by us in the street with all the marks
of the deepest affliction; and we are immediately told that he has
just received the news of the death of his father. It is impossible
that, in this case, we should not approve of his grief. Yet it
may often happen, without any defect of humanity on our part,
that, so far from entering into the violence of his sorrow, we
should scarce conceive the first movement of concern upon his
account. Both he and his father, perhaps, are entirely unknown
to us, or we happen to be employed about other things, and do
not take time to picture out in our imagination the different
circumstances of distress which must occur to him. We have
learned, however, from experience, that such a misfortune naturally excites such a degree of sorrow, and we know that if we
took time to consider his situation fully and in all its parts, we
should, without doubt, most sincerely sympathize with him. It
is upon the consciousness of this conditional sympathy, that our
approbation of his sorrow is founded, even in those cases in
which that sympathy does not actually take place; and the
general rules derived from our preceding experience of what,
upon most occasions, our sentiments would correspond with,
correct the impropriety of our present emotions.

The sentiment or affection of the heart from which any

action proceeds, and upon which its whole virtue or vice must ultimately depend, may be considered under two different aspects, or in two different relations; first, in relation to the cause that excites it, or the motive that gives occasion to it; and secondly, in relation to the end that it proposes, or the effect that it tends to produce.

In the suitableness or unsuitableness, in the proportion or disproportion which the affection seems to bear to the cause or object which excites it, consists the propriety or impropriety, the decency or ungracefulness of the consequent action.

In the beneficial or hurtful nature of the effects which the affection aims at, or tends to produce, consists the merit or demerit of the action, the qualities by which it is entitled to reward, or is deserving of punishment.

Philosophers have, of late years, considered chiefly the tendency of affections, and have given little attention to the relation which they stand in to the cause which excites them. In common life, however, when we judge of any person's conduct, and of the sentiments which directed it, we constantly consider them under both these aspects. When we blame in another man the excesses of love, of grief, of resentment, we not only consider the ruinous effects which they tend to produce, but the little occasion which was given for them. The merit of his favourite, we say, is not so great, his misfortune is not so dreadful, his provocation is not so extraordinary, as to justify so violent a passion. We should have indulged, we say; perhaps, have approved of the violence of his emotion, had the cause been in any respect proportioned to it.

When we judge in this manner of any affection, as proportioned or disproportioned to the cause which excites it, it is scarce possible that we should make use of any other rule or canon but the correspondent affection in ourselves. If, upon bringing the case home to our own breast, we find that the sentiments which it gives occasion to coincide and tally with our own, we necessarily approve of them as proportioned and suitable to their objects: if otherwise, we necessarily disapprove of them, as extravagant and out of proportion.

Every faculty in one man is the measure by which he judges

of the like faculty in another. I judge of your sight by my sight, of your ear by my ear, of your reason by my reason, of your resentment by my resentment, of your love by my love. I neither have, nor can have, any other way of judging about them.

We may judge of the propriety or impropriety of the sentiments of another person by their correspondence or disagreement with our own, upon two different occasions; either, first, when the objects which excite them are considered without any peculiar relation, either to ourselves or to the person whose sentiments we judge of; or, secondly, when they are considered as peculiarly affecting one or other of us.

1. With regard to those objects which are considered without any peculiar relation either to ourselves or to the person whose sentiments we judge of; wherever his sentiments entirely correspond with our own, we ascribe to him the qualities of taste and good judgment. The beauty of a plain, the greatness of a mountain, the ornaments of a building, the expression of a picture, the composition of a discourse, the conduct of a third person, the proportions of different qualities and numbers, the various appearances which the great machine of the universe is perpetually exhibiting, with the secret wheels and springs which produce them; in a word, all the general subjects of science and taste, are what we and our companion regard, as having no peculiar relation to either of us. We both look at them from the same point of view, and we have no occasion for sympathy, or for that imaginary change of situations from which it arises, in order to produce, with regard to these the most perfect harmony of sentiments and affections. If, notwithstanding, we are often differently affected, it arises either from the different degrees of attention, which our different habits of life allow us to give easily to the several parts of those complex objects, or from the different degrees of natural acuteness in the faculty of the mind to which they are addressed.

When the sentiments of our companion coincide with our own in things of this kind, which are obvious and easy, and in which, perhaps, we never found a single person who differed from us, though we, no doubt, must approve of them, yet he seems to deserve no praise or admiration on account of them.

But when they not only coincide with our own, but lead and direct our own; when in forming them he appears to have attended to many things which we had overlooked, and to have adjusted them to all the various circumstances of their objects; we not only approve of them but wonder and are surprised at their uncommon and unexpected acuteness and comprehensiveness, and he appears to deserve a very high degree of admiration and applause. For approbation heightened by wonder and surprise, constitutes the sentiment which is properly called admiration, and of which applause is the natural expression. The decision of the man who judges that exquisite beauty is preferable to the grossest deformity, or that twice two are equal to four, must certainly be approved of by all the world, but will not, surely, be much admired. It is the acute and delicate discernment of the man of taste, who distinguishes the minute, and scarce perceptible differences of beauty and deformity; it is the comprehensive accuracy of the experienced mathematician, who unravels, with ease, the most intricate and perplexed proportions; it is the great leader in science and taste, the man who directs and conducts our own sentiments, the extent and superior justness of whose talents astonish us with wonder and surprise, who excites our admiration and seems to deserve our applause: and upon this foundation is grounded the greater part of the praise which is bestowed upon what are called the intellectual virtues.

The utility of those qualities, it may be thought, is what first recommends them to us; and, no doubt, the consideration of this, when we come to attend to it, gives them a new value. Originally, however, we approve of another man's judgment, not as something useful, but as right, as accurate, as agreeable to truth and reality: and it is evident we attribute those qualities to it for no other reason but because we find that it agrees with our own. Taste, in the same manner, is originally approved of, not as useful, but as just, as delicate, and as precisely suited to its object. The idea of the utility of all qualities of this kind, is plainly an after-thought, and not what first recommends them to our approbation.

2. With regard to those objects, which affect in a particular

manner either ourselves or the person whose sentiments we judge of, it is at once more difficult to preserve this harmony and correspondence, and at the same time, vastly more important. My companion does not naturally look upon the misfortune that has befallen me, or the injury that has been done me, from the same point of view in which I consider them. They affect me much more nearly. We do not view them from the same station, as we do a picture, or a poem, or a system of philosophy, and are, therefore, apt to be very differently affected by them. But I can much more easily overlook the want of this correspondence of sentiments with regard to such indifferent objects as concern neither me nor my companion, than with regard to what interests me so much as the misfortune that has befallen me, or the injury that has been done me. Though you despise that picture, or that poem, or even that system of philosophy, which I admire, there is little danger of our quarrelling upon that account. Neither of us can reasonably be much interested about them. They ought all of them to be matters of great indifference to us both; so that, though our opinions may be opposite, our affections may still be very nearly the same. But it is quite otherwise with regard to those objects by which either you or I are particularly affected. Though your judgments in matters of speculation, though your sentiments in matters of taste, are quite opposite to mine, I can easily overlook this opposition; and if I have any degree of temper, I may still find some entertainment in your conversation, even upon those very subjects. But if you have either no fellow-feeling for the misfortunes I have met with, or none that bears any proportion to the grief which distracts me; or if you have either no indignation at the injuries I have suffered, or none that bears any proportion to the resentment which transports me, we can no longer converse upon these subjects. We become intolerable to one another. I can neither support your company, nor you mine. You are confounded at my violence and passion, and I am enraged at your cold insensibility and want of feeling.

In all such cases, that there may be some correspondence of sentiments between the spectator and the person principally concerned, the spectator must, first of all endeavour, as much as he can, to put himself in the situation of the other, and to bring home to himself every little circumstance of distress which can possibly occur to the sufferer. He must adopt the whole case of his companion with all its minutest incidents; and strive to render, as perfect as possible, that imaginary change of situation upon which his sympathy is founded.

After all this, however, the emotions of the spectator will still be very apt to fall short of the violence of what is felt by the sufferer. Mankind, though naturally sympathetic, never conceive, for what has befallen another, that degree of passion which naturally animates the person principally concerned. That imaginary change of situation, upon which their sympathy is founded, is but momentary. The thought of their own safety, the thought that they themselves are not really the sufferers, continually intrudes itself upon them; and though it does not hinder them from conceiving a passion somewhat analogous to what is felt by the sufferer, hinders them from conceiving any thing that approaches to the same degree of violence. The person concerned is sensible of this, and, at the same time. passionately desires a more complete sympathy. He longs for that relief which nothing can afford him but the entire concord of the affections of the spectators with his own. To see the emotions of their hearts, in every respect, beat time to his own, in the violent and disagreeable passions, constitutes his sole consolation. But he can only hope to obtain this by lowering his passion to that pitch, in which the spectators are capable of going along with him. He must flatten, if I may be allowed to say so, the sharpness of its natural tone, in order to reduce it to harmony and concord with the emotions of those who are about him. What they feel, will, indeed, always be, in some respects, different from what he feels, and compassion can never be exactly the same with original sorrow; because the secret consciousness that the change of situations, from which the sympathetic sentiment arises, is but imaginary, not only lowers it in degree, but in some measure, varies it in kind, and gives it a quite different modification. These two sentiments, however, may, it is evident, have such a correspondence with one another, as is sufficient for the harmony of society. Though they will never be unisons, they may be concords, and this is all that is wanted or required.

In order to produce this concord, as nature teaches the spectators to assume the circumstances of the person principally concerned, so she teaches this last in some measure to assume those of the spectators. As they are continually placing themselves in his situation, and thence conceiving emotions similar to what he feels; so he is as constantly placing himself in theirs, and thence conceiving some degree of that coolness about his own fortune, with which he is sensible that they will view it. As they are constantly considering what they themselves would feel, if they actually were the sufferers, so he is as constantly led to imagine in what manner he would be affected if he was only one of the spectators of his own situation. As their sympathy makes them look at it, in some measure, with his eyes, so his sympathy makes him look at it, in some measure, with theirs, especially when in their presence and acting under their observation: and as the reflected passion, which he thus conceives, is much weaker than the original one, it necessarily abates the violence of what he felt before he came into their presence, before he began to recollect in what manner they would be affected by it, and to view his situation in this candid and impartial light.

The mind, therefore, is rarely so disturbed but that the company of a friend will restore it to some degree of tranquillity and sedateness. The breast is, in some measure, calmed and composed the moment we come into his presence. We are immediately put in mind of the light in which he will view our situation, and we begin to view it ourselves in the same light; for the effect of sympathy is instantaneous. We expect less sympathy from a common acquaintance than from a friend: we cannot open to the former all those little circumstances which we can unfold to the latter: we assume, therefore, more tranquillity before him, and endeavour to fix our thoughts upon those general outlines of our situation which he is willing to consider. We expect still less sympathy from an assembly of strangers, and we assume, therefore, still more tranquillity before them, and always endeavour to bring down our passion to that pitch, which the particular company we are in may be expected to go along with. Nor is this merely an assumed appearance: for if we are at all masters of ourselves, the presence of a mere acquaintance will really compose us, still more than that of a friend; and that of an assembly of strangers still more than that of a mere acquaintance.

Society and conversation, therefore, are the most powerful remedies for restoring the mind to its tranquillity, if, at any time, it has unfortunately lost it; as well as the best preservatives of that equal and happy temper, which is so necessary to self-satisfaction and enjoyment. Men of retirement and speculation, who are apt to sit brooding at home over either grief or resentment, though they may often have more humanity, more generosity, and a nicer sense of honour, yet seldom possess that equality of temper which is so common among men of the world.

Of the Influence and Authority of the General Rules of Morality, and That They Are Justly Regarded as the Laws of the Deity

By Adam Smith

This selection is from Part III, Section III, of the first edition of Adam Smith's *The Theory of Moral Sentiments* (London: A. Millar, MDCCLIX), pp. 273–96. It deals with the sense of duty and the relation of the general moral laws regulating man's conduct to "the precepts that were prescribed to him by the infinite goodness of his Creator."

THE REGARD to those general rules of conduct, is what is properly called a sense of duty, a principle of the greatest consequence in human life, and the only principle by which the bulk of mankind are capable of directing their actions. Many men behave very decently, and through the whole of their lives avoid any considerable degree of blame, who yet, perhaps, never felt the sentiment upon the propriety of which we found our approbation of their conduct, but acted merely from a regard to what they saw were the established rules of behaviour. The man who has received great benefits from another person, may, by the natural coldness of his temper, feel but a very small degree of the sentiment of gratitude. If he has been virtuously educated, however, he will often have been made to observe how odious those actions appear which denote a want of this sentiment, and how amiable the contrary. Though his heart therefore is not warmed with any grateful affection, he will strive to act as if it was, and will endeavour to pay all those regards and attentions to his patron which the liveliest gratitude could suggest. He will visit him regularly; he will never talk of him but with expressions of the highest esteem, and of the many obligations which he owes to him. And what is more, he will cheerfully embrace every opportunity of making a proper return for past services. He may do all this too without any hypocrisy or blamable dissimulation, without any selfish intention of obtaining new favours, and without any design of imposing either upon his benefactor or the public. The motive of his actions may be no other than a reverence for the established rule of duty, a serious and earnest desire of acting, in every respect, according to the law of gratitude. A wife, in the same manner, may sometimes not feel that tender regard for her husband which is suitable to the relation that subsists between them. If she has been virtuously educated, however, she will endeavour to act as if she felt it, to be careful, officious, faithful, and sincere, and to be deficient in none of those attentions which the sentiment of conjugal affection could have prompted her to perform. Such a friend and such a wife, are neither of them, undoubtedly, the very best of their kinds; and though both of them may have the most serious and earnest desire to fulfil every part of their duty, yet they will fail in many nice and delicate regards, they will miss many opportunities of obliging, which they could never have overlooked if they had possessed the sentiment that is proper to their situation. Though not the very first of their kinds, however, they are perhaps the second; and if the regard to the general rules of conduct has been very strongly impressed upon them, neither of them will fail in any very essential part of their duty. None but those of the happiest mold are capable of suiting with exact justness, their sentiments and behaviour to the smallest difference of situation, and of acting upon all occasions with the most delicate and accurate propriety. The coarse clay of which the bulk of mankind are formed, cannot be wrought up to such perfection. There is scarce any man, however, who by discipline, education, and example, may not be so impressed with a regard to general rules, as to act upon almost every occasion with tolerable decency, and through the whole of his life avoid any considerable degree of blame.

Without this sacred regard to general rules, there is no man whose conduct can be much depended upon. It is this which constitutes the most essential difference between a man of principle and honour and a worthless fellow. The one adheres, upon all occasions, steadily and resolutely to his maxims, and preserves through the whole of his life one even tenor of conduct. The other, acts variously and accidentally, as humour, inclination, or interest chance to be uppermost. Nay, such are the inequalities of humour to which all men are subject, that without this principle, the man who, in all his cool hours, had the most delicate sensibility to the propriety of conduct, might often be led to act absurdly upon the most frivolous occasions, and when it was scarce possible to assign any serious motive for his behaving in this manner. Your friend makes you a visit when you happen to be in a humour which makes it disagreeable to receive him: in your present mood his civility is very apt to appear an impertinent intrusion; and if you were to give way to the views of things which at this time occur, though civil in your temper, you would behave to him with coldness and contempt. What renders you incapable of such a rudeness, is nothing but a regard to the general rules of civility and hospitality, which prohibit it. That habitual reverence which your former experience has taught you for these, enables you to act, upon all such occasions, with nearly equal propriety, and hinders those inequalities of temper, to which all men are subject, from influencing your conduct in any very sensible degree. But if without regard to these general rules, even the duties of politeness, which are so easily observed, and which one can scarce have any serious motive to violate, would yet be so frequently violated, what would become of the duties of justice, of truth, of chastity, of fidelity, which it is often so difficult to observe, and which there may be so many strong motives to violate? But upon the tolerable observance of these duties, depends the very existence of human society, which would crumble into nothing if mankind were not generally impressed with a reverence for those important rules of conduct.

This reverence is still further enhanced by an opinion which is first impressed by nature, and afterwards confirmed by reasoning and philosophy, that those important rules of morality, are the commands and laws of the Deity, who will finally reward the obedient, and punish the transgressors of their duty.

This opinion or apprehension, I say, seems first to be impressed by nature. Men are naturally led to ascribe to those mysterious beings, whatever they are, which happen in any country, to be the object of religious fear, all their own sentiments and passions. They have no other, they can conceive no other to ascribe to them. Those unknown intelligences which they imagine but see not, must necessarily be formed with some sort of resemblance to those intelligences of which they have experience. During the ignorance and darkness of pagan superstition, mankind seems to have formed the ideas of their divinities with so little delicacy, that they ascribed to them, indiscriminately, all the passions of human nature, those not excepted which do the least honour to our species, such as lust, hunger, avarice, envy, revenge. They could not fail, therefore, to ascribe to those beings, for the excellence of whose nature they still conceived the highest admiration, those sentiments and qualities which are the great ornaments of humanity, and which seem to raise it to a resemblance to divine perfection, the love of virtue and beneficence, and the abhorrence of vice and injustice. The man who was injured, called upon Jupiter to be witness of the wrong that was done to him, and could not doubt, but that divine being would behold it with the same indignation which would animate the meanest of mankind, who looked on when injustice was committed. The man who did the injury, felt himself to be the proper object of the detestation and resentment of mankind; and his natural fears led him to impute the same sentiments to those awful beings, whose presence he could not avoid, and whose power he could not resist. These natural hopes and fears, and suspicions, were propagated by sympathy, and confirmed by education; and the Gods were universally represented and believed to be the rewarders of humanity and mercy, and the avengers of perfidy and injustice. And thus religion, even in its rudest form, gave a sanction to the rules of morality, long before the age of artificial reasoning and philosophy. That the terrors of religion should thus enforce the natural sense of duty, was of too much importance to the happiness of mankind, for nature to leave it dependent upon the slowness and uncertainty of philosophical researches.

These researches, however, when they came to take place, confirmed those original anticipations of nature. Upon whatever we suppose that our moral faculties are founded, whether upon a certain modification of reason, upon an original instinct, called a moral sense, or upon some other principle of our nature, it cannot be doubted, that they were given us for the direction of our conduct in this life. They carry along with them the most evident badges of this authority, which denote that they were set up within us to be the supreme arbiters of all our actions, to superintend all our senses, passions, and appetites, and to judge how far each of them was either to be indulged or restrained. Our moral faculties are by no means, as some have pretended, upon a level in this respect with the other faculties and appetites of our nature, endowed with no more right to restrain these last, than these last are to restrain them. No other faculty or principle of action judges of any other. Love does not judge of resentment, nor resentment of love. Those two passions may be opposite to one another, but cannot, with any propriety, be said to approve or disapprove of one another. But it is the peculiar office of those faculties now under our consideration to judge, to bestow censure or applause upon all the other principles of our nature. They may be considered as a sort of senses of which those principles are the objects. Every sense is supreme over its own objects. There is no appeal from the eye with regard to the beauty of colours, nor from the ear with regard to the harmony of sounds, nor from the taste with regard to the agreeableness of flavours. Each of those senses judges in the last resort of its own objects. Whatever gratifies the taste is sweet, whatever pleases the eye is beautiful, whatever soothes the ear is harmonious. The very essence of each of those qualities consists in its being fitted to please the sense to which it is addressed. It belongs to our moral faculties, in the same manner to determine when the ear ought to be soothed, when the eye ought to be indulged, when the taste ought to be gratified, when and how far every other principle of our nature ought either to be indulged or restrained. What is agreeable to our moral faculties, is fit and right, and proper to be done; the contrary, wrong, unfit and improper. The sentiments which they approve of, are graceful and becoming: the contrary, ungraceful and unbecoming. The very words right and wrong, fit, improper, graceful, unbecoming, mean only what pleases or displeases those faculties.

Since these, therefore, were plainly intended to be the governing principles of human nature, the rules which they prescribe, are to be regarded as the commands and laws of the Deity, promulgated by those vicegerents which he has thus set up within us. All general rules are commonly denominated laws: thus the general rules which bodies observe in the communication of motion, are called the laws of motion. But those general rules which our moral faculties observe in approving or condemning whatever sentiment or action is subjected to their examination, may much more justly be denominated such. They have a much greater resemblance to what are properly called laws, those general rules which the sovereign lays down to direct the conduct of his subjects. Like them they are rules to direct the free actions of men; they are prescribed most surely by a lawful superior, and are attended too with the sanction of rewards and punishments. Those vicegerents of God within us, never fail to punish the violation of them, by the torments of inward shame, and self-condemnation; and on the contrary always reward obedience with tranquility of mind, with contentment, and self-satisfaction.

There are innumerable other considerations which serve to confirm the same conclusion. The happiness of mankind, as well as of all other rational creatures, seems to have been the original purpose intended by the Author of Nature, when he brought them into existence. No other end seems worthy of that supreme wisdom and divine benignity which we necessarily ascribe to him; and this opinion, which we are led to by the abstract consideration of his infinite perfections, is still more confirmed by the examination of the works of nature, which seem all intended to promote happiness, and to guard against misery. But by acting according to the dictates of our moral faculties, we necessarily pursue the most effectual means for promoting the happiness of mankind, and may therefore be said, in some sense, to co-operate with the Deity, and to advance as far as in our power the plan of Providence. By acting otherways, on the contrary, we seem to obstruct, in some measure, the scheme which the Author of Nature has established for the happiness and perfection of the world, and to declare ourselves, if I may say so, in some measure the enemies of God. Hence we are naturally encouraged to hope for his extraordinary favour and reward in the one case, and to dread his vengeance and punishment in the other.

There are besides many other reasons, and many other natural principles, which all tend to confirm and inculcate the same salutary doctrine. If we consider the general rules by which external prosperity and adversity are commonly distributed in this life, we shall find, that notwithstanding the disorder in which all things appear to be in this world, yet even here every virtue naturally meets with its proper reward, with the recompense which is most fit to encourage and promote it; and this too so surely, that it requires a very extraordinary concurrence of circumstances entirely to disappoint it. What is the reward most proper for encouraging industry, prudence, and circumspection? Success in every sort of business. And is it possible that in the whole of life these virtues should fail of attaining it? Wealth and external honours are their proper recompense, and the recompense which they can seldom fail of acquiring. What reward is most proper for promoting the practice of truth, justice, and humanity? The confidence, the esteem, and love of those we live with. Humanity does not desire to be great, but to be beloved. It is not in being rich that truth and justice would rejoice, but in being trusted and believed, recompenses which those virtues must almost always acquire. By some very extraordinary and unlucky circumstance, a good man may come to be suspected of a crime of which he was altogether incapable, and upon that account be most unjustly exposed for the remaining part of his life to the horror and aversion of mankind. By an accident of this kind he may be said to lose his all, notwithstanding his integrity and justice; in the same manner as a cautious man, notwithstanding his utmost circumspection, may be ruined by an earthquake or an inundation. Accidents of the first kind, however, are perhaps still more rare, and still more contrary to the common course of things than those of the second; and it still remains true, that the practice of truth, justice, and humanity, is a certain and almost infallible method of acquiring what those virtues chiefly aim at, the confidence and love of those we live with. A person may be very easily misrepresented with regard to a particular action; but it is scarce possible that he should be so with regard to the general tenor of his conduct. An innocent man may be believed to have done wrong: this, however, will rarely happen. On the contrary, the established opinion of the innocence of his manners, will often lead us to absolve him where he has really been in the fault, notwithstanding very strong presumptions. A knave, in the same manner may escape censure, or even meet with applause, for a

particular knavery, in which his conduct is not understood. But
no man was ever habitually such, without being almost universally known to be so, and without being even frequently suspected of guilt, when he was in reality perfectly innocent. And
so far as vice and virtue can be either punished or rewarded
by the sentiments and opinions of mankind, they both, according
to the common course of things, meet even here with something
more than exact and impartial justice.

But though the general rules by which prosperity and adversity are commonly distributed, when considered in this cool
and philosophical light, appear to be perfectly suited to the
situation of mankind in this life, yet they are by no means suited
to some of our natural sentiments. Our natural love and admiration for some virtues is such, that we should wish to bestow on
them all sorts of honours and rewards, even those which we
must acknowledge to be the proper recompenses of other qualities with which those virtues are not always accompanied. Our
detestation, on the contrary, for some vices is such, that we
should desire to heap upon them every sort of disgrace and dis-
aster, those not excepted which are the natural consequences of
very different qualities. Magnanimity, generosity, and justice
command so high a degree of admiration, that we desire to see
them crowned with wealth, and power, and honours of every
kind, the natural consequences of prudence, industry, and application; qualities with which those virtues are not inseparably
connected. Fraud, falsehood, brutality, and violence, on the
other hand excite in every human breast such scorn and abhorrence, that our indignation rouses to see them possess those
advantages which they may in some sense be said to have merited, by the diligence and industry with which they are sometimes attended. The industrious knave cultivates the soil; the
indolent good man leaves it uncultivated. Who ought to reap
the harvest? Who starve, and who live in plenty? The natural
course of things decides it in favor of the knave: the natural
sentiments of mankind in favour of the man of virtue. Man
judges, that the good qualities of the one are greatly over-recom-
pensed by those advantages which they tend to procure him,

and that the omissions of the other are by far too severely punished by the distress which they naturally bring upon him; and
human laws, the consequences of human sentiments, forfeit the
life and the estate of the industrious and cautious traitor, and
reward, by extraordinary recompenses, the fidelity and public
spirit of the improvident and careless good citizen. Thus man
is by nature directed to correct, in some measure, that distribution of things which she herself would otherwise have made.
The rules which for this purpose she prompts him to follow,
are different from those which she herself observes. She bestows
upon every virtue, and upon every vice, that precise reward or
punishment which is best fitted to encourage the one, or to
restrain the other. She is directed by this sole consideration, and
pays little regard to the different degrees of merit or demerit,
which they may seem to possess in the sentiments and passions
of man. Man, on the contrary, pays regard to this only, and
would endeavour to render the state of every virtue precisely
proportioned to that degree of love and esteem, and of every
vice to that degree of contempt and abhorrence which he himself conceives for it. The rules which she follows are fit for
her, those which he follows for him. But both are calculated to
promote the same great end, the order of the world, and the
perfection and happiness of human nature.

But though man is thus employed to alter that distribution
of things which natural events would make, if left to themselves; though like the Gods of the poets, he is perpetually
interposing, by extraordinary means, in favour of virtue, and in
opposition to vice, and like them, endeavours to turn away the
arrow that is aimed at the head of the righteous, but accel-
erates the sword of destruction that is lifted up against the
wicked; yet he is by no means able to render the fortune of
either quite suitable to his own sentiments and wishes. The
natural course of things cannot be entirely controlled by the
impotent endeavours of man: the current is too rapid and too
strong for him to stop it; and though the rules which direct
it appear to have been established for the wisest and best purposes, they sometimes produce effects which shock all his nat-

ural sentiments. That a great combination of men, should
prevail over a small one; that those who engage in an enterprise with forethought and all necessary preparation, should
prevail over such as oppose them without an end; and that every
end should be acquired by those means only which nature has
established for acquiring it, seems to be a rule not only necessary and unavoidable in itself, but even useful and proper for
rousing the industry and attention of mankind. Yet, when in
consequence of this rule, violence and artifice prevail over sincerity and justice, what indignation does it not excite in the
breast of every human spectator? What sorrow and compassion
for the sufferings of the innocent, and what furious resentment
against the success of the oppressor? We are equally grieved
and enraged, at the wrong that is done, but often find it altogether out of our power to redress it. When we thus despair
of finding any force upon earth which can check the triumph
of injustice, we naturally appeal to heaven, and hope, that the
great author of our nature will himself execute hereafter, what
all the principles which he has given us, for the direction of
our conduct, prompt us to attempt even here; that he will complete the plan which he himself has thus taught us to begin; and
will, in a life to come, render to every one according to the
works which he had performed in this world. And thus we are
led to the belief of a future state, not only by the weaknesses,
by the hopes and fears of human nature, but by the noblest
and best principles which belong to it, by the love of virtue, and
by the abhorrence of vice and injustice.

"Does it suit the greatness of God," says the eloquent and
philosophical bishop of Clermont, with that passionate and
exaggerating force of imagination, which seems sometimes to
exceed the bounds of decorum; "does it suit the greatness of
God, to leave the world which he has created in so universal
a disorder? To see the wicked prevail almost always over the
just; the innocent dethroned by the usurper; the father become
the victim of the ambition of an unnatural son; the husband
expiring under the stroke of a barbarous and faithless wife?
From the height of his greatness ought God to behold those

melancholy events as a fantastical amusement, without taking
any share in them? Because he is great, should he be weak, or
unjust, or barbarous? Because men are little, ought they to be
allowed either to be dissolute without punishment, or virtuous
without reward? O God! if this is the character of your Supreme
Being; if it is you whom we adore under such dreadful ideas;
can I any longer acknowledge you for my father, for my pro-
tector, for the comforter of my sorrow, the support of my weakness, the rewarder of my fidelity? You would then be no more
but an indolent and fantastical tyrant, who sacrifices mankind
to his insolent vanity, and who has brought them out of nothing,
only to make them serve for the sport of his leisure, and of his
caprice."

When the general rules which determine the merit and demerit of actions, come thus to be regarded, as the laws of an
All-powerful Being, who watches over our conduct, and who,
in a life to come, will reward the observance, and punish the
breach of them; they necessarily acquire a new sacredness from
this consideration. That our regard to the will of the Deity,
ought to be the supreme rule of our conduct, can be doubted
of by nobody who believes his existence. The very thought of
disobedience appears to involve in it the most shocking impropriety. How vain, how absurd would it be for man, either to
oppose or to neglect the commands that were laid upon him
by Infinite Wisdom, and Infinite Power! How unnatural, how
impiously ungrateful not to reverence the precepts that were
prescribed to him by the infinite goodness of his Creator, even
though no punishment was to follow their violation. The sense
of propriety too is here well supported by the strongest motives
of self-interest. The idea that, however, we may escape the
observation of man, or be placed above the reach of human
punishment, yet we are always acting under the eye, and
exposed to the punishment of God, the great avenger of injustice, is a motive capable of restraining the most headstrong
passions, with those at least who, by constant reflection, have
rendered it familiar to them.

It is in this manner that religion enforces the natural sense of duty: and hence it is, that mankind are generally disposed to place great confidence in the probity of those who seem deeply impressed with religious sentiments. Such persons, they imagine, act under an additional tie, besides those which regulate the conduct of other men. The regard to the propriety of action as well as to reputation, the regard to the applause of his own breast, as well as to that of others, are motives which they suppose have the same influence over the religious man, as over the man of the world. But the former lies under another restraint, and never acts deliberately but as in the presence of that Great Superior who is finally to recompense him according to his deeds. A greater truth is reposed, upon this account, in the regularity and exactness of his conduct. And wherever the natural principles of religion are not corrupted by the factious and party zeal of some worthless cabal; wherever the first duty which it requires, is to fulfil all the obligations of morality; wherever men are not taught to regard frivolous observances, as more immediate duties of religion, than acts of justice and beneficence; and to imagine, that by sacrifices and ceremonies, and vain supplications, they can bargain with the Deity for fraud, and perfidy, and violence, the world undoubtedly judges right in this respect, and justly places a double confidence in the rectitude of the religious man's behaviour.

CHAPTER IV

Thomas Reid
(1710–1796)

The Man and His Work

By NOAH PORTER

THOMAS REID, D.D., 1710–1796, was a native of Strachan, Scotland; student and subsequently Librarian of Marischal College, Aberdeen, in 1737; Pastor of New Machar, 1752; Professor of King's College, Aberdeen, in 1763; Professor of Moral Philosophy in the University of Glasgow, as successor of Adam Smith, from which he retired in 1787.

Dr. Reid was effectually aroused to philosophical activity, as Kant was somewhat later, by the speculations of Berkeley and Hume. Both had assumed and carried to their logical conclusions the scholastic doctrine of Representative Perception, or perception by means of intermediate ideas, so far as it was sanctioned by Locke, and Locke's definition of Knowledge, as the agreement of two ideas with one another, or an idea with its object.

Berkeley had shown that these assumptions involved the reduction of matter to ideas, and the universe of matter to a universe of ideas, permanently existing in the divine mind, and occasionally discerned by the finite mind. Hume had as logically concluded that the mind itself is no more than a bundle of ideas, and its phenomena are but a series of impressions.

Besides reducing matter to sensations and mind or spirit to ideas, Hume had resolved the connections between both into custom or subjective habits or experience. Custom he had explained by association. He had also formally called in question the *universality* of the relation of causation by making it dependent solely on experience, and had denied impliedly its *necessity a priori*. He had challenged the customary methods of reasoning to the existence and attributes of God from the evidences of design in the universe. He had also formally called in question the trustworthiness of all philosophical speculations whatever, by arguments in support of philosophical skepticism as the only possible position which reason could accept. Singularly enough he had used positive arguments against the trustworthiness of the Christian miracles and the credibility of the Christian history, which were founded on the very doctrine of causation which he had resolved into customary associations, and on the experience which his philosophical skepticism would compel him to distrust.

Reid was first aroused by these apparently legitimate conclusions from the received philosophy to reconsider the fundamental principles from which they were derived.

Against the special principles and inferences of Berkeley and Hume, and against the pronounced skepticism of Hume, he protested in the name of *Common Sense*. Many of the arguments of both he subjected to a critical revision. His conception of common sense was indefinite and inconsistently conceived, and his criticisms were applied with unequal acuteness and varied success. Common sense was at one time conceived and appealed to as the power of knowledge in general, as it is possessed and employed by a man of ordinary development and opportunities. At another it was treated as the Faculty of Reason—or the Source of Principles, the *Light of Nature*, etc. Perception was at one time defined as the power to know the external world and its relations, on occasion of some of the bodily senses; at another it was resolved into the capacity to suggest (following in this the language of Berkeley and Hutcheson) an existing world of matter as the cause of some or all of these sensations. Reid's analysis of the processes of sensation is, however, sometimes very acute, and his *Inquiry into the Human Mind* is a valuable contribution to this much vexed subject. He successfully exposed the groundlessness, inconsistency and contraditions of the ancient and modern theories of representative perception. He contended that the mind is active in sense-perception—that every act of sense-perception is an act of judgment. In his later writings, he attempted a more accurate statement of the nature of common sense, and its functions in philosophical speculation, as Buffier in his *Premières Vérités* had done before him, and not a few other philosophers—making common sense a capacity for certain original and intuitive judgments which may be used as the foundations of deductive reasoning. These first principles he divided into the two classes of contingent and necessary truths. He cited twelve examples of the first, and divided the latter into grammatical, logical, mathematical, aesthetical, ethical, and metaphysical. Of the last he made three—the principle of inherence, of causation, and design. He also asserted that the freedom of the will and the consequent responsibility of the individual soul are discerned by intuition. . . .

The first published work of Reid's was the brief "Essay on Quantity," 1748, in the *Transactions of the Royal Society of London*. It was designed as a Protest against the application of mathematical relations to ethical conceptions, such as had been made by Hutcheson in his *Ethical Treatises*, as the ground of determining the excellence and merit of a virtuous action. It consists of a brief statement of the kind of objects to which mathematical relations are applicable. Mathematics is defined as the science of measure. It is applicable to Quantity, or that which is measurable. Quantity is subdivided into the proper and the improper. Proper Quantity is that which is measured by its own kind. Improper is that which cannot be measured by its kind. Proper Quantity is of four species: Extension, Duration, Number and Proportion. Improper Quantity includes Velocity, Quantity of Motion, Density, Elasticity, *vis insita et impressa*, centripetal forces of all kinds, and the different orders of fluxions. Every kind of improper Quantity which is admitted into mathematics must first admit of degrees of greater and less, and second, must be associated with or related to something which has proper quantity, so that the one must be increased and diminished with the other. It follows that intellectual and moral activities, not being capable of being thus associated, or of being associated with that which is measurable, do not admit the relations of quantity.

The *Inquiry into the Human Mind on the Principles of Common Sense* was published in 1763. It was designed, as appears from the dedication, to set aside the hypothesis that nothing is perceived but what is in the mind which perceives it, with the inference that we do not perceive things that are external, but only certain images of them imprinted upon the mind, which are called impressions and ideas. The introduction treats (1) of the importance of the subject and the means of prosecuting it; (2) of the impediments to our knowledge of the mind; (3) of the present state of this part of philosophy, etc., in which Reid ascribes the skepticism of the times to the *ideal* system of Descartes. He proceeds to the analysis of the special sensations, beginning with smell, which he finds to be a pure subjective sensation, not involving the relations of figure or extension, and only known as proceeding from some cause other than the subject of it. In this connection he explains the difference between a sensation, and the remembrance and imagination of an object; the one being a knowledge of the present existence of a real object; the second, of its past existence; and the third, a simple apprehension of it without belief. He next interposes the position that judgment or belief may occur without a preceding simple apprehension, in this dissenting from Locke's definition of knowledge as an agreement between ideas. He next attacks the doctrine of Hume that there can be a sensation without a sentient. He adds that the conception or belief of a sentient being is *suggested* by our constitution as one of the axioms of common sense—a doctrine which had been in a sense already taught by Berkeley and Hutcheson, though not in the same application which Reid makes of it when he says, that it is a power "to which we owe many of our simple notions, as well as many original principles of belief." He next discusses the point whether the mind is active or only passive in sensation, and insists that it is active, as against the learned philosophers. In discussing Touch, he returns again to his doctrine of *suggestion,* under the head *natural signs,* and distinguishes the quality as of hardness in the body from the corresponding sensation by making the one to be interpreted or suggested by the other as its natural sign. In the same way extension is suggested by most of the tactual sensations; and the reality of the external world is made known to the mind as a first principle of common sense. In discussing vision, he contends that color is not the name of a sensation, but of a secondary quality, and proceeds to argue, as against Locke, that none of our sensations are resemblances of the qualities of bodies. Following Berkeley, Reid distinguishes visible figure and extension from tangible figure and extension, and presents an ingenious discussion of what he calls the geometry of visibles, i.e., a system of geometry such as might be constructed by the eye only if it were unaided by touch. After a careful statement of the physiological conditions of vision as known in his time, he proceeds to distinguish sensation from perception, describing the one as a state of feeling and the other as an act of knowing, and distinguishing perception as original and acquired, the first being determined by the constitution or capacity of man, and the second being an act of judgment by signs. He proceeds next to trace the analogy between our confidence in the operations of the two kinds of perception and our confidence in human testimony, there being an original tendency or necessity to an enlargement and improvement by experience. It is worthy of notice that he introduces here another principle of common sense as necessary to the acquired perceptions of natural powers, viz.: a confidence in the honesty of nature analogous to a similar confidence in the testimony of men, called by Reid *"the inductive principle."*

In 1774 Dr. Reid published, in the appendix to Lord Kames' *Sketches of Man,* a brief account of Aristotle's Logic. It was designed to abate what the author conceived to be an excessive estimate of the logical process as a source of knowledge, and to emphasize the importance of other sources of knowledge. It contains many superficial and incorrect representations of Aristotle's real opinions, although it rendered an important service

at the time when it was originally composed. It has been subjected to philosophical and critical annotations by the eminent
Aristotelian Sir William Hamilton, in his edition of Reid's works.

The *Essays on the Intellectual Powers of Man*, published in
1785, contains the substance of the lectures which Reid had
delivered for more than twenty years. We find in them sub-
stantially the same principles which were more briefly stated
in the *Inquiry*. The Preliminary Chapter in Essay I contains a
series of definitions or explanations of terms which give a tran-
script of the philosophical views which were held in his time.
Chapter II gives the principles taken for granted. These are
the existence of a subject of psychical operations—the existence
of any present psychical state of which we are conscious—the
agency of attention—the identity of the subject of our mental
states—the reality of inherence or the relation of substance and
attribute—the distinction of subject and object in mental operations—the truth of those principles in which there is common
agreement of competent judges in all generations—the trustworthiness of the faculties of sane men. Chapter VII treats of the division of the Powers of the Mind. Reid follows the prevalent
twofold division into powers of the understanding, and powers of
the will. He criticizes and sets aside the division in books of logic
of the intellectual powers into simple apprehension, judgment
and reasoning, and proposes, as an incomplete division, the Powers we have by the External Senses—Memory—Conception—
Abstraction—Judgment—Reasoning—Taste—Moral Perception and
Consciousness. To these he subjoins the Social operations of
the mind. In treating of the External Senses, he sharply distinguishes the impressions on the brain and nerve from the perceptions of which they are the condition—more sharply than
from the sensations; he analyzes the act of perception into the
attaining or having a notion of the object, and an irresistible
belief of its present existence, which is also independent of
reasoning, i.e., is immediate. After an extended statement and
criticism of the theories of representative perception he treats
of sensations in chapter XVI, asserting that sensations and perceptions are known by the same names, and yet are distinguish-

able in thought. The sensations are confined to the soul, are painful, pleasant, or indifferent, and are distinguishable from the desires. In this analysis, however, sensations are confounded by Reid with emotions. The primary and secondary qualities are distinguished thus: of the first we have a direct notion, of the second a relative and obscure notion. Neither the primary nor the secondary resemble any sensation, as Locke asserted of the primary qualities. Passing next to matter, he teaches that the existence of a material substance, in addition to the sensible qualities, is directly discerned by the mind, though its relation to its qualities can only be obscurely apprehended. The infinite divisibility of matter must also be received as an axiom, and there are other axioms concerning its relation to space which cannot be perceived by the senses. *Space* and its relations, with the axioms concerning its existence and its relations, are known directly in connection with the senses of touch and sight, but not as objects of these senses. Returning to the evidence of sense, and the belief which rests upon it, he distinguishes it from the evidence of reasoning and from the evidence of what are technically called axioms, though it is analogous to the latter.

The senses can be improved in respect to the acuteness of the sensations and the range and variety of the perceptions. The sensations as such are not fallacious, but only the acquired perceptions and other conclusions arising from rashness, or ignorance of the laws of nature.

Memory Reid treats as an original faculty, which involves a belief of past duration and an immediate knowledge of the actual existence of objects in the past. The knowledge of limited duration involves the belief of a duration which is unlimited, just as limited extension involves unlimited space. Both time and space are objects *sui generis*. They are not things, but rather *receptacles* of things, without which these could not possibly have existed. Memory involves a belief of past identity as well as of past duration, and identity is known directly. Identity has different senses as applied to different objects. The discussion of *time, space,* etc., introduces an extended criticism of Locke's account of the origin of these notions by means of sensation and reflection, in which Reid implies that he considers these two sources of knowledge, as they are defined by Mr. Locke, to be inadequate.

Conception, Reid calls also *simple apprehension,* in this confounding the representation of individual and general ideas or notions, and this confusion runs through the entire discussion of the subject. Our conceptions are of three kinds: of individual things, of the meaning of general words and the creations of our own imagination. The term imagination, when distinguished from conception, he limits to mental pictures of visible objects. The relation of conceptions to their originals leads Reid to discuss again the falseness of the theory of representative ideas. A chapter on mistakes concerning conception strikingly illustrates the confused and equivocal senses in which the author uses the term. The power and laws of association he adverts to under the title of the train of thoughts in the mind, but professes to add nothing to what Hume and Lord Kames had written, to whom he refers for a full exposition of the subject.

In Essay V, "Of Abstraction," Reid treats first of General Words, in which he notices and explains their *extension* and *comprehension* and the relation of the one to the other. He next discusses general conceptions, and shows that such are possible of the attributes of things and the genera and species of things. In treating Chapter III, "Of Abstraction and Generalization," he observes that the general conceptions which are formed by compounding objects do not become simple by blending their constituents into one. In other words, the compounds of nature and those formed by the mind are strikingly contrasted. In the formation and application of these universals we impliedly assume the orderly procedure and arrangement of nature. Of the nature of universals, as discussed by Nominalists, Conceptualists, and Realists, Reid expresses the following opinion: Universals have no real existence except in the mind. They are not objects of the imagination proper. Locke, who represents the Conceptualists, and Berkeley and Hume, who represent the Nominalists, divide the truth between themselves.

"Of Judgment," in Essay VI, Reid's doctrine is summed in

the three propositions: (1) It is an act specifically distinct from simple apprehension. (2) There are notions which should be referred to the faculty of judgment as their source, as those of affirmation, negation, truth, falsehood, knowledge and belief, indeed of relations of every kind. (3) In mature persons, judgment accompanies sensation, consciousness and memory; as also in the formation of abstract and general conceptions. Judgment, so far from supposing simple apprehension or ideas as the material with which it operates, is necessary to provide ideas and simple apprehensions. This is true of the natural judgments of sensations, and consciousness, as well as of the relations which are involved in the act of judgment itself. That *common* sense is a particular description of judgment is obvious from the use of the term by many writers. It follows from this corrected conception of the nature of judgment, that all knowledge is not limited to the agreement or disagreement of ideas. Immediate knowledge cannot be thus defined. Some judgments are, in the proper sense of the word, intuitions. Such are termed *axioms, first principles, principles of common-sense, self-evident truths.* All knowledge obtained by reasoning must be built upon first principles. Some of these are certain, others are probable only. It is important and practicable to determine these principles— for, first, every man is a competent judge of them; second, opinions which contradict first principles are not merely false, they are also absurd. The consent of men of all ages and conditions is of great authority in establishing them. Opinions that appear very early and are absolutely necessary in the conduct of life are to be received as first principles. These first principles are of two classes: the first principles of contingent truths, and the first principles of necessary truths. Reid enumerates *twelve* of the first class, viz.: Everything exists of which we are conscious. The thoughts of which I am conscious are the thoughts of a being called myself, etc. The things which I remember did really happen. We may be certain of our identity as far as we remember. The things which we perceive exist, and are what we perceive them to be. We have some power over our actions and the determinations of our wills. The natural faculties by which we discriminate truth from error are not fallacious. There is life and intelligence in our fellow-men. Certain features and gestures indicate certain thoughts and dispositions of the mind. Human testimony naturally awakens confidence. In respect to events depending on human volition, there is a self-evident probability, greater or less. In the phenomena of nature, what is to be will probably be like to what has been in similar circumstances. Necessary truths are grammatical, logical, mathematical, maxims of taste, first principles of morals and metaphysical truths. Of the last, three are conspicuous. (1) The qualities which we perceive belong to a subject which we call body; those of which we are conscious belong to a subject which we call mind. (2) Whatever begins to exist must have a cause which produced it. (3) Design and intelligence in the cause may be inferred with certainty from the marks or signs of it in the effect. Next follows a brief statement of criticism of the received doctrines in respect to first principles; also a chapter on prejudices and the causes of error.

Essay VII is "Of Reasoning," which is allied to judgment and is divided into probable and demonstrative, the first being limited to truths which are probable, and the second, to those which are necessary. So far as in morality there are truths which are necessary or intuitive, so far is morality capable of demonstration. The skeptical distrust of Reason can only apply to Reasoning, but the belief in first principles is not an act of the reasoning power. Hume is in error in asserting that our reasonings of causes and effects are derived from custom, and are acts of the sensitive rather than the cogitative part of our nature.

"Of Taste," Essay VIII, Reid's doctrine is that, like one of the senses, it is founded on an internal capacity to be pleased or displeased, coupled with the power of judgment. The qualities in objects which affect this sensibility are grouped under novelty, grandeur and beauty. Each of these are illustrated at length.

The "Essays on the Active Powers of Man" commence with an essay on Active Power in general. The conception of power, like other original conceptions, cannot be defined, but we may assert that power is not an object of sense or consciousness, as Locke contends and Hume denies. We have only a relative notion of it. It requires a subject in which it inheres. Power may exist and not be exerted. The notion of power has no contrary. After criticizing Locke's and Hume's explanation of the notion and of our belief in it, Reid contends that power *probably* belongs only to beings possessed of understanding and will; all that the science of nature investigates is the laws of nature. The powers of man are limited.

The will is appropriate to the power and act of determining. It should be distinguished from the sensations, affections and desires. Every act of will must have an object. It must concern itself immediately with some act of a man's own, believed to be within our power. The will affects the acts of the understanding in Attention, Deliberation, and Resolution or Purpose. Some acts of will are transient and others permanent. Nothing is virtuous or immoral which is not voluntary. Virtue in habit consists in the purpose.

Principles of action are whatever excites to action. They are threefold: mechanical, animal and rational. The mechanical principles are twofold: instincts and habits. Besides the commonly accepted instincts there are instincts of belief, as in testimony, and the uniformity of laws of nature. Habit is a facility acquired by repetition. The animal principles are the appetites which are corporeal in their occasion and are neither social nor selfish— the desires, of which there are three: the desire of esteem, of power and of knowledge, all which are social; the benevolent affections, general and special, the last comprising the domestic, the grateful, the pitiful, the respectful, the friendly and the sexual, and public spirit. Of the malevolent affections, there are two: emulation and resentment. All these become passions when excessively excited. Disposition describes a permanent subjective tendency to the excitement of certain of these principles.

The Rational Principles of action are such as imply judgment. There are two: a regard for our good upon the whole, and a regard to duty. The last of these is grounded on the possession of an original power of the mind, which we call the Moral Faculty, by which we distinguish actions as right and wrong, and discern the First Principles of Morals, attendant upon which are the feelings of moral approbation and disapprobation. Conscience comes into maturity by gradual growth. It is peculiar to man; it is intended as a guide; it is both an active and an intellectual power.

The liberty of a moral agent is a power over the determinations of the will. It supposes some *practical judgment* or Reason. Necessity is the want of such moral liberty. Liberty is used in three senses: (1) of confinement of the body; (2) of obligation from law; (3) as opposed to necessity as defined. This is conceivable because every man knows that he possesses it. The words cause and effect, action and active power, are used in more than one meaning, and hence are used ambiguously when applied to material and spiritual agents.

Necessity is not proved by the influence of motives, unless it can be proved that the existence of motives compels to a particular determination. The arguments for the fact of Liberty are: (1) We are naturally convinced that we act freely. (2) The fact of moral responsibility implies it. (3) Liberty is essential to the deliberate choice and execution of plans *that are deliberately chosen*. Against Liberty it is urged (A) that liberty of determination is impossible because, (1) there must be a sufficient reason for every existence and every event; and (2) because it would imply that an event may occur without a cause. (B) It would be hurtful to man. (C) Man has no such liberty, because every human action is foreseen. But the foreknowledge of God does not involve necessity. It should be granted that foreknowledge of contingent events is impossible for man, but it is not for this reason impossible for God. On the other hand, upon the scheme of necessity God is made the author of sin.

The first Principles of Morals relate (A) to virtue in general; (B) to the different branches of virtue; (C) to the comparison of virtues. The first are, some things in human conduct merit approbation and praise, others blame and punishment.

That which is involuntary deserves neither. What is necessary cannot be the object of praise or blame. Men are culpable for omitting as well as for performing acts. We ought to use the best means to learn our duty. We ought to fortify ourselves against temptation. The second are, we ought to prefer a greater to a less good. We should follow the intuitions of nature. No man is born for himself only. We ought to act towards another as we should wish him to act towards us. Veneration and submission to God are obligatory on all. Of the third class are, unmerited generosity should be secondary to gratitude, and both to justice. Unmerited beneficence should yield to compassion to the miserable. External acts of piety to works of mercy. An act deserving moral approbation must be believed by the agent to be morally good. Justice and its obligations are naturally approved as morally good—and are not the results of artificial arrangements. These positions are against Hume. Moral approbation is an act of judgment as well as of feeling.

The Correspondence Between David Hume and Thomas Reid

In *The Works of Thomas Reid*, edited by Sir William Hamilton, Volume I, pages 7 f., is a copy of a letter from David Hume to Thomas Reid, and on page 91, a copy of one from Reid to Hume. Dugald Stewart gives this explanation of this exchange of letters: "As the refutation of Mr. Hume's Sceptical theory was the great and professed object of Dr. Reid's *Inquiry* he was anxious, before taking the field as a controversial writer, to guard against the danger of misapprehending or misrepresenting the meaning of his adversary, by submitting his reasonings to Mr. Hume's private examination. With this view he availed himself of the good offices of Dr. Blair, with whom both he and Mr. Hume had long lived in habits of friendship. The communications which he at first transmitted, consisted only of detached parts of the work, and appear evidently, from a correspond-

ence which I have perused, to have conveyed a very imperfect idea
of his general system. In one of Mr. Hume's letters to Dr. Blair, he
betrays some want of his usual good humour, in looking forward to
his new antagonist. 'I wish,' says he, 'that the parsons would confine
themselves to their old occupation of worrying one another, and
leave philosophers to argue with temper, moderation, and good manners.' After Mr. Hume, however, had read the manuscript, he addressed himself directly to the author, in terms so candid and liberal,
that it would be unjust to his memory to withhold from the public
so pleasing a memorial of his character." (From *Collected Works of
Dugald Stewart,* Volume X, p. 256.) Stewart does not give the date
of this letter, February 25, 1763. See the editor's comments in the
Introduction.

DAVID HUME'S LETTER TO THOMAS REID

By Dr. Blair's means I have been favoured with the perusal of
your performance, which I have read with great pleasure and
attention. It is certainly very rare, that a piece so deeply philosophical is wrote with so much spirit, and affords so much
entertainment to the reader; though I must still regret the disadvantages under which I read it, as I never had the whole
performance at once before me, and could not be able fully
to compare one part with another. To this reason, chiefly, I
ascribe some obscurities, which, in spite of your short analysis
or abstract, still seem to hang over your system. For I must
do you the justice to own, that when I enter into your ideas,
no man appears to express himself with greater perspicuity
than you do; a talent which, above all others, is requisite in
that species of literature which you have cultivated. There are
some objections which I would willingly propose to the chapter,
"Of Sight," did I not suspect that they proceed from my not
sufficiently understanding it; and I am the more confirmed in
this suspicion, as Dr. Blair tells me, that the former objections
I made had been derived chiefly from that cause. I shall, therefore, forbear till the whole can be before me, and shall not at
present propose any farther difficulties to your reasonings. I
shall only say, that if you have been able to clear up these

abstruse and important subjects, instead of being mortified, I shall be so vain as to pretend to a share of the praise; and shall think that my errors, by having at least some coherence, had led you to make a more strict review of my principles, which were the common ones, and to perceive their futility.

As I was desirous to be of some use to you, I kept a watchful eye all along over your style; but it is really so correct, and so good English, that I found not anything worth the remarking. There is only one passage in this chapter, where you make use of the phrase *hinder to do,* instead of *hinder from doing,* which is the English one; but I could not find the passage when I sought for it. You may judge how unexceptionable the whole appeared to me, when I could remark so small a blemish. I beg my compliments to my friendly adversaries, Dr. Campbell and Dr. Gerard, and also to Dr. Gregory, whom I suspect to be of the same disposition, though he has not openly declared himself such.

THOMAS REID'S LETTER TO DAVID HUME

King's College (Aberdeen),
18th March, 1763.

Sir, On Monday last, Mr. John Farquhar brought me your letter of February 25th, enclosed in one from Dr. Blair. I thought myself very happy in having the means of obtaining at second hand, through the friendship of Dr. Blair, your opinion of my performance: and as you have been pleased to communicate it directly in so polite and friendly a manner, as merits great acknowledgment on my part. Your keeping a watchful eye over my style, with a view to be of use to me, is an instance of candour and generosity to an antagonist, which would affect me very sensibly, although I had no personal concern in it, and I shall always be proud to show so amiable an example. Your judgment of the style, indeed, gives me great consolation, as I was very diffident of myself in regard to English, and have been indebted to Drs. Campbell and Gerard for many corrections of that kind.

In attempting to throw some new light upon those abstruse subjects, I wish to preserve the due mean betwixt confidence and despair. But whether I have any success in this attempt or not, I shall always avow myself your disciple in metaphysics. I have learned more from your writings in this kind, than from all others put together. Your system appears to me not only coherent in all its parts, but likewise justly deduced from principles commonly received among philosophers; principles which I never thought of calling in question, until the conclusions you draw from them in the *Treatise of Human Nature* made me suspect them. If these principles are solid, your system must stand; and whether they are or not, can better be judged after you have brought to light the whole system that grows out of them, than when the greater part of it was wrapped up in clouds and darkness. I agree with you, therefore, that if this system shall ever be demolished, you have a just claim to a great share of the praise, both because you have made it a distinct and determined mark to be aimed at, and have furnished proper artillery for the purpose.

When you have seen the whole of my performance, I shall take it as a very great favour to have your opinion upon it, from which I make no doubt of receiving light, whether I receive correction or no. Your friendly adversaries Drs. Campbell and Gerard as well as Dr. Gregory, return their compliments to you respectfully. A little philosophical society here, of which all the three are members, is much indebted to you for its entertainment. Your company would, although we are all good Christians, be more acceptable than that of St. Athanasius; and since we cannot have you upon the bench, you are brought oftener than any other man to the bar, accused and defended with great zeal, but without bitterness. If you write no more in morals, politics, or metaphysics, I am afraid we shall be at a loss for subjects. I am, respectfully, Sir, you most obliged, humble servant,

THOMAS REID

Of Mr. Hume's Opinion of the Idea of Power

By THOMAS REID

This selection is from *The Works of Thomas Reid*, edited by Sir William Hamilton (Edinburgh: Maclachlan and Stewart, 1863), Vol. II, pp. 520–22. It is Chapter IV of Essay I, of the *Essays on the Intellectual Powers of Man*, 1785. It is a fair sample of Reid's criticisms of Hume.

THIS VERY INGENIOUS AUTHOR adopts the principle of Mr. Locke before mentioned—That all our simple ideas are derived either from sensation or reflection. This he seems to understand even in a stricter sense than Mr. Locke did. For he will have all our simple ideas to be copies of preceding impressions, either of our external senses or of consciousness. "After the most accurate examination," says he, "of which I am capable, I venture to affirm, that the rule here holds without any exception, and that every simple idea has a simple impression which resembles it, and every simple impression a correspondent idea. Every one may satisfy himself in this point, by running over as many as he pleases."

I observe here, by the way, that this conclusion is formed by the author rashly and unphilosophically. For it is a conclusion that admits of no proof but by induction; and it is upon this ground that he himself founds it. The induction cannot be perfect till every simple idea that can enter into the human mind be examined, and be shown to be copied from a resembling impression of sense or of consciousness. No man can pretend to have made this examination of all our simple ideas without exception; and, therefore, no man can, consistently with the rules of philosophising, assure us, that this conclusion holds without any exception.

The author professes, in his title page, to introduce into moral subjects, the experimental method of reasoning. This was a very laudable attempt; but he ought to have known that it is a rule in the experimental method of reasoning—That conclusions established by induction ought never to exclude exceptions, if any such should afterwards appear from observation or experiment. Sir Isaac Newton, speaking of such conclusions, says, "*Et si quando in experiundo postea repreiatur aliquid, quod a parte contraria faciat; tum demum, non sine istis exceptionibus affirmetur conclusio opportebit.*" "But," says our author, "I will venture to affirm that the rule here holds without any exception."

Accordingly, throughout the whole treatise, this general rule is considered as of sufficient authority, in itself, to exclude, even from a hearing, everything that appears to be an exception to it. This is contrary to the fundamental principles of the experimental method of reasoning, and, therefore, may be called rash and unphilosophical.

Having thus established this general principle, the author does great execution by it among our ideas. He finds, that we have no idea of *substance*, material or spiritual; that body and mind are only certain trains of related impressions and ideas, that we have no idea of *space* or *duration*, and no idea of *power*, active or intellectual.

Mr. Locke used his principle of sensation and reflection with greater moderation and mercy. Being unwilling to thrust the ideas we have mentioned into the *limbo* of non-existence, he stretches sensation and reflection to the very utmost, in order to receive these ideas within the pale: and draws them into it, as it were, by violence.

But this author, instead of showing them any favour, seems fond to get rid of them.

Of the ideas mentioned, it is only that of *power* that concerns our present subject. And, with regard to this, the author boldly affirms, "That we never have any idea of Power; that we deceive ourselves when we imagine we are possessed of any idea of this kind."

He begins with observing, "That the terms *efficacy, agency, power, force, energy,* are all nearly synonymous; and, therefore, it is an absurdity to employ any of them in defining the rest. By this observation," says he, "we reject at once the vulgar definitions which philosophers have given of *power* and *efficacy*."

Surely this author was not ignorant that there are many things of which we have a clear and distinct conception, which are so simple in their nature, that they cannot be defined any other way than by synonymous words. It is true that this is not a logical definition; but that there is, as he affirms, an absurdity in using it, when no better can be had, I cannot perceive.

He might here have applied to *power* and *efficacy*, what he says, in another place, of *pride* and *humility*. "The passions of *pride* and *humility*," he says, "being simple and uniform impressions, it is impossible we can ever give a just definition of them. As the words are of general use, and the things they represent the most common of any, every one, of himself, will be able to form a just notion of them without danger of mistake."

He mentions Mr. Locke's account of the idea of Power—that, observing various changes in things, we conclude that there must be somewhere a power capable of producing them, and so arrive at last, by this reasoning, at the idea of Power and Efficacy.

"But," says he, "to be satisfied that this explication is more popular than philosophical, we need but reflect on two very obvious principles, first, *That Reason alone can never give rise to any original idea;* and, secondly, *That Reason, as distinguished from Experience, can never make us conclude that a cause, or productive quality, is absolutely requisite to every beginning of existence.*"

Before we consider the two principles which our author opposes to the popular opinion of Mr. Locke, I observe:

First, That there are some *popular* opinions, which, on that very account, deserve more regard from philosophers than this author is willing to bestow.

That things cannot begin to exist, nor undergo any change, without a cause that hath power to produce that change, is indeed so popular an opinion that, I believe, this author is the first of mankind that ever called it in question. It is so popular that there is not a man of common prudence who does not act from this opinion, and rely upon it every day of his life. And any man who should conduct himself by the contrary opinion, would soon be confined as insane, and continue in that state till a sufficient cause was found for his enlargement.

Such a popular opinion as this stands upon a higher authority than that of philosophy; and philosophy must strike sail to it, if she would not render herself contemptible to every man of common understanding.

For though, in matters of deep speculation, the multitude must be guided by philosophers, yet, in things that are within the reach of every man's understanding, and upon which the whole conduct of human life turns, the philosopher must follow the multitude, or make himself perfectly ridiculous.

Secondly, I observe, that whether this popular opinion be true or false, it follows, from men's having this opinion, that they have an idea of power. A false opinion about power, no less than a true, implies an idea of power; for how can men have any opinion, true or false, about a thing of which they have no idea?

The *first* of the very obvious principles which the author opposes to Mr. Locke's account of the idea of power, is—that *Reason alone can never give rise to any original idea.*

This appears to me so far from being a very obvious principle, that the contrary is very obvious.

Is it not our reasoning faculty that gives rise to the idea of reasoning itself? As our idea of sight takes its rise from our being endowed with that faculty, so does our idea of reasoning. Do not the ideas of demonstration, of probability, our ideas of a syllogism, of major, minor and conclusion, of an enthymeme, dilemma, sorites, and all the various modes of reasoning, take their rise from the faculty of reason? Or is it possible that a being, not endowed with the faculty of reasoning, should have these ideas? This principle, therefore, is so far from being obviously true, that it appears to be obviously false.

The *second* obvious principle is, *That Reason, as distinguished from Experience, can never make us conclude, that a cause, or productive quality, is absolutely requisite to every beginning of existence.*

In some *Essays on the Intellectual Powers of Man,* I had occasion to treat of this principle—That every change in nature must have a cause; and, to prevent repetition, I beg leave to refer the reader to what is said upon this subject, Essay vi, Chap. 6. I endeavoured to show that it is a first principle, evident to all men come to years of understanding. Besides its having been universally received, without the least doubt, from the beginning of the world, it has this sure mark of a first principle, that the belief of it is absolutely necessary in the ordinary affairs of life, and, without it, no man could act with common prudence, or avoid the imputation of insanity. Yet a philosopher, who acted upon the firm belief of it every day of his life, thinks fit, in his closet, to call it in question.

He insinuates here that we may know it from *experience.* I endeavoured to show, that we do not learn it from experience, for two reasons.

First—*Because it is a necessary truth, and has always been received as a necessary truth. Experience gives no information of what is necessary, or of what must be.*

We may know from experience, what is, or what was, and from that may probably conclude what shall be in like circumstances; but, with regard to what must necessarily be, experience is perfectly silent.

Thus we know, by unvaried experience, from the beginning of the world, that the sun and stars rise in the east and set in the west. But no man believes, that it could not possibly have been otherwise, or that it did not depend upon the will and power of Him who made the world, whether the earth should revolve to the east or to the west.

In like manner, if we had experience, ever so constant, that every change in nature we have observed, actually had a cause, this might afford ground to believe, that, for the future, it shall be so; but no ground at all to believe that it must be so, and cannot be otherwise.

Another reason to show that this principle is not learned from experience is—*That experience does not show us a cause of one in a hundred of those changes which we observe, and therefore can never teach us that there must be a cause of all.*

Of all the paradoxes this author has advanced, there is not one more shocking to the human understanding than this, That things may begin to exist without a cause. This would put an end to all speculation, as well as to all the business of life. The employment of speculative men, since the beginning of the world, has been to investigate the causes of things. What pity is it, they never thought of putting the previous question, Whether things have a cause or not? This question has at last been stated; and what is there so ridiculous as not to be maintained by some philosopher?

Enough has been said upon it, and more, I think, than it deserves. But, being about to treat of the active powers of the human mind, I thought it improper to take no notice of what has been said by so celebrated a Philosopher, to show that there is not in the human mind, any idea of power.

Philosophy and Common Sense

By Thomas Reid

This selection is from *The Works of Thomas Reid,* edited by Sir William Hamilton (sixth ed., 1863), pp. 100–101, 105–8, and 110–11. It comprises a part of Section III of Chapter I and Sections II–VII of Chapter II of Reid's *An Inquiry into the Human Mind.*

Descartes, Malebranche, and Locke, have all employed their genius and skill to prove the existence of a material world; and with very bad success. Poor untaught mortals believe undoubtedly that there is a sun, moon, and stars; an earth, which we inhabit; country, friends, and relations, which we enjoy; land, houses, and moveables, which we possess. But philosophers, pitying the credulity of the vulgar, resolve to have no faith but what is founded upon reason. They apply to philosophy to furnish them with reasons for the belief of those things which all mankind have believed, without being able to give any reason for it. And surely one would expect, that, in matters of such importance, the proof would not be difficult: but it is the most difficult thing in the world. For these three great men, with the best good will, have not been able, from all the treasures of philosophy, to draw one argument that is fit to convince a man that can reason, of the existence of any one thing without him. Admired Philosophy! daughter of light! parent of knowledge and wisdom! if thou art she, surely thou hast not yet arisen upon the human mind, nor blessed us with more of thy rays than are sufficient to shed a darkness visible upon the human faculties, and to disturb that repose and security which happier mortals enjoy, who never approached thine altar, nor felt thine influence! But if, indeed, thou hast not power to dispel these clouds and phantoms which thou hast discovered or created, withdraw this penurious and malignant ray; I despise Philosophy, and renounce its guidance—let my soul dwell with Common Sense. . . .

It may be observed, that the defects and blemishes in the received philosophy concerning the mind, which have most exposed it to contempt and ridicule of sensible men, have chiefly been owing to this—that the votaries of this Philosophy, from a natural prejudice in her favour, have endeavoured to extend her jurisdiction beyond its just limits, and to call to her bar the dictates of Common Sense. But these decline this jurisdiction; they disdain the trial of reasoning, and disown its authority; they neither claim its aid, nor dread its attacks.

In this unequal contest betwixt Common Sense and Philosophy, the latter will always come off both with dishonour and loss; nor can she ever thrive till this rivalship is dropt, these encroachments given up, and a cordial friendship restored: for, in reality, Common Sense holds nothing of Philosophy, nor needs her aid. But, on the other hand, Philosophy (if I may be permitted to change the metaphor) has no other root but the principles of Common Sense; it grows out of them, and draws its nourishment from them. Severed from this root, its honours wither, its sap is dried up, it dies and rots.

The philosophers of the last age, whom I have mentioned, did not attend to the preserving this union and subordination so carefully as the honour and interest of philosophy required: but those of the present have waged open war with Common Sense, and hope to make a complete conquest of it by the subtilties of Philosophy—an attempt no less audacious and vain than that of the giants to dethrone almighty Jove. . . .

Let us now attend carefully to what the mind is conscious of when we smell a rose or a lily; and, since our language affords no other name for this sensation, we shall call it a *smell* or *odour*, carefully excluding from the meaning of those names everything but the sensation itself, at least till we have examined it.

Suppose a person who never had this sense before, to receive it all at once, and to smell a rose—can he perceive any similitude or agreement between the smell and the rose, or indeed between it and any other object whatsoever? Certainly he cannot. He finds himself affected in a new way, he knows not why or from what cause. Like a man that feels some pain or pleasure formerly unknown to him, he is conscious that he is not the cause of it himself; but cannot, from the nature of the thing, determine whether it is caused by body or spirit, by something near, or by something at a distance. It has no similitude to anything else, so as to admit of a comparison; and, therefore, he can conclude nothing from it, unless, perhaps, that there must be some unknown cause for it.

It is evidently ridiculous to ascribe to it figure, colour, extension, or any other quality of bodies. He cannot give it a place, any more than he can give a place to melancholy or joy, nor can he conceive it to have any existence, but when it is smelled. So that it appears to be a simple and original affection or feeling of the mind, altogether inexplicable and unaccountable. It is, indeed, impossible that it can be in any body: it is a sensation, and a sensation can only be in a sentient thing.

The various odours have each their different degrees of strength or weakness. Most of them are agreeable or disagreeable; and frequently those that are agreeable when weak, are disagreeable when stronger. When we compare different smells together, we can perceive very few resemblances or contrarieties, or, indeed, relations of any kind between them. They are all so simple in themselves, and so different from each other, that it is hardly possible to divide them into *genera* and *species*. Most of the names we give them are particular; as the smell of a *rose,* of a *jessamine,* and the like. Yet there are some general names—as *sweet, stinking, musty, putrid, cadaverous, aromatic.* Some of them seem to refresh and animate the mind, others to deaden and depress it.

So far we have considered this sensation abstractly. Let us next compare it with other things to which it bears some relation. And first I shall compare this sensation with the remembrance, and the imagination of it.

I can think of the smell of a rose when I do not smell it; and it is possible that when I think of it, there is neither rose nor smell anywhere existing. But when I smell it, I am necessarily determined to believe that the sensation really exists. This is common to all sensations, that, as they cannot exist but in being perceived, so they cannot be perceived but they must exist. I could as easily doubt of my own existence, as of the existence of my sensations. Even those profound philosophers who have endeavoured to disprove their own existence, have yet left their sensations to stand upon their own bottom, stript of a subject, rather than call in question the reality of their existence.

Here, then, a sensation, a smell for instance, may be presented to the mind three different ways: it may be smelled, it may be remembered, it may be imagined or thought of. In the first case, it is necessarily accompanied with a belief of its present existence; in the second, it is necessarily accompanied with a belief of its past existence; and in the last, it is not accompanied with belief at all, but is what the logicians call a *simple apprehension.*

Why sensation should compel our belief of the present existence of the thing, memory, a belief of its past existence, and imagination no belief at all, I believe no philosopher can give a shadow of reason, but that such is the nature of these operations: they are all simple and original, and therefore inexplicable acts of the mind.

Suppose that once, and only once, I smelled a tuberose in a certain room, where it grew in a pot and gave a very grateful perfume. Next day I relate what I saw and smelled. When I attend as carefully as I can to what passes in my mind in this case, it appears evident that the very thing I saw yesterday, and the fragrance I smelled, are now the immediate objects of my mind, when I remember it. Further, I can imagine this pot and flower transported to the room where I now sit, and yielding the same perfume. Here likewise it appears, that the individual thing which I saw and smelled, is the object of my imagination.

Philosophers indeed tell me, that the immediate object of my memory and imagination in this case, is not the past sensation, but an idea of it, an image, phantasm, or species, of the odour I smelled; that this idea now exists in my mind, or in my sensorium; and the mind, contemplating this present idea, finds it a representation of what is past, or of what may exist; and accordingly calls it memory, or imagination. This is the doctrine of the ideal philosophy; which we shall not now examine, that we may not interrupt the thread of present investigation. Upon the strictest attention, memory appears to me to have things that are past and not present ideas, for its object. We shall afterwards examine this system of ideas, and endeavour to make it appear, that no solid proof has ever been advanced of the existence of ideas; that they are a mere fiction and hypothesis, contrived to solve the phenomena of the human understanding; that they do not at all answer this end; and that this hypothesis of ideas or images of things in the mind, or in the sensorium, is the parent of those many paradoxes so shocking to common sense, and of that scepticism which disgrace our philosophy of the mind, and have brought upon it the ridicule and contempt of sensible men.

In the meantime, I beg leave to think, with the vulgar, that, when I remember the smell of the tuberose, that very sensation which I had yesterday and which has now no more any existence, is the immediate object of my memory; and when I imagine it present, the sensation itself, and not any idea of it, is the object of my imagination. But, though the object of my sensation, memory, and imagination, be in this case the same, yet these acts or operations of the mind are as different, and as easily distinguishable, as smell, taste, and sound. I am conscious of a difference in kind between sensation and memory, and between both and imagination. I find this also, that the sensation compels my belief of the present existence of the smell, and memory of my belief of its past existence. There is a smell, is the immediate testimony of sense; there was a smell, is the immediate testimony of memory. If you ask me, why I believe that the smell exists, I can give no other reason, nor shall ever be able to give any other, than that I smell it. If you ask, why I believe that it existed yesterday, I can give no other reason but that I remember it.

Sensation and memory, therefore, are simple, original, and perfectly distinct operations of the mind, and both of them are original principles of belief. Imagination is distinct from both, but is no principle of belief. Sensation implies the present existence of its object, memory its past existence, but imagination views its object naked, and without any belief of its existence or non-existence, and is therefore what the schools call *Simple Apprehension*.

But here, again, the ideal system comes in our way: it teaches us that the first operation of the mind about its ideas, is simple apprehension—that is, the bare conception of a thing without any belief about it: and that, after we have got simple apprehensions, by comparing them together, we perceive agreements or disagreements between them; and that this perception of the agreement or disagreement of ideas is all that we call belief, judgment, or knowledge. Now, this appears to me to be all fiction, without any foundation in nature; for it is acknowledged by all, that sensation must go before memory and imagination; and hence it necessarily follows, that apprehension,

accompanied with belief and knowledge, must go before simple apprehension, at least in the matters we are now speaking
of. So that here, instead of saying that the belief or knowledge
is got by putting together and comparing the simple apprehensions, we ought rather to say that the simple apprehension is
performed by resolving and analysing a natural and original
judgment. And it is with the operations of the mind, in this
case, as with natural bodies, which are, indeed, compounded
of simple principles or elements. Nature does not exhibit these
elements separate, to be compounded by us; she exhibits them
mixed and compounded in concrete bodies, and it is only by
art and chemical analysis that they can be separated.

But what is this belief or knowledge which accompanies sensation and memory? Every man knows what it is, but no man
can define it. Does any man pretend to define sensation, or to
define consciousness? It is happy, indeed, that no man does. And
if no philosopher had endeavoured to define and explain belief,
some paradoxes in philosophy, more incredible than ever were
brought forth by the most abject superstition or the most frantic
enthusiasm, had never seen the light. Of this kind surely is that
modern discovery of the ideal philosophy, that sensation, memory, belief, and imagination, when they have the same object,
are only different degrees of strength and vivacity in the idea.
Suppose the idea be that of a future state after death: one man
believes it firmly—this means no more than that he hath a strong
and lively idea of it; another neither believes nor disbelieves—
that is, he has a weak and faint idea. Suppose, now, a third
person believes firmly that there is no such thing, I am at a loss
to know whether his idea be faint or lively: if it is faint, then
there may be a firm belief where the idea is faint; if the idea
is lively, then the belief of a future state and the belief of no
future state must be one and the same. The same arguments that
are used to prove that belief implies only a stronger idea of the
object than simple apprehension, might as well be used to prove
that love implies only a stronger idea of the object than indifference. And then what shall we say of hatred, which must upon
this hypothesis be a degree of love, or a degree of indifference?

If it should be said, that in love there is something more than an idea—to wit, an affection of the mind—may it not be said with equal reason, that in belief there is something more than an idea—to wit, an assent or persuasion of the mind?

But perhaps it may be thought as ridiculous to argue against this strange opinion, as to maintain it. Indeed, if a man should maintain that a circle, a square, and a triangle differ only in magnitude, and not in figure, I believe he would find nobody disposed either to argue against him; and yet I do not think it less shocking to common sense, to maintain that sensation, memory, and imagination differ only in degree, and not in kind. I know it is said, that, in a delirium, or in dreaming, men are apt to mistake one for the other. But does it follow from this, that men who are neither dreaming nor in a delirium cannot distinguish them? I cannot tell: neither can I tell how a man knows that he exists. But, if any man seriously doubts whether he is in a delirium, I think it highly probable that he is, and that it it time to seek for a cure, which I am persuaded he will not find in the whole system of logic.

I mentioned before Locke's notion of a belief of knowledge; he holds that it consists in a perception of the agreement or disagreement of ideas; and this he values himself upon as a very important discovery.

We shall have occasion afterwards to examine more particularly this grand principle of Locke's philosophy, and to show that it is one of the main pillars of modern scepticism, although he had no intention to make that use of it. At present let us only consider how it agrees with the instances of belief now under consideration; and whether it gives any light to them. I believe that the sensation I have exists; and that the sensation I remember does not now exist, but did exist yesterday. Here, according to Locke's system, I compare the idea of a sensation with the ideas of past and present existence: at one time I perceive that this idea agrees with that of present existence, but disagrees with that of past existence; but, at another time, it agrees with the idea of past existence, and disagrees with that of present existence. Truly these ideas seem to be very capricious in their agreements and disagreements. Besides, I cannot, for my heart, conceive what is meant by either. I say a sensation exists, and I think I understand clearly what I mean. But you want to make the thing clearer, and for that end tell me, that there is an agreement between the idea of that sensation and the idea of existence. To speak freely, this conveys to me no light, but darkness; I can conceive no otherwise of it, than as an odd and obscure circumlocution. I conclude, then, that the belief which accompanies sensation and memory, is a simple act of the mind, which cannot be defined. It is, in this respect, like seeing and hearing, which can never be so defined as to be understood by those who have not these faculties; and to such as have them, no definition can make these operations more clear than they are already. In like manner, every man that has any belief—and he must be a curiosity that has none—knows perfectly what belief is, but can never define or explain it. I conclude, also, that sensation, memory, and imagination, even where they have the same object, are operations of a quite different nature, and perfectly distinguishable by those who are sound and sober. A man that is in danger of confounding them, is indeed to be pitied; but whatever relief he may find from another art, he can find none from logic or metaphysic. I conclude further, that it is no less a part of the human constitution, to believe the present existence of our sensations, and to believe the past existence of what we remember, than it is to believe that twice two make four. The evidence of sense, the evidence of memory, and the evidence of the necessary relations of things, are all distinct and original kinds of evidence, equally grounded on our constitution: none of them depends upon, or can be resolved into another. To reason against any of these kinds of evidence is absurd, nay, to reason for them is absurd. They are first principles; and such fall not within the province of reason, but of common sense. . . .

Leaving this philosophy, therefore, to those who have occasion for it, and can use it discreetly as a chamber exercise, we may still inquire how the rest of mankind, and even the adepts themselves, except in some solitary moments, have got so strong and irresistible a belief, that thought must have a subject, and be the act of some thinking being; how every man believes himself to be something distinct from his ideas and impressions—something which continues the same identical self when all his ideas and impressions are changed. It is impossible to trace the origin of this opinion in history; for all languages have it interwoven in their original construction. All nations have always believed it. The constitution of all laws and governments, as well as the common transactions of life, suppose it.

It is no less impossible for any man to recollect when he himself came by this notion; for, as far back as we can remember, we were already in possession of it, and as fully persuaded of our own existence, and the existence of other things, as that one and one make two. It seems, therefore, that this opinion preceded all reasoning, and experience, and instruction, and this is the more probable, because we could not get it by any of these means. It appears, then, to be an undeniable fact, that, from thought or sensation, all mankind, constantly and invariably, from the first dawning of reflection, do infer a power or faculty of thinking, and a permanent being or mind to which that faculty belongs; and that we as invariably ascribe all the various kinds of sensation and thought we are conscious of, to one individual mind or self.

But by what rules of logic we make these inferences, it is impossible to show; nay, it is impossible to show how our sensations and thoughts can give us the very notion and conception either of a mind or of a faculty. The faculty of smelling is something very different from the actual sensation of smelling; for the faculty may remain when we have no sensation. And the mind is no less different from the faculty; for it continues the same individual being when the faculty is lost. Yet this sensation suggests to us both a faculty and a mind; and not only suggests the notion of them, but creates a belief of their existence; although it is impossible to discover, by reason, any tie or connection between one and the other.

What shall we say, then? Either those inferences which we draw from our sensations—namely, the existence of a mind, and of powers or faculties belonging to it—are prejudices of philosophy or education, mere fictions of the mind, which a wise man should throw off as he does the belief of fairies; or they are judgments of nature—judgments not got by comparing ideas, and perceiving agreements and disagreements, but immediately inspired by our constitution.

If this last is the case, as I apprehend it is, it will be impossible to shake off those opinions, and we must yield to them at last, though we struggle hard to get rid of them. And if we could, by a determined obstinacy, shake off the principles of our nature, this is not to act the philosopher, but the fool or the madman. It is incumbent upon those who think that these are not natural principles, to show, in the first place, how we can otherwise get the notion of a mind and its faculties; and then to show how we come to deceive ourselves into the opinion that sensation cannot be without a sentient being.

It is the received doctrine of philosophers, that our notions of relations can only be got by comparing the related ideas: but, in the present case, there seems to be an instance to the contrary. It is not by having first the notion of mind and sensation, and then comparing them together, that we perceive the one to have the relation of a subject or substratum, and the other that of an act or operation: on the contrary, one of the related things—to wit, sensation—suggests to us both the correlate and the relation.

I beg leave to make use of the word *suggestion*, because I know not one more proper, to express a power of the mind, which seems entirely to have escaped the notice of philosophers, and to which we owe many of our simple notions which are neither impressions nor ideas, as well as many original principles of belief. I shall endeavour to illustrate, by an example, what I understand by this word. We all know, that a certain kind of sound suggests immediately to the mind, a coach passing in the street; and not only produces the imagination, but the belief, that a coach is passing. Yet there is here no comparing of ideas, no perception of agreements or disagreements, to produce this belief; nor is there the least similitude between the sound we hear and the coach we imagine and believe to be passing.

It is true that this suggestion is not natural and original; it is the result of experience and habit. But I think it appears, from what hath been said, that there are natural suggestions: particularly, that sensation suggests the notion of present exist- ence, and the belief that what we perceive or feel does now exist; that memory suggests the notion of past existence, and the belief that what we remember did exist in time past; and that our sensations and thoughts do also suggest the notion of a mind, and the belief of its existence, and of its relation to our thoughts. By a like natural principle it is, that a beginning of existence, or any change in nature, suggests to us the notion of a cause and compels our belief of its existence. And, in like manner, as shall be shown when we come to the sense of touch, certain sensations of touch, by the constitution of our nature, suggest to us extension, solidity, and motion, which are nowise like to sen- sation, although they have been hitherto confounded with them

CHAPTER V

Dugald Stewart
(1753–1828)

The Man and His Work

By NOAH PORTER

DUGALD STEWART, son of Rev. Matthew Stewart, Professor of
Mathematics, University of Edinburgh, born November 22,
1753; educated at University of Edinburgh, also at Glasgow,
1771–2; elected successor to his father, 1785, also Professor of
Moral Philosophy as successor to Adam Ferguson; in 1810 re-
linquished active duties; died June 11, 1828.

Dugald Stewart followed Reid very closely in his methods
of analysis and his accumulation of the discriminated facts of
experience, but went far beyond him in the exactness and reach
of his philosophical principles and method. He illustrated his
opinions from a very wide range of reading, which, if it was not
in the eminent sense learned and profound, was careful and
comprehensive, and never failed to set them forth in an elaborate and elegant diction. In his lectures he is said to have been
eminently attractive and eloquent. These lectures attracted many
pupils from the Continent and America, and excited an enthusi-
astic interest in philosophical investigations, and did much to
awaken nobler ideals and a more spiritual and ethical faith in
the young men of his time. The reaction which was awakened in
France by the influence of Reid upon Royer-Collard was furth-
ered by the influence of Stewart's writings upon Prevost and
Jouffroy. Indeed, we may confidently assert that the so-called
eclectic school of Cousin rests upon the elements and influences

which were largely furnished by the Scottish philosophers. Says Lord Cockburn: "Dugald Stewart was one of the greatest of didactic orators. Had he lived in ancient times, his memory would have descended to us as that of one of the finest of the old eloquent sages. Flourishing in an age which required all the dignity of morals to counteract the tendencies of physical pursuits and political convulsions, he has exalted the character of his country and generation. No intelligent pupil of his ever ceased to respect philosophy or was ever false to his principles without feeling the crime aggravated by the recollection of the morality which Stewart taught him."

Prof. Veitch says of him: "Among Scottish philosophers Mr. Stewart stands pre-eminently out as a psychological observer. On questions properly metaphysical he has left little which can be regarded as essentially his own. The field within which he labored was that of the phenomena of the mind, intellectual, moral, and aesthetical, as these appear under the modifications imposed on them by the general circumstances of human life—education and society. In careful, delicate, and original observations within this sphere he has seldom been equalled."

Stewart's contributions to psychology are abundant and various, and they give the principal charm and value of his writings. The value and extent of his contributions of this description is less obvious, from the circumstances that his psychological writings appear more frequently in the form of comments on the opinions of others than as his own observations and conclusions.

He recognizes the influence of the laws of Association far more distinctly than Reid had done, and goes so far as to resolve our belief in the extension of colored *visibilia* into "an inseparable association." In this he prepares the way for the more extended application of the associational power to the solution of psychical phenomena which was adopted by his successor, Dr. Thomas Brown.

In metaphysics, while Stewart followed Reid in general, he substituted for the phrases, "the Principle of Common Sense," and "Metaphysical Axioms": "the Fundamental Laws of Human Belief," and "the Principles of Human Knowledge." Among the primary qualities of material bodies he distinguishes (*Phil. Essays*) the "mathematical affections," and recognizes the truth that these imply the existence of space and time.

In respect to causation and the principle of causality it is to be observed, however, that in respect to the nature of this relation or notion he agrees with Hume, though he dissents from the conclusions which Hume derives from this definition. . . .

As an historian of philosophy Stewart is elegant rather than erudite, although his *Dissertation on the Progress of Metaphysical Philosophy* contains many just observations and much curious knowledge. He barely recognized the existence of the School of Kant, the terminology of which offended his taste, if it did not somewhat perplex his understanding.

In 1792 Stewart published *Elements of Philosophy of the Human Mind*, vol. 1; vol. 2 in 1814; both in several editions; vol. 3, with additions to vol. 1, in 1827; Edinburgh and London. In 1793 he published *Outlines of Moral Philosophy*, and in many editions, in 1795, Dr. Adam Smith's essays, with account of his life and writings; in 1801, *Account of Life and Writings of William Robertson, D. D.;* in 1803, *Life and Writings of Thomas Reid, D. D.;* in 1805, *A Short Statement of Some Important Facts Relative to the Late Election of a Mathematical Professor* (Leslie), etc.; in 1806, *Postscript* to the same; in 1810, *Philosophical Essays;* in 1812, *Some Account of a Boy Born Blind;* in 1815, Part I of *A General View of the Progress of Metaphysical, Ethical, and Political Philosophy, Since the Revival of Letters in Europe;* Part II, 1821, prefixed to the supplement to the 4th and 5th editions of the *Encyclopaedia Britannica,* also separately, Edin. 1821, Bost. 1822; in 1828, *The Philosophy of the Active and Moral Powers of Man,* 2 vols., 8vo, Edin., Bost., 1828, 2 vols. in French, by Dr. L. Simon, 1824. *Complete Works,* Cambridge, Mass., in 7 vols., 1829, also 1831. The collected works with additions and memoir by Sir William Hamilton, 11 vols., 1854–58, Edin.

The *Elements of the Human Mind,* Vols. 1, 2, 3 (II, III, IV, collected works)—published respectively in 1792, 1814, 1827—

contain Stewart's most important psychological observations, and
to a large extent his ablest metaphysical disquisitions. As these
volumes appeared at intervals somewhat remote from one another, they also furnish much instructive information in respect
to the progress of psychology and philosophy during Stewart's
lifetime. The Introduction, Vol. I, discusses philosophy in general, from the Baconian standpoint, and vindicates the application of the experimental or inductive method to the phenomena
of the human mind. It might properly be called an apology for
philosophical and psychological studies, from the charge of
being necessarily metaphysical. Stewart contends that our knowledge of matter and mind is relative only and limited to their
so-called attributes, while yet a reflective examination of the
processes and principles which are fundamental to all inductive
inquiries must be of eminent service in studying the laws of
spirit. His treatment of "External Perception" is limited to a
few comments upon the errors which have prevailed among
philosophers and the explanation of these errors. His own doctrine is stated almost within a single page, and seems to suppose
the reader to be acquainted with the analyses of Reid, which
Stewart implies that he accepts as altogether satisfactory. Attention is assumed to be a familiar experience without being
explained, and its relations to memory only are discussed. The
possibility that voluntary actions should become automatic is
explained by the law of association, and the doctrine is advanced
that we can attend to no more than one object at a time. Conception is employed by Stewart to designate the object of the
representative power or phantasy, and Stewart maintains that
there never can be such an object without the momentary belief
of its real existence. Under Abstraction, Stewart treats of the
formation and nature of general conceptions, which are often
called by him *ideas,* and treated as the equivalent to the ideas
of the ancient schools. Stewart is himself a conceptionalist. In
Chapter V of the Association of Ideas, Stewart goes far beyond
Reid, finding in Hume the ablest expounder of the laws of association, but notices that our associations are not confined to
the three relations recognized by Hume, but rest upon every

possible relation. He discusses the power which the mind has over its trains of association, and then proceeds to explain, by means of prevalent association, the phenomena of wit, rhyming, poetical fancy, invention, dreaming, and adds an extended discussion of the influence of habits of association upon speculative conclusions, judgments of taste, and morality. Memory and imagination are both treated with great fulness of practical illustration. The second volume of the *Elements* treats of three principal topics: Reason and the Fundamental Laws of Human Belief, Reasoning and Deductive Evidence, and The Experimental or Inductive Logic. In these discussions Stewart proves himself to be an able and acute metaphysician in spite of himself, treating as he does, of the *a priori* elements or conditions of all scientific knowledge. The views expressed are in general the same as those of Reid, but with greater exactness of statement and nicety of discrimination. The essential differences between several classes of the so-called principles of common sense, the ambiguity and consequent infelicity of the appellation, and the great variety of distinct processes which are indiscriminately huddled together, not only by popular writers, but by the most careful philosophers, under the designations of reason and reasoning, these are all commented on with no little acuteness, making the volume a valuable contribution to philosophy. One serious defect in it is not to be disguised or overlooked: Stewart had not the courage of his opinions. He had not the confidence in the distinctions which he made, and in the principles on which he proposed to build them up into a consistent system, nor did he follow them out in their minute and ramified applications. He was characteristically cautious of what he considered excessive refinement and broad generalizations. For a metaphysical philosopher he was afraid of what he styled the subtleties of metaphysics when stated into forms too refined to be readily apprehended by men of general culture in the scholastic language of abstract terminology. He preferred to concern himself with the application of his principles to special cases, and the illustrations of them by concrete examples. The third volume of the *Elements* consists of a disquisition upon language in general, and its relations to thought, upon the Principle or Law of Sympathetic Imitation, and upon the several varieties of intellectual character as exemplified in the metaphysician, the mathematician, the poet, and the sexes; also a comparison between the faculties of man and those of the lower animals, with a very curious and valuable Appendix concerning James Mitchell, a boy born deaf and blind.

The *Philosophical Essays,* originally published in 1810, 4to, afterwards 1816, 1818, 8vo, are by far the most important contributions of Stewart to philosophy proper. The "Preliminary Dissertation" treats of prevalent errors in respect to the philosophy of the mind, among which he criticizes the physiological theories of Hartley, Bentham, Priestley, and Darwin (the elder), and vindicates for the Philosophy of the Mind a place among investigations properly philosophical. The first essay, Part I, treats with great critical ability of the defects in Locke's account of the origin of knowledge, showing that the applications made of his theory by Berkeley and Hume were entirely legitimate and logical. The second essay treats with equal ability of the Idealism of Berkeley and our belief in the existence of the material world. In this essay Stewart introduces his view of the mathematical affections of matter. In the third he treats of the actual influence of Locke's authority upon the French illuminati and encyclopedists. In the fourth he discusses the theories of Hartley, Priestley and Darwin; and in the fifth treats of the argument for materialism supposed by Horne Tooke to be furnished from the etymological significations of many words. Part II contains four essays relative to matters of taste; 1. On the beautiful; 2. On the sublime; 3. On the (faculty or habit) of taste; 4. On the culture of certain intellectual habits connected with the first elements of taste. These essays in respect to principle and illustrations follow in the line of Burke, Price and Alison, the last of whom explains the aesthetic emotions by the operation of the associative power.

The *Philosophy of the Active and Moral Powers of Man,* first published in 1828, contains a psychological analysis of the emotions, Stewart's theory of the moral faculty and of the will, with some contributions to natural theology. He follows the views of Reid very closely upon all these topics, although his analysis is more refined and exact, and his critical and philosophical discussions of metaphysical questions are more various and learned. The treatise deserves greater consideration because there are so few treatises in the English language that treat of the emotions. It is characterized by the defect that is universal in the writings of Stewart, rather discoursing of the opinions of others than defining and defending his own. It abounds in interesting matter, and is one of the most attractive of Stewart's works. The *Dissertation on the Progress of Metaphysical Ethical and Political Philosophy Since the Revival of Letters in Europe,* Part I, 1815—Part II, 1821—is very incomplete and unequal. The portion most thoroughly elaborated is that on Locke and Leibnitz. His remarks on the Scottish school of metaphysicians are acute and valuable. His notice of Kant's philosophy is chiefly instructive as it shows how inadequately the reach and import of the critical philosophy was appreciated by one of the ablest philosophers and critics of Great Britain. The *Lectures on Political Economy* were published for the first time in 1855 in the *Collected Works* by Sir William Hamilton. They were printed from the earlier MS. notes of the author, with additions from the notes of those of his pupils. They fill two volumes and follow in general the topics and modes of discussion of the school of Adam Smith. The *Elements of the Philosophy of the Human Mind* and *The Philosophy of the Active and Moral Powers* have been extensively used as textbooks in their original and abridged forms in Great Britain and America.

Four Objections to Reid's Philosophy of Common Sense Answered

By DUGALD STEWART

This selection is from the memoir by Dugald Stewart entitled "An Account of the Life and Writings of Thomas Reid," which was read at different meetings of the Royal Society of Edinburgh in 1802. It is taken from *The Collected Works of Dugald Stewart*, Vol. X, pp. 281–86, 289–94, and 303–7. (See the editor's note, p. 82.) The title is supplied by the editor, and was suggested by the author's first two sentences.

A SLIGHT REVIEW of some of the more important and fundamental objections which have been proposed to Dr. Reid's doctrines may, I hope, be useful. Of these objections, the four following appear to me to be chiefly entitled to attention.

1. That he has assumed gratuitously, in all his reasonings, that theory concerning the human soul, which the scheme of Materialism calls in question.

2. That his views tend to damp the ardour of philosophical curiosity, by stating as ultimate facts, phenomena which may be resolved into principles more simple and general.

3. That by an unnecessary multiplication of original or instinctive principles, he has brought the science of mind into a state more perplexed and unsatisfactory, than that in which it was left by Locke and his successors.

4. That his philosophy, by sanctioning an appeal from the decisions of the learned to the voice of the multitude, is unfavorable to a spirit of free inquiry, and lends additional stability to popular errors.

1. With respect to Dr. Reid's supposed assumption of a doubtful hypothesis concerning the nature of the thinking and sentient principle, it is almost sufficient for me to observe, that the charge is directed against that very point of his philosophy

in which it is most completely invulnerable. The circumstance which peculiarly characterizes the inductive science of mind is, that it professes to abstain from all speculations concerning its nature and essence, confining the attention entirely to *phenomena,* for which we have the evidence of consciousness, and to the laws by which these phenomena are regulated. In this respect, it differs equally, in its scope, from the pneumatological discussions of the schools, and from the no less visionary theories, so loudly vaunted by the physiological metaphysicians of more modern times. Compared with the first, it differs, as the inquiries of the *mechanical* philosophers concerning the laws of moving bodies, differ from the discussions of the ancient sophists concerning the existence and nature of motion. Compared with the other, the difference is analogous to what exists between the conclusions of Newton concerning the law of gravitation, and his *query* concerning the invisible, either of which he supposed it might possibly be the effect. The facts which this inductive science aims at ascertaining, rest on their own proper evidence—an evidence unconnected with all these hypotheses, and which would not, in the smallest degree, be affected, although the truth of any one of them should be fully established. It is not, therefore, on account of its inconsistency with any favorite opinions of my own, that I would oppose the disquisitions either of scholastic pneumatology, or of physiological metaphysics; but because I consider them as an idle waste of time and genius on questions where our conclusions can neither be verified nor overturned by an appeal to experiment or observation. Sir Isaac Newton's query concerning the cause of gravitation was certainly not *inconsistent* with his own discoveries concerning its laws; but what would have been the consequences to the world, if he had indulged himself in the prosecution of hypothetical theories with respect to the former, instead of directing his astonishing powers to an investigation of the latter?

That the general spirit of Dr. Reid's philosophy is hostile to the conclusions of the Materialist, is indeed a fact. Not, however, because his system rests on the contrary hypothesis as a fundamental principle, but because his inquiries have a powerful tendency to wean the understanding gradually from those obstinate associations and prejudices, to which the common mechanical theories of mind owe all their plausibility. It is, in truth, much more from such examples of sound research concerning the laws of thought, than from any direct metaphysical refutation, that a change is to be expected in the opinions of those who have been accustomed to confound together two classes of phenomena, so completely and essentially different. But this view of the subject does not belong to the present argument.

It has been recommended of late, by a Medical author of great reputation, to those who wish to study the human mind, to begin with preparing themselves for the task by the study of anatomy. I must confess, I cannot perceive the advantages of this order of investigation, as the anatomy of the body does not seem to me more likely to throw light on the philosophy of the mind, than an analysis of the mind to throw light on the physiology of the body. To ascertain, indeed, the general laws of their connexion, from facts established by observation or experiment, is a reasonable and most interesting object of philosophical curiosity; and in this inquiry (which was long ago proposed and recommended by Lord Bacon), a knowledge of the constitution both of mind and body is indispensably requisite; but even here, if we wish to proceed on firm ground, the two classes of facts must be kept completely distinct, so that neither of them may be warped or distorted, in consequence of theories suggested by their supposed relations or analogies.[1] Thus, in many of the phenomena connected with custom and habit, there is ample scope for investigating general laws, both with respect to our mental and our corporeal frame; but what light do we derive from such information concerning this part of our constitution, as is contained in the following sentence of Locke? "Habits seem to be but trains of motion in the animal spirits, which, once set a-going, continue in the same steps they had

---

[1] *Elements of the Philosophy of the Human Mind,* pp. 11, 12, 2d edit. (Introd. *supra, Works,* Vol. II, pp. 52, 53.)

been used to, which, by often treading, are worn into a smooth path." [2] In like manner, the laws which regulate the connexion between the mind and our external organs, in the case of Perception, have furnished a very fertile subject of examination to some of the best of our modern philosophers; but how impotent does the genius of Newton itself appear, when it attempts to shoot the gulf which separates the sensible world, and the sentient principle? "Is not the Sensorium of animals," he asks in one of his Queries, "the place where the sentient substance is present, and to which the sensible Species of things are brought through the nerves and brain, that they may be perceived by the mind present in that place?"

It ought to be remembered also, that this inquiry, with respect to the laws regulating the connexion between our bodily organization, and the phenomena subjected to our own consciousness, is but one particular department of the philosophy of the mind, and that there still remains a wide and, indeed, boundless region, where all our *data* must be obtained from our own mental operations. In examining, for instance, the powers of judgment and reasoning, let any person of sound understanding, after perusing the observations of Bacon on the different classes of our prejudices, or those of Locke on the abuse of words, turn his attention to the speculations of some of our contemporary theorists, and he will at once perceive the distinction between the two modes of investigation which I wish at present to contrast. "Reasoning," says one of the most ingenious and original of these, "is that operation of the *sensorium,* by which we excite two or many tribes of ideas, and then re-excite the ideas in which they differ or correspond. If we determine this difference, it is called Judgment; if we in vain endeavour to determine it, it is called Doubting. If we re-excite the ideas in which they differ, it is called Distinguishing; if we re-excite those in which they correspond, it is called Comparing." [3] In what acceptation the word *idea* is to be understood in the foregoing passage,

---

[2] *Essay,* &c., Book II, chap. xxxiii, section 6.
[3] Darwin's *Zoonomia,* vol. i, p. 181, 3d edit.

may be learned from the following definition of the same author: "The word *idea* has various meanings in the writers of metaphysic. It is here used simply for those notions of external things which our organs of sense bring us acquainted with originally; and is defined, a contraction, or motion, or configuration of the fibres, which constitute the immediate organ of sense." [4] Mr. Hume, who was less of a physiologist than Dr. Darwin, has made use of a language by no means so theoretical and arbitrary, but still widely removed from the simplicity and precision essentially necessary in studies, where everything depends on the cautious use of terms. "*Belief,*" according to him, is "a lively idea related to or associated with a present impression." [5] "*Memory* is the faculty by which we repeat our impressions, so as that they retain a considerable degree of their first vivacity, and are somewhat intermediate betwixt an *idea* and an *impression.*" [6]

According to the views of Dr. Reid, the terms which express the simple powers of the mind, are considered as unsusceptible of definition or explanation; the words Feeling, for example, Knowledge, Will, Doubt, Belief, being, in this respect, on the same footing with the words Green or Scarlet, Sweet or Bitter. To the names of these mental operations, all men annex some notions more or less distinct; and the only way of conveying to them notions more correct, is by teaching them to exercise their own powers of reflection. The definitions quoted from Hume and Darwin, even if they were more unexceptionable in point of phraseology, would, for these reasons, be unphilosophical, as attempts to simplify what is incapable of analysis; but as they are actually stated, they not only envelop truth in mystery, but lay a foundation, at the very outset, for an erroneous theory. It is worth while to add, that of the two theories in question, that of Darwin, how inferior soever, in the estimation of competent judges, as a philosophical work, is by far the best calculated to impose on the very wide circle of readers, by the

---

[4] *Ibid.*, vol. i, pp. 11, 12.

[5] *Treatise on Human Nature,* Part III, sect. vii, Vol. I, p. 172, orig. edit.

[6] *Ibid.,* Part I, sect. iii. Vol. I, p. 23, *seq.*

mixture it exhibits of crude and visionary metaphysics, with those important facts and conclusions which might be expected from the talents and experience of such a writer, in the present advanced state of medical and physiological science. The questions which have been hitherto confined to a few, prepared for such discussions by habits of philosophical study, are thus submitted to the consideration, not only of the cultivated and enlightened minds which adorn the medical profession, but of the half-informed multitude who follow the medical trade; nor is it to be doubted, that many of these will give the author credit, upon subjects of which they feel themselves incompetent to judge, for the same ability which he displays within their own professional sphere. The hypothetical principles assumed by Hume are intelligible to those only who are familiarized to the language of the schools; and his ingenuity and elegance, captivating as they are to men of taste and refinement, possess slight attractions to the majority of such as are most likely to be misled by his conclusions. . . .

2. To allege, that in this circumscription of the field of our inquiries concerning the mind, there is any tendency to repress a reasonable and philosophical curiosity, is a charge no less unfounded than the former; inasmuch as every physical inquiry concerning the material world is circumscribed by limits precisely analogous. In all our investigations, whatever their subject may be, the business of philosophy is confined to a reference of particular facts to other facts more general; and our most successful researches must at length terminate in some law of nature, of which no explanation can be given. In its application to Dr. Reid's writings, this objection has, I think, been more pointedly directed against his reasonings concerning the process of nature in Perception; a part of his writings which (as it is of fundamental importance in his general system) he has laboured with peculiar care. The result is, indeed, by no means flattering to the pride of those theorists who profess to explain everything; for it amounts to an acknowledgment, that after all the lights which anatomy and physiology supply, the information we obtain by means of our senses, concerning the existence

and the qualities of matter, is no less incomprehensible to our faculties, than it appears to the most illiterate peasant; and that all we have gained is a more precise and complete acquaintance with some particulars in our animal economy—highly interesting indeed when regarded in their proper light, as accessions to our physical knowledge, but, considered in connexion with the philosophy of the mind, affording only a more accurate statement of the astonishing phenomena which we would vainly endeavour to explain. This language has been charged, but most unjustly and ignorantly, with *mysticism;* for the same charge may be brought, with equal fairness, against all the most important discoveries in the sciences. It was in truth the very objection urged against Newton, when his adversaries contended, that *gravity* was to be ranked with the *occult qualities* of the schoolmen, till its mechanical cause should be assigned; and the answer given to this objection by Sir Isaac Newton's commentator, Mr. Maclaurin, may be literally applied, in the instance before us, to the inductive philosophy of the human mind.

> The opponents of Newton, finding nothing to object to his observations and reasonings, pretended to find a resemblance between his doctrines and the exploded tenets of the scholastic philosophy. They triumphed mightily in treating gravity as an occult quality, because he did not pretend to deduce this principle fully from its cause. . . . I know not that ever it was made an objection to the circulation of the blood, that there is no small difficulty in accounting for it mechanically. They, too, who first extended gravity to air, vapour, and to all bodies round the earth, had their praise; though the cause of gravity was as obscure as before, or *rather appeared more mysterious*, after they had shown, that there was no body found near the earth, exempt from gravity, that might be supposed to be its cause. Why, then, were his admirable discoveries, by which this principle was extended over the universe, so ill relished by some philosophers? The truth is, he had, with great evidence, overthrown the boasted schemes by which they pretended to unravel all the mysteries of nature; and the philosophy he introduced, in place of them, carrying with it a sincere confession of our

being far from a complete and perfect knowledge of it, could not please those who had been accustomed to imagine themselves possessed of the eternal reasons and primary causes of all things.

It was, however, no new thing that this philosophy should meet with opposition. All the useful discoveries that were made in former times, and particularly in the seventeenth century, had to struggle with the prejudices of those who had accustomed themselves not so much as to think, but in a certain systematic way; who could not be prevailed on to abandon their favourite schemes, while they were able to imagine the least pretext for continuing the dispute. Every art and talent was displayed to support their falling cause; no aid seemed foreign to them that could in any manner annoy their adversary; and such often was their obstinacy, that truth was able to make little progress, till they were succeeded by younger persons who had not so strongly imbibed their prejudices. (*Account of Newton's Discoveries.*)

These excellent observations are not the less applicable to the subject now under consideration, that the part of Dr. Reid's writings which suggested the quotation, leads only to the correction of an inveterate prejudice, not to any new general conclusion. It is probable, indeed (now that the ideal theory has in a great measure disappeared from our late metaphysical systems), that those who have a pleasure in detracting from the merits of their predecessors, may be disposed to represent it as an idle waste of labour and ingenuity, to have entered into a serious refutation of an hypothesis at once gratuitous and inconceivable. A different judgment, however, will be formed by such as are acquainted with the extensive influence which, from the earliest accounts of science, this single prejudice has had in vitiating almost every branch of the philosophy of the mind; and who, at the same time, recollect the names of the illustrious men by whom, in more modern times, it has been adopted as an incontrovertible principle. It is sufficient for me to mention those of Berkeley, Hume, Locke, Clarke, and Newton. To the two first of these, it has served as the basis of their sceptical conclusions, which seem indeed to follow from it as necessary consequences; while the other repeatedly refer to it in their reasonings, as one of those facts concerning the mind, of which it would be equally superfluous to attempt a proof or a refutation.

I have enlarged on this part of Dr. Reid's writings the more fully, as he was himself disposed, on all occasions, to rest upon it his chief merit as an author. In proof of this, I shall transcribe a few sentences from a letter of his to Dr. (James) Gregory, dated 20th August 1790.

> It would be want of candour not to own, that I think there is some merit in what you are pleased to call *my Philosophy;* but I think it lies chiefly in having called in question the common theory of *Ideas* or *Images of things in the mind* being the only objects of thought; a theory founded on natural prejudices, and so universally received as to be interwoven with the structure of language. Yet were I to give you a detail of what led me to call in question this theory, after I had long held it as self-evident and unquestionable, you would think, as I do, that there was much of chance in the matter. The discovery was the birth of time, not of genius; and Berkeley and Hume did more to bring it to light than the man that hit upon it. I think there is hardly anything that can be called *mine* in the philosophy of the mind, which does not follow with ease from the detection of this prejudice.
>
> I must, therefore, beg of you most earnestly to make no contrast in my favour to the disparagement of my predecessors in the same pursuit. I can truly say of them, and shall always avow, what you are pleased to say of me, that but for the assistance I have received from their writings, I never could have wrote or thought what I have done.

3. Somewhat connected with the last objection, are the censures which have been so frequently bestowed on Dr. Reid, for an unnecessary and unsystematical multiplication of original or instinctive principles.

In reply to these censures, I have little to add to what I have remarked on the same topic, in the *Philosophy of the Human Mind.*[7] That the fault which is thus ascribed to Dr. Reid has

---

[7] *Elements,* Vol. I, Chap. i, sect. 3; *Works,* Vol. II, p. 108, *seq.*

been really committed by some ingenious writers in this part of
the island, I most readily allow; nor will I take upon me to
assert, that he has, in no instance, fallen into it himself. Such
instances, however, will be found, on an accurate examination
of his works, to be comparatively few, and to bear a very trifling
proportion to those, in which he has most successfully and
decisively displayed his acuteness, in exposing the premature
and flimsy generalizations of his predecessors.

A certain degree of leaning to that extreme to which Dr.
Reid seems to have inclined, was, at the time when he wrote,
much safer than the opposite bias. From the earliest ages, the
sciences in general, and more particularly the science of the
human mind, have been vitiated by an undue love of simplicity;
and, in the course of the last century, this disposition, after having been long displayed in subtle theories concerning the Active
Powers, or the Principles of Human Conduct, has been directed
to similar refinements with respect to the Faculties of the Understanding, and the Truths with which they are conversant. Mr.
Hume himself has coincided so far with the Hartleian school,
as to represent the "principle of union and cohesion among our
simple ideas as a kind of *attraction*, of as universal application
in the Mental world as in the Natural;" [8] and Dr. Hartley, with
a still more sanguine imagination, looked forward to an era,
"when future generations shall put all kinds of evidences and
inquiries into mathematical forms; reducing Aristotle's ten categories, and Bishop Wilkin's forty *summa genera*, to the head of
quantity alone, so as to make mathematics and logic, natural
history and civil history, natural philosophy and philosophy of
all other kinds, coincide *omni ex parte*."[9]

It is needless to remark the obvious tendency of such premature generalizations to withdraw the attention from the study
of particular phenomena; while the effect of Reid's mode of
philosophizing, even in those instances where it is carried to an
excess, is to detain us, in this preliminary step, a little longer
than is absolutely necessary. The truth is, that when the phenom-

[8] *Treatise of Human Nature*, Vol. I, p. 30 (orig. ed.).
[9] Hartley, *On Man*, p. 207, 4to edition, London, 1791.

ena are once ascertained, generalization is here of comparatively
little value, and a task of far less difficulty than to observe facts
with precision, and to record them with fairness.

In no part of Dr. Reid's writings, I am inclined to think,
could more plausible criticisms be made on this ground, than in
his classification of our Active Principles; but even there, the
facts are always placed fully and distinctly before the reader.
That several of the benevolent affections which he has stated
as ultimate facts in our constitution, might be analyzed into the
same general principle differently modified, according to circumstances, there can, in my opinion, be little doubt. This, however
(as I have elsewhere observed),[10] notwithstanding the stress
which has been sometimes laid upon it, is chiefly a question of
arrangement. Whether we suppose these affections to be all ultimate facts, or some of them to be resolvable into other facts
more general, they are equally to be regarded as constituent
parts of human nature; and, upon either supposition, we have
equal reason to admire the wisdom with which that nature is
adapted to the situation in which it is placed. The laws which
regulate the acquired perceptions of Sight, are surely as much
a part of our frame, as those which regulate any of our original
perceptions; and, although they require, for their development,
a certain degree of experience and observation in the individual,
the uniformity of the result shows, that there is nothing arbitrary
nor accidental in their origin. In this point of view, what can be
more philosophical, as well as beautiful, than the words of Mr.
Ferguson, that "natural affection springs up in the soul of the
mother, as the milk springs in her breast, to furnish nourishment
to her child!" "The effect is here to the race," as the same author
has excellently observed, "what the vital motion of the heart
is to the individual, too necessary to the preservation of nature's
works, to be entrusted to the precarious will or intention of those
most nearly concerned." [11]

The question, indeed, concerning the origin of our different

---

[10] *Outlines of Moral Philosophy*, pp. 70, 80. Second edition. Edinburgh,
1801. (*Supra, Works*, Vol. VI, pp. 21, 13.)

[11] *Principles of Moral and Political Science*, Part I, chap. i, sect. 3.

affections, leads to some curious analytical disquisitions, but is of very subordinate importance to those inquiries which relate to their laws, and uses, and mutual references. In many ethical systems, however, it seems to have been considered as the most interesting subject of disquisition which this wonderful part of our frame presents. . . .

4. The criticisms which have been made on what Dr. Reid has written concerning the intuitive truths which he distinguishes by the title of *Principles of Common Sense*, would require a more ample discussion than I can now bestow on them; not that the importance of these criticisms (of such of them, at least, as I have happened to meet with) demands a long or elaborate refutation; but because the subject, according to the view I wish to take of it, involves some other questions of great moment and difficulty, relative to the foundations of human knowledge. Dr. Priestley, the most formidable of Dr. Reid's antagonists, has granted as much in favour of this doctrine as it is worth while to contend for on the present occasion. "Had these writers," he observes with respect to Dr. Reid and his followers, "assumed, as the elements of their Common Sense, certain truths which are so plain that no man could doubt of them (without entering into the ground of our assent to them), their conduct would have been liable to very little objection. All that could have been said would have been, that, without any necessity, they had made an innovation in the received use of a term. For no person ever denied that there *are* self-evident truths, and that these must be assumed as the foundation of all our reasoning. I never met with any person who did not acknowledge this, or heard of any argumentative treatise that did not go upon the supposition of it." [12] After such an acknowledgment, it is impossible to forbear asking (with Dr. Campbell), "What is the great point which Dr. Priestley would controvert? Is it, whether such self-evident truths shall be denominated Principles of Common Sense, or be distinguished by some other appellation?" [13]

That the doctrine in question has been, in some publications,

---

[12] *Examination of Dr. Reid's Inquiry*, &c., p. 119.
[13] *Philosophy of Rhetoric*, Vol. I, p. lll. See Note E.

presented in a very exceptionable form, I most readily allow; nor would I be understood to subscribe to it implicitly, even as it appears in the works of Dr. Reid. It is but an act of justice to him, however, to request, that his opinions may be judged of from his own works alone, not from those of others who may have happened to coincide with him in certain tenets, or in certain modes of expression and that, before any ridicule be attempted on his conclusions concerning the authority of Common Sense, his antagonists would take the trouble to examine in what acceptation he has employed that phrase.

The truths which Dr. Reid seems, in most instances, disposed to refer to the judgment of this tribunal, might, in my opinion, be denominated more unexceptionably, "Fundamental Laws of Human Belief." [14] They have been called by a very ingenious foreigner (M. Trembley of Geneva), but certainly with a singular infelicity of language, *Préjugés Légitimes*. Of this kind are the following propositions: *I am the same person today that I was yesterday; The material world has an existence independent of that of percipient beings; There are other intelligent beings in the universe beside myself; The future course of nature will resemble the past.* Such truths no man but a philosopher ever thinks of stating to himself in words; but all our conduct and all our reasonings proceed on the supposition that they are admitted. The belief of them is essential for the preservation of our animal existence; and it is accordingly coeval with the first operations of the intellect.

One of the first writers who introduced the phrase *Common Sense* into the technical or appropriate language of logic, was Father Buffier, in a book entitled, *Traité des Primières Vérités*. It has since been adopted by several authors of note in this country, particularly by Dr. Reid, Dr. Oswald, and Dr. Beattie; by all of whom, however, I am afraid, it must be confessed, it has been occasionally employed without a due attention to precision. The last of these writers uses it to denote that power by which the mind perceives the truth of any intuitive proposi-

---

[14] *Elements,* Vol. II, chap. i. section 2; *supra, Works,* Vol. III, p. 45.

tion; whether it be an axiom of abstract science, or a statement of some fact resting on the immediate information of consciousness, or perception, or of memory, or one of those fundamental laws of belief which are implied in the application of our faculties to the ordinary business of life. The same extensive use of the word may, I believe, be found in the other authors just mentioned. But no authority can justify such a laxity in the employment of language in philosophical discussions; for, if mathematical axioms be (as they are manifestly and indisputably) a class of propositions essentially distinct from the other kinds of intuitive truth now described, why refer them all indiscriminately to the same principle in our constitution? If this phrase, therefore, be at all retained, precision requires that it should be employed in a more limited acceptation; and, accordingly, in the works under our consideration, it is appropriated most frequently, though by no means uniformly, to that class of Intuitive Truths which I have already called "Fundamental Laws of Belief." When thus restricted, it conveys a notion, unambiguous at least, and definite; and, consequently, the question about its propriety or impropriety turns entirely on the coincidence of this definition with the meaning of the word as employed in ordinary discourse. Whatever objections, therefore, may be stated to the expression as now defined, will apply to it with additional force when used with the latitude which has been already censured.

I have said, that the question about the propriety of the phrase *Common Sense,* as employed by philosophers, must be decided by an appeal to general practice. For although it be allowable and even necessary for a philosopher, to limit the acceptation of words which are employed vaguely in common discourse, it is always dangerous to give to a word a scientific meaning essentially distinct from that in which it is usually understood. It has, at least, the effect of misleading those who do not enter deeply into the subject; and of giving a paradoxical appearance to doctrines, which, if expressed in more unexceptionable terms, would be readily admitted.

It appears to me that this has actually happened in the

present instance. The phrase *Common Sense,* as it is generally
understood, is nearly synonymous with *Mother-wit;* denoting
that degree of sagacity (depending partly on original capacity,
and partly on personal experience and observation) which qual-
ifies an individual for those simple and essential occupations
which all men are called on to exercise habitually by their common nature. In this acceptation, it is opposed to those mental
acquirements which are derived from a regular education and
from the study of books; and refers, not to the speculative convictions of the understanding, but to that prudence and dis-
cretion which are the foundation of successful conduct. Such
is the idea which Pope annexes to the word, when, speaking of
good sense (which means only a more than ordinary share of
common sense), he calls it

> . . . the gift of Heaven,
> And though no science, fairly worth the seven.

To speak, accordingly, of appealing from the conclusions of
philosophy to common sense, had the appearance, to title-page
readers, of appealing from the verdict of the learned to the voice
of the multitude; or of attempting to silence free discussion,
by a reference to some arbitrary and undefinable standard,
distinct from any of the intellectual powers hitherto enumerated
by logicians. Whatever countenance may be supposed to have
been given by some writers to such an interpretation of this
doctrine, I may venture to assert, that none is afforded by the
works of Dr. Reid. The standard to which he appeals is neither
the creed of a particular sect, nor the inward light of enthusi-
astic presumption, but that constitution of human nature without which all the business of the world would immediately cease;
and the substance of his argument amounts merely to this, that
those essential laws of belief, to which sceptics have objected
when considered in connexion with our scientific reasonings,
are implied in every step we take as active beings; and if called
in question by any man in his practical concerns, would expose
him universally to the charge of insanity.

Concerning the Fundamental Laws
of Human Belief

By DUGALD STEWART

This selection is from *The Collected Works of Dugald Stewart*, Vol. III, *Elements of the Philosophy of the Human Mind*, Vol. II, pp. 36–38 and 40–45. (See the editor's note, p. 82.) Instead of naming the elemental constituents of the human mind "the principles of common sense," as Reid had done, Stewart calls them "the fundamental laws of human belief," because of an ambiguity which he points out in the word "principle."

THERE IS AN AMBIGUITY in the word *principle*. In its proper acceptation, it seems to me to denote an assumption (whether resting on fact or on hypothesis) upon which, as a *datum*, a train of reasoning proceeds; and for the falsity or incorrectness of which no logical rigour in the subsequent process can compensate. Thus the gravity and the elasticity of the air are *principles of reasoning* in our speculation about the barometer. . . . In a sense perfectly analogous to this, the *definitions* of geometry (all of which are merely *hypothetical*) are the *first principles* of reasoning in the subsequent demonstrations, and the basis on which the whole fabric of the science rests.

I have called this the *proper* acceptation of the word, because it is that in which it is most frequently used by the best writers. It is also most agreeable to the literal meaning which its etymology suggests, expressing the original point from which our reasoning sets out or commences.

Dr. Reid often uses the word in this sense, as, for example, in the following sentence: "From three or four axioms, which he calls *regulae philosophandi*, together with *the phenomena observed by the senses, which he likewise lays down as first principles*, Newton deduces, by strict reasoning, the propositions contained in the third book of his *Principia,* and in his *Optics.*"

On other occasions, he uses the same word to denote those *elemental* truths (if I may use the expression) which are virtually taken for granted or assumed in every step of our reasoning, and without which, although no *consequences* can be directly inferred from them, a train of reasoning would be impossible. Of this kind, in mathematics are the *axioms,* or (as Mr. Locke and others frequently call them) the *maxims;* in physics, a belief of *the continuance of the Laws of Nature;* in all our reasonings, without exception, a belief in *our own identity,* and in the *evidence of memory.* Such truths are the *last elements* into which reasoning resolves itself when subjected to a metaphysical analysis, and which no person but a metaphysician or a logician ever thinks of stating in the form of a proposition, or even of expressing verbally to himself. It is to truths of this description that Locke seems in general to apply the name of *maxims;* and, in this sense, it is unquestionably true, that no science (not even geometry) is founded on maxims as its first principle.

In one sense of the word *principle,* indeed, maxims may be called principles of reasoning; for the words *principles* and *elements* are sometimes used as synonymous. Nor do I take upon me to say that this mode of speaking is exceptionable. All that I assert is, that they cannot be called *principles of reasoning,* in the sense which has just now been defined; and that accuracy requires that the word on which the whole question hinges, should not be used in both senses in the course of the same argument. It is for this reason that I have employed the phrase *principles of reasoning* on the one occasion, and *elements of reasoning* on the other.

It is difficult to find unexceptionable language to mark distinctions so completely foreign to the ordinary purposes of speech; but, in the present instance, the line of separation is strongly and clearly drawn by this criterion—that from *principles of reasoning* consequences may be deduced; from what I have called *elements of reasoning,* none ever can.

A process of logical reasoning has been often likened to a chain supporting a weight. If this similitude be adopted, the *axioms* or *elemental truths* now mentioned may be compared to the successive concatenations which connect the different links immediately with each other; the *principles* of our reasoning resemble the hook, or rather the beam, from which the whole is suspended. . . .

It is by the immediate evidence of consciousness that we are assured of the *present existence* of our various sensations, whether pleasant or painful; of all our affections, passions, hopes, fears, desires, and volitions. It is thus, too, we are assured of the *present existence* of those thoughts which, during our waking hours, are continually passing through the mind, and of all the different effects which they produce in furnishing employment to our intellectual faculties.

According to the common doctrine of our best philosophers, it is by the evidence of *consciousness* we are assured that we ourselves exist. The proposition, however, when thus stated, is not accurately true; for our own existence (as I have elsewhere observed) is not a direct or immediate object of consciousness, in the strict and logical meaning of that term. We are conscious of sensation, thought, desire, volition; but we are not conscious of the existence of Mind itself; nor would it be possible for us to arrive at the knowledge of it (supposing us to be created in the full possession of all the intellectual *capacities* which belong to human nature), if no impression were ever to be made on our external senses. The moment that, in consequence of such an impression, a sensation is excited, we learn two facts at once—the existence of the sensation, and our own existence as sentient beings—in other words, the very first exercise of consciousness necessarily implies a belief, not only of the present existence of what is felt, but of the present existence of *that* which feels and thinks: or (to employ plainer language) the present existence of that being which I denote by the words *I* and *myself*. Of these facts, however, it is the former alone of which we can properly be said to be conscious, agreeably to the rigorous interpretation of the expression. A conviction of the latter, although it seems to be so inseparable from the exercise of consciousness that it can scarcely be considered as posterior to it in the order of *time,* is yet (if I may be allowed to make use of a scholastic distinction) posterior to it in the order of *nature;* not only as it supposes consciousness to be already awakened by some sensation, or some other mental affection; but as it is evidently rather a judgment accompanying the exercise of that power, than one of its immediate intimations concerning its appropriate class of internal phenomena. It appears to me, therefore, more correct to call the belief of our own existence a concomitant or accessory of the exercise of consciousness, than to say, that our existence is a fact falling under the immediate cognizance of consciousness, like the existence of the various agreeable or painful sensations which external objects excite in our minds.

That we cannot, without a very blamable latitude in the use of words, be said to be *conscious* of our personal identity, is a proposition still more indisputable; inasmuch as the very idea of personal identity involves the idea of *time,* and consequently presupposes the exercise not only of *consciousness,* but of *memory.* The belief connected with this idea is implied in every thought and every action of the mind, and may be justly regarded as one of the simplest and most essential elements of the understanding. Indeed, it is impossible to conceive either an intellectual or an active being to exist without it. It is, however, extremely worthy of remark, with respect to this belief, that, universal as it is among our species, nobody but a metaphysician ever thinks of expressing it in words, or of reducing into the shape of a proposition the truth to which it relates. To the rest of mankind, it forms not an object of knowledge; but a condition or supposition, necessarily and unconsciously involved in the exercise of all their faculties. On a part of our constitution, which is obviously one of the last or primordial elements at which it is possible to arrive in analyzing our intellectual operations, it is plainly unphilosophical to suppose, that any new light can be thrown by metaphysical discussion. All that can be done with propriety, in such cases, is to state the fact.

And here, I can not help taking notice of the absurd and inconsistent attempts which some ingenious men have made, to explain the gradual process by which they suppose the mind to be led to the knowledge of its own existence, and of that continued identity which our constitution leads us to ascribe to it. How (it has been asked) does a child come to form the very abstract and metaphysical idea expressed by the pronoun *I* or *moi?* In answer to this question, I have only to observe, that when we set about the explanation of a phenomenon, we must proceed on the supposition that it is possible to resolve it into some more general law or laws with which we are already acquainted. But, in the case before us, how can this be expected, by those who consider that all our knowledge of mind is derived from the exercise of reflection; and that every act of this power implies a conviction of our own existence as reflecting and intelligent beings? Every theory, therefore, which pretends to account for this conviction, must necessarily involve that sort of paralogism which logicians call a *petitio principii;* inasmuch as it must resolve the thing to be explained into some law or laws, the evidence of which rests ultimately on the assumption in question. From this assumption, which is necessarily implied in the joint exercise of consciousness and memory, the philosophy of the human mind, if we mean to study it analytically, must of necessity set out; and the very attempt to dig deeper for its foundation, betrays a total ignorance of the logical rules, according to which alone it can ever be prosecuted with any hopes of success.

It was, I believe, first marked by M. Prevost of Geneva (and the remark, obvious as it may appear, reflects much honour on his acuteness and sagacity), that the inquiries concerning the mind, founded on the hypothesis of the *animated statue*—inquiries which both Bonnet and Condillac professed to carry on analytically—were in truth altogether synthetical. To this criticism it may be added, that their inquiries, in so far as they had for their object to explain the origin of our belief of our own existence, and of our personal identity, assumed, as the principles of their synthesis, facts at once less certain and less familiar than the problem which they were employed to resolve.

Nor is it to the metaphysician only that the ideas of identity and of personality are familiar. Where is the individual who has not experienced their powerful influence over his imagination, while he was employed in reflecting on the train of events which have filled up the past history of his life; and on that internal world, the phenomena of which have been exposed to his own inspection alone? On such an occasion, even the wonders of external nature seem comparatively insignificant; and one is tempted (with a celebrated French writer) in contemplating the spectacle of the universe, to adopt the words of the Doge of Genoa, when he visited Versailles—"*Ce qui m'étonne le plus ici, c'est de m'y voir.*"

The belief which all men entertain of the existence of the material world (I mean their belief of its existence independently of that of percipient beings) and their expectation of the continued uniformity of the laws of nature, belong to the same class of ultimate or elemental laws of thought, with those which have been just mentioned. The truths which form their objects are of an order so radically different from what are commonly called *truths,* in the popular acceptation of that word, that it might perhaps be useful for logicians to distinguish them by some appropriate appellation, such, for example, as that of *metaphysical* or *transcendental* truths. They are not *principles* or *data* (as will afterwards appear) from which any consequence can be deduced; but form a part of those original *stamina* of human reason, which are equally essential to all the pursuits of science, and to all the active concerns of life.

I shall only take notice farther, under this head, of the confidence which we must necessarily repose in the evidence of memory (and, I may add, in the continuance of our personal identity) when we are employed in carrying on any process of deduction or argumentation—in following out, for instance, the steps of a long mathematical demonstration. In yielding our assent to the conclusion to which such a demonstration leads, we evidently trust to the fidelity with which our memory has connected the different links of the chain together. The reference which is often made, in the course of a demonstration, to propositions formerly proved, places the same remark in a light still stronger; and shows plainly that, in this branch of knowledge, which is justly considered as the most certain of any, the authority of the same laws of belief which are recognised in the ordinary pursuits of life, is tacitly acknowledged. Deny the evidence of memory as a ground of certain knowledge, and you destroy the foundations of mathematical science as completely as if you were to deny the truth of the axioms assumed by Euclid.

The foregoing examples sufficiently illustrate the nature of that class of truths which I have called *Fundamental Laws of Human Belief,* or *Primary Elements of Human Reason.* A variety of others, not less important, might be added to the list: such, for example, as our belief of the existence of *efficient* causes; our belief of the existence of other intelligent beings besides ourselves, etc. . . .

From such propositions as these—*I exist; I am the same person today that I was yesterday; the material world has an existence independent of my mind; the general laws of nature will continue, in future, to operate uniformly as in time past*—no inference can be deduced, any more than from the intuitive truths prefixed to the *Elements* of Euclid. Abstracted from other *data,* they are perfectly barren in themselves; nor can any possible combination of them help the mind forward one single step in its progress. It is for this reason that, instead of calling them, with some other writers, *first principles,* I have distinguished them by the title of *Fundamental laws of belief;* the former word seeming to denote, according to common usage, some *fact,* or some *supposition,* from which a series of consequences may be deduced.

Dugald Stewart on Hindu Philosophy

By Daniel Sommer Robinson

THE CHIEF SOURCE of Dugald Stewart's knowledge of Hindu Philosophy was the writings of the distinguished orientalist and philologist, Sir William Jones (1746–94) whose *Works* were published in six volumes in London (1799). (Citations from his *Works* quoted below will be abbreviated with the initials WJ, and those from *The Collected Works of Dugald Stewart* will be abbreviated WS.) Sir William Jones founded The Asiatic Society in Calcutta in 1784, and served as its president until his untimely death in 1794, at the age of forty-eight years.

The reader should keep in mind the fact that Sir William Jones was not a philosopher but a philologist and a jurist who had a sympathetic interest in and a deep understanding of Hindu culture, whereas Dugald Stewart was an original thinker with an extensive knowledge of the whole history of Western philosophy and was especially well informed on the entire development of British Empiricism. Nevertheless, Stewart had a genuine respect for the scholarly achievements of Sir William Jones, who translated into English and interpreted a good deal of classic Hindu literature. However, as we shall see presently, Stewart did not always agree with these interpretations.

Perhaps what aroused Stewart's interest most was the claim of Sir William Jones that Hindu Philosophy contained a conception of the material world that was identical with that of Bishop Berkeley and David Hume. He quotes from the *Works* of Jones the following three interesting passages that elaborate this conception:

The difficulties attending the vulgar notion of material substances, induced many of the wisest among the ancients, and some of the most enlightened among the moderns, as well as the Hindu philosophers, to believe that the whole creation was rather an energy than a work, by which the infinite mind, who is present at all times, and in all places, exhibits to his creatures a set of perceptions like a wonderful picture, or piece of music, always varied, yet always uniform. (WS, Vol. V, p. 180. From the Introduction to a translation of some Hindu verses.)

The Vedantis, unable to form a distinct idea of brute matter independent of mind, or to conceive that the work of supreme goodness was left a moment to itself, imagine that the Deity is ever present to his work, and constantly supports a series of perceptions, which in one sense they call illusory, *though they can not but admit the reality of all created forms, as far as the happiness of creatures can be affected by them.* (WS, Vol. V, p. 108, from WJ, Vol. I, p. 249. The italics are Stewart's.)

The word MAYA, or *Delusion,* has a subtile and recondite sense in the *Vedanta* philosophy, where it signifies the system of *perceptions,* whether of secondary or of primary qualities, which the Deity was believed by Epicharmus, Plato, and many truly pious men, to raise, by his omnipresent spirit, in the minds of his creatures; but which had not, in their opinion, any existence independent of mind. (WS, Vol. V, p. 108, from WJ, Vol. I, p. 231.)

Elsewhere, in Note B to his chapter entitled "Fundamental Laws of Belief," Stewart makes this significant comment: "The prevalence in India of an opinion bearing *some* resemblance to the Berkeleian Theory, may be urged as an objection to the reasoning in the text; but, on examination, this resemblance will be found much slighter than has been generally apprehended. On this point the following passage from Sir William Jones is decisive; and the more so, as he himself has fallen into the common mistake of identifying the Hindu belief with the conclusion of Berkeley and Hume." (WS, Vol. III, p. 370.)

He then quotes a fourth passage from Sir William Jones:

The fundamental tenet of the *Vedanti* school . . . consisted, *not in denying the existence of matter, that is, of solidity, impenetrability, and extended figure (to deny which would be lunacy) but in correcting the popular notion of it,* and in contending, that it has no essence independent of mental perception, that existence and perceptibility are convertible terms, that external appearances and sensations are illusory, and *would vanish into nothing, if the divine energy, which alone sustains them, were suspended but for a moment;* an opinion which Epicharmus and Plato seem to have adopted, and which has been maintained in the present century with great eloquence, but with little public applause; partly because it has been misunderstood, and partly because it has been misapplied by the false reasoning of some unpopular writers who are said to have disbelieved in the moral attributes of God, whose omnipresence, wisdom, and goodness, are the basis of the Indian philosophy. I have not sufficient evidence on the subject to profess a belief in the doctrine of the *Vedanta,* which human reason alone could, perhaps, neither fully demonstrate, nor fully disprove; but it is manifest that nothing can be farther removed from impiety than a system wholly built on the purest devotion. (WS, Vol. III, pp. 370 f., from WJ, Vol. I, pp. 165–66. Most of the italics are Stewart's.)

Commenting on this fourth passage, Stewart first points out that Jones confuses two conceptions of the relation of the material universe to the Deity. He writes: "Sir William Jones here evidently confounds the system which represents the material universe as not only at first *created,* but as every moment *upheld* by the agency of Divine Power, with that of Berkeley and Hume, which, denying the distinction between primary and secondary qualities, asserts that extension, figure, and impenetrability, are not less inconceivable without a *percipient* mind than our sensations of heat and cold, sounds and odours. According to both systems, it may undoubtedly be said that the material universe has no existence independent of *mind;* but it ought not to be overlooked, that in the *one,* this word refers to the Creator, and in the *other,* to the created percipient." (WS, Vol. III, p. 371n.)

In justification of Sir William Jones, it must be admitted that Bishop Berkeley was himself, at least to some extent, guilty of this same confusion. In his celebrated new proof for the existence of God he argues that the world of nature is kept in existence by God's acting as a perceiver, when creaturely perceivers are not functioning, but he also argues that the material world operates according to natural laws ordained by the Creator. Stewart does not name a representative of the view that the material universe is "every moment *upheld* by the agency of divine power," but he might have named Jonathan Edwards. In his *A History of American Philosophy,* Professor Schneider designates this theory "Edwards' doctrine of omnificence" and adds "Edwards' idealism was opposed to Berkeley's." In support of this he quotes Edwards as follows:[1]

> God's *preserving* of created things in being, is perfectly equivalent to a *continued creation,* or to his creating those things out of nothing at *each moment* of their existence. . . . For it does not at all *necessarily* follow, that because there was sound, or light, or colour, or resistance, or gravity, or thought, or consciousness, or any other dependent thing the last moment, that therefore there shall be the like at the next. All dependent existence whatsoever is in a constant flux, ever passing and returning; renewed every moment, as the colours of bodies are every moment renewed by the light that shines upon them; and all is constantly proceeding from God, as light from the sun. *In him we live, and move, and have our being.*

Presumably Schneider would agree with Stewart that Berkeley's conception of the relation of the material world to Deity was not precisely what Sir William Jones says it was. Berkeley was not an advocate of omnificence—the doctrine that God continually and from moment to moment recreates the material world out of nothing. In *Siris* he explicitly denies that God has sense organs as do creaturely percipients: "There is no sense, nor sensory, nor anything like a sense or sensory in God. . . . God knoweth all things as pure mind or intellect but nothing by sense, nor in nor through a sensory." (*Siris,* paragraph 289.) Hence, Stewart was right in denying that Berkeley's idealism was identical with that of the Hindus.

Stewart has another interesting argument against this identification. Referring to the tenets of the Hindus quoted above, he writes: "These tenets were rather articles of a theological creed than of a philosophical system; or, at least, the two were

---

[1] Herbert W. Schneider, *A History of American Philosophy* (New York: Columbia University Press), p. 20. See the interesting article "Other Dates," by R. J. Butler, in *Mind,* Jan., 1959, pp. 16–33.

so blended together, as sufficiently to account for the hold
which, independently of any refined reasoning, they had taken
of the popular belief." (WS, Vol. III, p. 371.) In support of this
contention, Stewart quotes a personal letter he received from
Sir James Mackintosh, who was Recorder of Bombay when he
wrote Stewart:[2]

> . . . I had yesterday a conversation with a young Bramin of no
> great learning, the son of the Pundit (or assessor for Hindu law)
> of my Court. He told me that, besides the myriads of gods
> whom their creed admits, there was one whom they know by
> the name of BRIM, or the great one, without form or limits,
> whom no created intellect could make any approach towards
> conceiving; that in reality, there were no trees, no houses, no
> land, no sea, but all without was Maia, or illusion, the act of
> BRIM; that whatever we saw or felt was only a dream, or, as
> he expressed it in his imperfect English, thinking in one's sleep;
> and that the reunion of the soul to BRIM, from whom it originally
> sprung, was the awakening from the long sleep of finite existence.
> All this you have heard and read before as Hindu speculation.
> What struck me was, that speculations so refined and abstruse
> should, in a long course of ages, have fallen through so great a

---

[2] Sir James Mackintosh (1765–1832) was the author of important
essays. He was Stewart's choice for his successor to the Chair of Moral
Philosophy in the University of Edinburgh when Dr. Thomas Brown was
elected. Sir James would not accept the position. According to the *Dictionary of National Biography*, Sir James was "a friend and in some degree
a disciple," but he had "apparently not heard Stewart's lectures at Edinburgh" (Vol. XII, p. 617). Sir James Mackintosh was appointed to the
Recordership at Bombay in 1803, sailed on February 14, 1804, and arrived
on May 26. He served in this position until 1811. He was knighted at the
time of his appointment. On November 26, 1805, he founded the Literary
Society of Bombay. Noah Porter devotes two paragraphs to Sir James
Mackintosh as an important member of the Scottish School, following his
account of Dr. Thomas Brown. Originally written for the 7th ed. of the
Encyclopaedia Britannica (1830–42), Sir James Mackintosh's *Dissertation
on the Progress of Ethical Philosophy* was separately published in 1836. It
was severely criticised by James Mill in his *Fragment on Mackintosh*, 1835.
A second edition of the *Dissertation* was published in 1862 (Edinburgh,
Adam and Charles Black), with a preface by the editor, William Whewell,
who charges James Mill with "captiousness, contumely and buffoonery."

space as that which separates the genius of their original inventor from the mind of this weak and unlettered man. The names of these inventors have perished; but their ingenious and beautiful theories, blended with the most monstrous superstitions, have descended to men very little exalted above the most ignorant populace, and are adopted by them as a sort of articles of faith, without a suspicion of their philosophical origin, and without the possibility of comprehending any part of the premises from which they were deduced. I intend to investigate a little the history of these opinions, for I am not altogether without apprehension, that we may all the while be mistaking the hyperbolical effusions of mystical piety, for the technical language of a philosophical system. Nothing is more usual than for fervent devotion to dwell so long and so warmly on the meanness and worthlessness of created things, and on the all-sufficiency of the Supreme Being, that it slides insensibly from comparative to absolute language, and, in the eagerness of its zeal to magnify the Deity, seems to *annihilate* everything else. To distinguish between the very different import of the same words in the mouth of a mystic and of a sceptic, requires more philosophical discrimination than most of our Sanscrit investigators have hitherto shown. (WS, Vol. III, pp. 371–72.)

No doubt the fact that Stewart made such use of this letter from his friend Sir James Mackintosh, is itself sufficient proof that he was in full accord with its contents, but this is made still more evident by his referring to the letter as "the authority of so enlightened and philosophical an observer." However, whether he was in complete agreement with the theory of his friend or not, he is certainly correct in his own opinion that the tenets of Hindu philosophy have a theological origin, or, as he puts it, are the outcome of "high theological speculation."

On the other hand, the Berkeley-Hume idealism is "deduced as a sceptical consequence from a particular hypothesis concerning the origin of our knowledge, inculcated by the Schoolmen, and adopted by Locke and his followers." (WS, Vol. V, p. 107.) This is the empirical hypothesis clearly expressed in the maxim of Francis Bacon, "All our knowledge is derived from experience," but still more clearly in Diderot's rule: "Every expression which cannot find an external and a sensible object to which it can thus establish its affinity, is destitute of signification." Stewart quotes this rule from Diderot's works, and adds the following comment in a footnote: "In this *philosophical rule,* Diderot goes much further than Hume, in consequence of the different interpretation which he has given to Locke's principle." (See WS, Vol. V, p. 125.) With the contemporary logical positivists, this rule has become the fixed dogma of empirical verification. Stewart sharply contrasts the Hindu principle with this empirical principle in these words: "The scepticism of Hume, on the contrary, proceeds entirely on a scholastic hypothesis concerning perception, which, when followed out to its logical consequences, leaves no evidence for the existence either of the Divine Mind or of any other; nor, indeed, for that of anything whatever, but of our own impressions and ideas." (WS, Vol. V, p. 109.) Thus on this important issue Sir William Jones and Dugald Stewart were more or less at loggerheads.

In his third presidential discourse delivered before the Asiatic Society in Calcutta on February 2, 1786, Sir William Jones claimed that most of the philosophy of the Greeks was borrowed from the Hindus. He said:

> In more retired scenes, in groves, and in seminaries of learning, we may perceive the *Brahmans* and the *Sermanes* mentioned by Clemens, *disputing in the forms of logic,* or discoursing on the vanity of human enjoyments, on the immorality of the soul, her emanation from the eternal mind, her debasement, wanderings, and final union with her source. The six philosophical schools, whose principles are explained in the *Dersana Sastra,* comprise all the metaphysics of the old *Academy,* the *Stoa* and the *Lyceum;* nor is it possible to read the *Vedanta,* or the many fine compositions in illustration of it, without believing, that Pythagoras and Plato derived their sublime theories from the same fountain with the sages of India. (WJ, Vol. I, p. 28. Quoted by Stewart, WS, Vol. III, p. 225.)

And in his eleventh anniversary discourse delivered on February 20, 1794, he made the following statement: "Here I cannot refrain from introducing a singular tradition, which prevailed, according to the well-informed author of the *Dabistan,* in the *Panjab,* and in several Persian provinces, that, among other *Indian* curiosities, which Callisthenes transmitted to his uncle, was *a technical system of logic,* which the Brahmans had communicated to the inquisitive Greek, and which the Mohammedan writer supposes to have been the ground-work of the famous *Aristotelian* method. If this be true," continues Sir William Jones—and none will dispute the justness of his remark—"it is one of the most interesting facts that I have met with in *Asia.*" (WJ, Vol. I, p. 165. Quoted by Stewart, WS, Vol. III, pp. 225 f.) Both of these passages are quoted by Stewart in support of his contention that Aristotle borrowed a considerable portion of his logic from the Hindus. Stewart was a severe critic of Aristotelian Logic, and his use of these two passages to justify his criticisms is of considerable interest. But before quoting Sir William Jones he called attention to the fact that "Father Pons, a Jesuit missionary, was (I believe) the first person who communicated to the learned of Europe the very interesting fact, that the use of the Syllogism is, at this day, familiarly known to the Brahmins of India." (WS, Vol. III, p. 225.) The letter of Father Pons is dated 1740. Stewart says that "this information does not seem to have attracted much attention in England, until it was corroborated by the indisputable testimony of Sir William Jones," who said "I can only assure you, that I have frequently seen perfect syllogisms in the philosophical writings of the *Brahmins,* and have often heard them used in their verbal controversies." (WJ, Vol. I, p. 165.)

Stewart writes:

Of the soundness of the opinion concerning the origin of the Greek philosophy, to which these quotations give the sanction of an authority so truly respectable, our stock of facts is as yet too scanty to enable us to form a competent judgment. Some may perhaps think, that the knowledge of the Aristotelian logic which exists in India, may be sufficiently accounted for by the Mohammedan conquests; and by the veneration in which Aristotle was held, from a very early period, by the followers of the prophet. On the other hand, it must be acknowledged, that this part of Aristotle's work contains some intrinsic evidence of aid borrowed from a more ancient school. . . . Should future researches verify the suspicions of Sir William Jones and others, that the first rudiments of the art were imported into Greece from the East, it would contribute to vindicate his [Aristotle's] character against that charge of plagiarism, and of unfairness towards his predecessors, which has been admitted even by some who speak with the most unbounded reverence of his intellectual endowments. (WS, Vol. III, pp. 226 f. and 229.)

It is quite obvious that Dugald Stewart wanted to believe what Sir William Jones said about Aristotle's borrowings from the Hindu thinkers, but he certainly did so with some important qualifications, and he also added in parentheses this confession about his suggestions: "which I hazard with much diffidence." But, it should also be emphasized that Sir William Jones introduced this idea as "a singular tradition." Presumably he was unable to verify it.

Stewart makes use of a number of other passages from the writings of Sir William Jones, which do not especially deal with Hindu Philosophy, but which are here briefly summarized for the benefit of readers who may have a special interest in one or more of these items. The two scholars are in complete agreement as to the fallacies of etymologies, and Stewart quotes Jones at some length in support of his critique of etymological researches that are especially erudite and concerned with languages known only to a few experts (WS, Vol. IV, p. 67). They are also in full accord in thinking that the close similarities between the Greek and the Sanscrit, and between the Sanscrit and the Latin languages indicate that all three originated from an older language that no longer exists, Latin being considered as the oldest of the Greek dialects. (WS, Vol. V. p. 78–105.)

In his discussion of the idea of Sublimity, Stewart calls attention to the almost universal fact that when men worship they look *"upwards* towards the objects of their worship," and he quotes Sir William Jones' *Dissertation on the Gods of Greece, Italy, and India* in support of this argument (WS, Vol. V, pp.

291 ff.). Stewart also refers to Sir William Jones' translation of the *Hindu Hymn to Narrayana* (WS, Vol. VII, p. 34), and he quotes Jones as opposed to his own theory that monotheism arose from polytheism because of Biblical Revelation (WS, Vol. VII, p. 79). Sir William Jones found in the *Laws of Manu* a notable modification of the law of usury which exempted adventures at sea from usury, and Stewart makes effective use of this in his discussions of commerce and trade (WS, Vol. IX, p. 152).

The Collected Works of Dugald Stewart are worthy of the attention of every student of philosophy. His numerous references to the writings of Sir William Jones are of special significance in that they indicate how extensive was the influence of this distinguished orientalist on the thinking of one of the ablest of his British contemporaries. The intercultural contact and fertilization of ideas that we find expressed in these writings undoubtedly were of momentous importance to both cultures. Surely the writings of Stewart and Jones deserve a great deal more attention from serious students than they have thus far received.

CHAPTER VI

Thomas Brown

(1778–1820)

The Man and His Work

By Noah Porter

Thomas Brown, M. D., born at Kirkmabreck, Scotland, 1778. Student of Law, then of Medicine, Edinburgh. M. D., 1803. Associate Professor with Dugald Stewart in Moral Philosophy, 1810. Died 1820.

He was distinguished as an author in other departments than philosophy. At the age of 18 he published an able criticism, or "Observations on the Zoonomia of E. Darwin," and at different periods of his life various poetical compositions. In 1804, Edinburgh, he gave to the public *An Inquiry into the Relation of Cause and Effect,* 2 ed., 1806, 3d, with additions, 1818. After his death, *Lectures on the Philosophy of the Human Mind,* 1820, 4 vols. 8vo, Edinburgh. Compare *Accounts of the Life and Writings of Thomas Brown, M.D.,* by David Welch, Edinburgh, 1825.

Dr. Brown was distinguished for acute and subtle analysis and eloquent exposition. His *Inquiry,* etc., was his most elaborate work, and is written in an eloquent but sober diction. His Lectures were published after his death, in the form in which they were delivered to his classes. They were designed for a somewhat miscellaneous and susceptible audience, which was ready to respond to brilliant rhetorical exhibitions. Being composed by a writer distinguished for a luxuriant imagination no less than for philosophical acuteness, it is not surprising that their diction should be diffuse and ornate, and that they abound in original passages of splendid declamation as well as in copious extracts from eminent writers. The effect of these lectures during the lifetime of their author was very decided, and the influence upon the course of subsequent speculation of some of the doctrines which he set forth so impressively has been most manifest. Brown retains the doctrine insisted on by Reid and Stewart, that there are certain original intuitions which in a system of knowledge take the place of unproved first principles. Such are the belief in causation and "the irresistible feeling of identity" of the self, or soul. He contends that the Scottish philosophers extended far too widely the number of their first principles, and he followed the example of Stewart, of resolving into frequent and inseparable associations many beliefs which had been considered as original and incapable of analysis. He rejects the doctrine of consciousness which had been accepted by Reid and Stewart, and in this was followed by Hamilton, at least in part. He contemplates the phenomena of the soul as *successive states*, which he usually designates as feelings, and by introducing this appellation he practically set aside the distinction between knowledge and belief on the one hand, and sensation and emotion on the other. The term suggestion, which had been used by Berkeley and Reid in a special metaphysical meaning of *a priori* affirmation, as well as in the ordinary sense of association, he first limits to the last in what he calls *simple suggestion*, and then enlarges it as relative suggestion, so as to include all the processes in which comparison or judgment is involved, and thus provides, in a way of his own, for the suggestion—*i.e.*, the *relative suggestion—of being, self, space, and time.* But comparison and all the forms of relative suggestion are still *feelings* of likeness and unlikeness, etc. Brown's analysis of the processes of sense-perception is acute and subtle; and he attaches great importance to the *muscular sense*, not only for the special sensations which it gives, but also for its supposed significance in the generation of the relations of externality and of extension. His views of the generation or origination of the relations of space by means of relations of time, and of externality as the joint products of the muscular sensations and causality—*i.e.*, of uniform succession—are not unlike those of the school of Herbart, and have been reproduced in part by John Stuart Mill.

In respect to *causation*, he agrees with Hume, that the relation itself is resolved into invariable succession, but resists entirely his resolution of our belief in its universal presence into customary associations, contending that the belief is a first truth or intuitive belief. In his analyses of psychological phenomena, he makes a more liberal use than Stewart of the associative power; and the influence of Brown's terminology and of his methods and conclusions has been potent in the formation and consolidation of the Associational Psychology—represented by J. Mill, J. S. Mill, Alexander Bain, and Herbert Spencer.

Brown's philosophy is characterized by Sir J. Mackintosh as "an open revolt against the authority of Reid." He openly disputed the merit of Reid as to his supposed exposure and refutation of the ideal theories of sense-perception; he limited the number and importance of the principles of common sense, and greatly extended the sphere of association, in evolving apparently simple and indecomposable products from manifold elements of experience and feeling. In these particulars his teachings and influence differ from those of Reid.

The *Inquiry into the Relation of Cause and Effect* appears in its modified and completed form in the third edition in 1818. The first edition, 1804, was limited to an examination into the theory of Hume. The second, 1806, entered into the discussion of the correct theory and its applications. The third edition is divided into 4 Parts: 1st, "On the Real Import of the Relation of Cause and Effect," in which a cause is defined as "that which immediately precedes any change, and which existing at any time in similar circumstances has been always, and will be always, immediately followed by a similar change." Brown justifies this definition by considering all the classes of events to which the appellation is applied, whether these events are bodily or mental. Among the latter, special importance has been attached to the volitions, and Brown in analyzing the volitions is led to resolve them into permanent and prevailing desires consequent upon deliberation. Part 2 treats of the sources of delusion with respect to this relation. The author first asserts that substances are nothing diverse from their qualities, although we are tempted to regard the two as diverse. Language by its metaphors increases the illusion, as when we speak of the *bond of connection* between cause and effect. The conception of power as latent is next noticed. The exercise of power is, in fact, only a name for the presence of certain antecedent circumstances. Our senses are so imperfect as to fail to reveal many of these circumstances. Part 3 discusses the circumstances, in which the belief of the relation arises. Experience is the first named, the author contending that only after the experience of an antecedence and succession of two events does the belief occur— that one event is the cause of another. This belief is not the result of reasoning, nor does it proceed from the *a priori* axiom of the *sufficient reason* or any other axiom which expresses independent certainty concerning the physical forces. Part 4 is devoted to Mr. Hume's theory of our belief of this relation. He notices first the relation of Hume's special theory of causation to his general theory of the relation of ideas to impressions. He next inquires why frequent experiences seem to be necessary to ground the belief in a special connection of two events as cause and effect. To this question he replies that they are necessary only to enable us to separate the events from all superfluous circumstances; and that customary occurrence, which Hume contends is the only explanation of the belief, is only necessary to enable us to effect this separation. But the way in which this customary occurrence contributes to this belief is not by effecting a ready transition from one idea to another, as Hume contends.

Next, Dr. Brown seeks to show that Dr. Reid errs in accepting Hume's idea of power, viz., that of invariable antecedence; while Dr. Reid is right in ascribing the belief in this necessary connection to an intuitive principle. He concludes with an argument and with notes, to show that his own doctrine of causation is entirely consistent with belief in God and the possibility of miraculous events, both of which Hume denies.

The *Lectures on the Philosophy of the Mind* contain Dr. Brown's psychological analyses, as given in the lecture-room. Dr. Brown was a physician, and he contemplated writing a treatise on the physiology of the mind. He devotes several preliminary lectures to the consideration of the methods appropriate to physical inquiry. He then proceeds to inquire how far the same methods are applicable to the mind. To this question he answers: Of mind and matter our knowledge is only relative—*i.e.*, we know only the phenomena of either; of the essence and possible capacities of either we know nothing. "Of the essence of the mind we know nothing but in relation to the states or feelings that form or have formed our momentary consciousness." But yet "it is the same individual mind which in intellectual investigation is at once the object and the observer." "But the noble endowment of memory with which the Creator has blessed us solves all the mystery of this singular paradox." By this faculty philosophy is possible; the mind, though simple, is extended and multiplied, the relation of thought to thought becomes possible, and we class the phenomena of spirit as we do the phenomena of matter. In Lecture 10, the author observes, that by the constitution of our nature we ascribe the phenomena of matter and of mind to one permanent subject. Our business is to analyze the phenomena of mind, as we analyze the phenomena of matter; but there is a difference, in that what we call a complex phenomenon of the mind is in itself indivisible. In Lecture 12 he treats of consciousness as equivalent "to the whole series of states of the mind, whatever the individual momentary states may be," and denies that there is a power by which the mind knows its own states, or that to this power the name of consciousness is applied, as is implicitly held by Locke and explicitly by Reid and Stewart. The direct experience of any mental state again does not imply the self as its subject. This comes only after the remembrance of several states "by that irresistible law of our nature which impresses us with the conviction of our identity." This belief in mental identity is defended against objections, and in this connection the doctrine of first truths, or truths of intuition generally, is distinctly emphasized. Lecture 16 he devotes to the classification of mental phenomena. After considering and criticizing that commonly received, viz., the intellectual and active powers of understanding and will, he proposes a division into *external and internal affections,* i.e., the affections occasioned by external agents and those which spring from the mind's overt activity. The internal affections he again subdivides into the intellectual states and the emotions. The external affections also include those which are commonly termed *sensations.* These sensations he subjects to a special analysis, more extended and apparently more subtle than any to be found in any previous English psychology. He begins with smell, which gives sensation only, or at the utmost, a sensation, with the suggestion of *a cause,* but nothing further— neither externality nor extension. The same is true of hearing and taste. The belief of the external and the extended world he limits to touch only. In analyzing the phenomena of this sense, he groups its affections into the two classes of resistance and extension.

The experience of resistance he ascribes, not to the tactual experiences, but to those of the muscular sense. But even these would be regarded as purely subjective, did they not occur in a different causal (i.e., time) order. Such a different order of cause and effects might be conceived in the act of stretching the arm, with or without pressure against a resisting object, and this would suggest the existence of an object differing from the mind itself—i.e., as external. Extension is analyzed by a resort to the relations of time—i.e., to the successive experiences of the muscular and other sensations. In connection with this analysis he considers—Lectures 26, 7—Reid's supposed confutation of the Ideal system in which he charges him with ignorance of the system as originally held and with ignorance that it had been abandoned. (Cf. Hamilton's refutation of this critique, *Ed. Review,* vol. 52, No. 103. Discussion II.) Lectures 27–28 are devoted to an analysis of the Feelings ascribed to Vision, in which Brown denies that the experience of visual sensations necessarily suggests extension in any of its relations, but contends that the internal and apparently inseparable connection of the two is to be explained by the process of association.

The Internal Intellectual states of the mind, Brown holds, are "all referable to two generic susceptibilities—those of simple suggestion and relative suggestion." Simple suggestion is equivalent to association as usually conceded. Relative suggestion occurs on the perception of two objects, when we have a feeling of any relation between them. The laws of simple suggestion are of two classes, primary and secondary. The primary laws are three, viz., Resemblance, Contrast, and nearness of Place and Time. The secondary laws are those which respect the circumstances which modify the action of the simple laws. Of these there are nine, as the original feelings are (1) of longer or shorter continuance, (2) more or less lively, (3) more or less often present, (4) more or less recent, (5) more or less pure from mixture, (6) variable with original constitution, (7) *do.* with temporary emotions, (8) *do.* with changes in the body, (9) *do.* with previous habits. To simple suggestion are reduced certain supposed Faculties of the mind, as Conception, Memory, Imagination, and Habit.

The feelings of *Relative Suggestion* are excited by objects which are co-existing and successive. Objects are really co-existent as those which are material, and seemingly such as the mental. To both belong the relations of position, resemblance, or difference, proportion, degree, and comprehension. The relation of resemblance explains the possibility of general notions, and of classification, the exercise of judgment, and Reasoning. Brown professes to be himself a Conceptualist, though he prefers the appellations Notionist or Relationist, and charges against the Nominalist that he overlooks the relation of resemblance. The syllogistic method he criticizes as setting up what is a form of successful proof to others as the method of universal investigation. Reasoning is but a succession of judgments. The process is but a series of relative suggestions, of which the subjects are mutually related. We reason from particulars to particulars, when these mutual relations are discerned, as truly as from generals to particulars.

The Relations of succession, when they are invariable, comprehend all that we usually recognize as the relations of causes and effects. They provide for all the judgments of causality. The exclusive occupation of the mind with certain relative suggestions, is the same with the process usually called *abstraction*.

The next class of internal states of mind are *the emotions*. These differ from the intellectual feelings "by that peculiar vividness of feeling which every one understands, but which it is impossible to express by any verbal definition," etc. The Emotions are classed as Immediate, Retrospective, and Prospective. The immediate emotions are subdivided into those which do not, and those which do, involve moral affections. Under the first are Cheerfulness and Melancholy, Wonder at what is strange, Languor at what is tedious, Beauty and Deformity, Sublimity, Ludicrousness. Under the second are feelings distinctive of Vice and Virtue, Love and Hate, Sympathy, Pride, and Humility. The Retrospective Emotions having relations to others are Anger and Gratitude. The Retrospective Emotions which have reference to ourselves are Regret and its opposite, and Remorse and its opposite.

The Prospective Emotions comprehend the desire for Continued Existence, the desire of Pleasure, the desire of Action, the desire of Society, the desire of Knowledge, the desire of Power in the two forms of Ambition and of Power, the desire of the Affection of others, the desire of Glory, the desire of Happiness of others, the desire of Evil to others.

The ethical theory of Brown starts with the principle that moral distinctions are original—i.e., that there are certain feelings which are followed by approbation and the opposite. The foresight of certain actions not yet performed as respectively approvable and the contrary explains the sense of obligation; when we think of such actions as already past, we conceive of them as having merit.[1]

---

[1] In his *Realistic Universe* (Revised Edition), p. 84, John Elof Boodin accepts Brown's modification of Reid's theory of sense perception. (Editor's note.)

The Sceptical System of Berkeley and Hindu Philosophy

By Thomas Brown

This selection is from Thomas Brown's *Lectures on the Philosophy of Mind* (in four vols.; Edinburgh: Adam and Charles Black, 1851), Vol. II, pp. 14–22. Brown claims that Berkeley is really a sceptic even though he thought his philosophy was "an antidote to scepticism." Compare Brown's discussion of Sir William Jones' comments with that of Stewart above, pp. 180 ff. The title has been supplied.

IF THERE WERE, indeed, any sceptic as to the existence of an external world, who could seriously profess that his practical conduct was in accordance with his speculative disbelief, we might very justly exercise, with respect to his own profession, that philosophic doubt or disbelief which he recommends. Pyrrho, the great founder of this philosophy, is, indeed, said to have acted so truly on his principles, that if a cart ran against him, or a dog attacked him, or if he came upon a precipice, he would not stir a foot to avoid the danger. "But his attendants," says Dr. Reid, "who, happily for him, were not so great sceptics, took care to keep him out of harm's way: so that he lived till he was ninety years of age." [1] In all these cases, we may safely take for granted that this venerable sceptic, when he exhibited himself with his train of domestics, knew, at least, as well as the spectators, the nature of the comedy which he was acting, for their entertainment and his own imagined glory; that he could discriminate, with perfect accuracy, the times when it would be safe, and the times when it would be unsafe, for him to be consistent; and that he would never feel, in so strong and lively a manner, the force of his own principles, as when he was either absolutely alone, or with attendants within a very few inches of the ground on which he was philosophizing. We are

---

[1] Reid's *Inquiry into the Human Mind*, chap. i, sect. 5.

told, accordingly, that when his passions were too strongly roused to allow him to remember the part which he was acting, he entered with sufficient readiness into his native character of a mere human being. Of this, one ludicrous instance is recorded, in which his anger against his cook so completely got the better, both of his moral and physical philosophy, that, with the spit in his hand, and the meat on it, which had been roasting, he pursued him to the very market-place. Many stories of this sort, however, we may well suppose would be invented against philosophers of a class that at once challenged the opposition of the whole mob of mankind, and afforded subjects of that obvious and easy ridicule which the mob of mankind, even without the provocation of such a challenge, are always sufficiently ready to seize.

Into a detail of the sceptical system of Berkeley it is unnecessary to enter at any length; since, notwithstanding the general acuteness which its truly illustrious author has displayed in this, and in all his works, I cannot but consider his ideal system as presenting a very imperfect and inaccurate view, not merely of the real phenomena of the mind, but even of the sceptical argument against the existence of matter. It was not as a sceptic, however, that this most devout and aimable of philosophers, to whom Pope scarcely paid a higher compliment than was strictly due, in ascribing to him "every virtue under heavens" [2]—it was not as a sceptic that he was desirous of being ranked. On the contrary, I have no doubt that his system seemed to him valuable, chiefly for being, as he conceived, an antidote to scepticism; and that he was far less anxious to display acuteness than to expose the sophistry of materialism, and to present, as he thought, an additional argument for the existence of a divine omnipresent mind, which unquestionably it would have afforded, and an argument, too, it must be owned, completely irresistible, if our mere ideas were what he conceived them to be. These he evidently considered not as states of the individual mind, but as separate things existing in it, and capable of existing in

---

[2] "Epilogue to the Satires," Dial. II. v.73.

other minds, but in them alone; and it is in consequence of these assumptions that his system, if it were to be considered as a system of scepticism, is chiefly defective. But having, as he supposed, these ideas, and conceiving that they did not perish when they ceased to exist in his mind, since the same ideas recurred at intervals, he deduced, from the necessity which there seemed for some omnipresent mind, in which they might exist during the intervals of recurrence, the necessary existence of the Deity; and if, indeed, as he supposed, ideas be something different from the mind itself, recurring only at intervals to created minds, and incapable of existing but in mind, the demonstration of some infinite omnipresent mind, in which they exist during these intervals of recurrence to finite minds, must be allowed to be perfect. The precise nature of the argument, and its demonstrative force, if the hypothetical circumstances, which Berkeley himself was far from considering as hypothetical, be admitted, have not been sufficiently regarded by philosophers, when they express their astonishment that a system, which, if not scepticism, is, at least, so much akin to it, or so favourable, at least, to the general sceptical spirit, should yet have been brought forward, as its truly pious author informs us, for the express purpose of combating scepticism. He is not, indeed, always a very perspicuous unfolder of his own opinions; but, in a passage of his third Dialogue, the series of propositions which I have now stated as constituting his demonstration, are delivered by himself with great distinctness and brevity. "When I deny," says Philonous to Hylas, "when I deny sensible things an existence out of the mind, I do not mean my mind in particular, but all minds. Now, it is plain they have an existence exterior to my mind, since I find them, by experience, to be independent of it. There is, therefore, some other mind wherein they exist during the intervals between the times of my perceiving them as likewise they did before my birth, and would do after my supposed annihilation. And as the same is true with regard to all other finite created spirits, it necessarily follows there is an Omnipresent Eternal Mind, which knows and comprehends all things, and exhibits them to our view in such a manner, and according to such rules, as he himself hath ordained, and are by us all termed the Laws of Nature." [3]

The existence of ideas as separate from the mind, and the permanent existence of these when they have ceased to exist in the individual mind, are evidently assumptions as gratuitous as the assumption of the external existence of matter itself could have been; or rather, the permanent and independent ideas are truly matter, under another name; and to believe that these foreign independent substances, which pass from mind to mind, exist in the mind, is not to intellectualize matter, but to materialize intellect. A mind containing, or capable of containing, something foreign within itself, and not merely one foreign substance, but a multitude of foreign substances at the same moment, is no longer that simple indivisible existence, which we termed spirit. Any of the elementary atoms of matter is, indeed, more truly spiritual; the very notion of recipiency of any kind being as little consistent with our notion of mind as the notion of hardness or squareness.

The whole force of the pious demonstration, therefore, which Berkeley flattered himself with having urged irresistibly, is completely obviated by the simple denial that ideas are anything more than the mind itself affected in a certain manner; since, in this case, our ideas exist no longer than our mind is affected in that particular manner which constitutes each particular idea; and to say that our ideas exist in the divine mind, would thus be to say, only, that our mind itself exists in the divine mind. There is not the sensation of colour in addition to the mind, nor the sensation of fragrance in addition to the mind, but, according to that juster view of the mental phenomena which I have repeatedly endeavoured to impress on you, the sensation of colour is the mind existing in a certain state, and the sensation of fragrance is the mind existing in a different state.

The most philosophic scepticism, as to the existence of external things, is unquestionably that which is founded on this very view of the phenomena of the mind. All the terms which

---

[3] *Three Dialogues*, &c., pp. 109–10.

we use to express our knowledge, sensations, perceptions, ideas, notions, propositions, judgments, intuitions, conclusions, or whatever other terms we may employ to express particular varieties of thought, are significant, it may be said, and truly said, of states or affections of the mind, and of nothing more. What I term my perception of the colour, or softness, or shape, or fragrance, or taste of a peach, is a certain state of my own mind: for my mind surely can be conscious only of its own feelings; or rather, as the consciousness of present feelings is a redundancy of language, my mind, affected in a certain manner, whether it be with what is termed sensation or knowledge, or belief, can still be nothing more than my mind itself affected in a certain manner—my mind itself existing in a certain state. Against this argument, I confess that I know no mere argument which can be adduced in opposition, any more than I know any mere argument which can be adduced against the strange conclusions that are most legitimately drawn from the doctrine of the infinite divisibility of matter, and various other physical and mathematical applications of the notion of infinity. In no one of these cases, however, do we feel our belief shaken; because it is founded either on associations so early, and strong, and indissoluble, as those which we have been endeavouring to trace, or, if not on those, on principles of direct intuition, in that species of internal revelation which gives to reason itself, in the primary truths on which every argument proceeds, its divine authority; and we only smile at conclusions, in which it is impossible for us to find a single logical error, but which, from the constitution of our nature, it is physically impossible for us to admit, or to admit, at least, without an instant dissent, which renders our momentary logical admission as nugatory as if the direct existence of an external world had been established by the clearest logical demonstration.

In one of the Anniversary Orations of Sir William Jones, of which the subject is the philosophy of the Asiatics, he informs us that a system of idealism, very similar to that of Berkeley, is to be found in the metaphysics of Hindustan. The fundamental tenet of one great school of the philosophers of that ancient

land of philosophy, is the disbelief of the existence of matter;
the phenomena of the seeming material universe being conceived by them to be only an illusive representation which the
Deity presents to the mind (and which they distinguish by the
name of *Maja*): while the opposite species of scepticism is to be
found in another sect of their philosophers, who disbelieve the
existence of mind, and reduce all the phenomena of thought to
material organization. The same subtlety and refinement of scepticism, which have led to the systems of materialism and idealism in our Western World, are to be found, we are told, in
the corresponding systems of the East.[4]

Why is it that we are struck with no common emotion on
finding, in the metaphysics of that distant country, systems of
opinions so similar to our own? Is it that the notion of the
immense space which separates us, unites with our conception,
and impresses us, as it were, with the omnipresence of our own
intellectual nature—when we recognise, on scenes so remote, and
in circumstances of society so different, the same thoughts, and
doubts, and errors, which have perplexed, and occupied, and
delighted ourselves? This recognition, in whatever circumstances
it may occur, gives to us a feeling of more than kindred—a sort
of identity with the universal nature of man, in all its times and
places. The belief which others share with us seems to be our
own belief, which has passed from each to each, or is present to
all, like those permanent ideas of which Berkeley speaks, that
quit one intellect to exist in another. We cannot separate the
thought which we remember from the notion of the mind which
we remember to have conceived it; and it seems to us, therefore, not as if similar doubts and errors, but almost as if the very
doubts and errors of our own mind, and its ardour of inquiry,
and frequent disappointments, and occasional, but rare felicities
of discovery, had spread and renewed themselves in a remote
existence. It is this recognition of our common nature, which
gives the chief interest to scenes that have been occupied with
the passions of beings like ourselves. The mountains which the

---

[4] WJ, Vol. I, pp. 165–66, 4to Edit.

Titans were fabled to have heaped up in their war against Jupiter, must have excited, even in the most devout believer of Grecian mythology, emotions far less ardent and immediate than the sight of the humbler cliffs, at which the small Spartan host, and their gallant leader, devoted themselves in the defensive war against the Persian invaders. The races of men may perish, but the remembrance of them still lives imperishable, and seems to claim kindred with us as often as we tread the same soil, or merely think of those who have trod it.

> Turn thy sight eastward, o'er the time-hush'd plains
> Now graves of vanish'd empire, once gleam'd o'er
> From flames on hallow'd altars, hail'd by hymns
> Of seers, awakeners of the worshipp'd Sun!
> Ask silent Tigris—Bid Euphrates tell
> Where is the grove-crown'd Baal to whose stern frown
> Bow'd haughty Babylon?—Chaldea, famed
> For star-taught sages—hard Phoenicia's sons,
> Fierce, fear-surmounting curbers of the deep,
> Who stretch'd a floating sceptre o'er the seas,
> And made mankind one empire?—Where is now
> Egypt's wide-homaged Isis? where the Thors,
> That shook the shakers of the Roman world? [5]

The very gods of all these countries have perished but the mortals who bent the knee before them still survive them in the immortality of our common nature—in that universal interest which gives to us a sort of intellectual existence in scenes and times the most remote, and makes the thoughts and emotions of others as it were a part of our own being—uniting the past, the present, and the future, and blending man with man wherever he is to be found.

---

[5] Aaron Hill's *Free Thoughts on Faith,* 220–27.

The Nature of Consciousness

By Thomas Brown

This selection is from Lecture VII of Thomas Brown's *Lectures on the Philosophy of Mind,* Vol. I, pp. 294–303 and p. 305.

IN THE SYSTEMS of philosophy, which have been most generally prevalent, especially in this part of the island, consciousness has always been classed as one of the intellectual powers of the mind, differing from its other powers, as these mutually differ from each other. It is accordingly ranked by Dr. Reid, as separate and distinct, in his catalogue of the intellectual powers; and he says of it, that "it is an operation of the understanding of its own kind, and cannot be logically defined. The objects of it are our present pains, our pleasures, our hopes, our fears, our desires, our doubts, our thoughts of every kind; in a word, all the passions, and all the actions and operations of our own minds, while they are present." And in various parts of his works, which it would be needless to quote, he alludes to its radical difference from the other powers of the mind, as if it were a point on which there could be no question. To me, however, I must confess, it appears, that this attempt to double, as it were, our various feelings, by making them not to constitute our consciousness, but to be the objects of it, as of a distinct intellectual power, is not a faithful statement of the phenomena of the mind, but is founded, partly on a confusion of thought, and still more on a confusion of language. Sensation is not the object of consciousness different from itself, but a particular sensation is the consciousness of the moment; as a particular hope, or fear, or grief, or resentment, or simple remembrance, may be the actual consciousness of the next moment. In short, if the mind of man, and all the changes which take place in it, from the first feeling with which life commenced, to the last with which it closes, could be made visible to any other thinking being, a certain series of feelings alone, that is to say, a certain number of successive states of the mind, would be distinguishable in it, forming, indeed, a variety of sensations, and thoughts, and passions, as momentary states of the mind, but all of them existing individually, and successively to each other. To suppose the mind to exist in two different states, in the same moment, is a manifest absurdity. To the whole series of states of the mind, then, whatever the individual momentary successive states may be, I give the name of our consciousness—using that term, not to express any new state additional to the whole series (for to that, which is already the whole, nothing can be added, and the mind, as I have already said, cannot be conceived to exist at once in two different states) but merely as a short mode of expressing the wide variety of our feelings; in the same manner as I use any other generic word for expressing briefly the individual varieties comprehended under it. There are not sensations, thoughts, passions, and also consciousness, any more than there is quadruped or animal, as a separate being, to be added to the wolves, tigers, elephants, and other living creatures, which I include under those terms.

The fallacy of conceiving consciousness to be something different from the feeling, which is said to be its object, has arisen, in a great measure, from the use of the personal pronoun *I*, which the conviction of our identity, during the various feelings, or temporary consciousnesses of different moments, has led us to employ, as significant of our permanent self—of that being, which is conscious, and variously conscious, and which continues, after these feelings have ceased, to be the subject of other consciousnesses, as transient as the former. *I* am *conscious* of a certain feeling, really means, however, no more than this—I feel in a certain manner, or, in other words, my mind exists in that state which constitutes a certain feeling; the mere existence of that feeling, and not any additional and distinguishable feeling that is to be termed consciousness, being all which is essential to the state of my mind, at the particular moment of sensation; for a pleasure, or pain, of which we are not conscious, is a pleasure or pain, that, in reference to us at least, has no existence. But when we say, I am conscious of a particular feeling, in the usual paraphrastic phraseology of our language, which has no mode of expressing, in a single word, the mere existence of a feeling, we are apt, from a prejudice of grammar, to separate the sentient *I* and the feeling, as different—not different, as they really are, merely in this respect, that the feeling is one momentary and changeable state of the permanent substance I, that is capable of existing also, at other moments, in other states—but so radically different, as to justify our classing the feeling in the relation of an object, to that sentient principle which we call I—and an obejct to it, not in retrospect only, as when the feeling is remembered, or when it is viewed in relation to other remembered feelings—but in the very moment of the primary sensation itself; as if there could truly be two distinct states of the same mind, at that same moment, one of which states is to be termed sensation, and the other different state of the same mind to be termed consciousness.

To estimate more accurately the effect which this reference to self produces, let us imagine a human being to be born with his faculties perfect as in mature life, and let us suppose a sensation to arise for the first time in his mind. For the sake of greater simplicity, let us suppose the sensation to be of a kind as little complex as possible; such, for example, as that which the fragrance of the rose excites. If, immediately after this first sensation, we imagine the sentient principle to be extinguished, what are we to call that feeling which filled and constituted the brief moment of life? It was a simple sensation, and nothing more; and if only we say, or do not say, that the mind was conscious of the sensation—we shall convey precisely the same meaning; the consciousness of the sensation being, in that case, only a tautological expression of the sensation itself. There will be, in this first momentary state, no separation of self and the sensation—no little proposition formed in the mind, *I feel* or *I am conscious of a feeling*—but the feeling, and the sentient I, will, for the moment, be the same. It is this simple feeling, and this alone, which is the whole consciousness of the first moment; and no reference can be made of this to a self, which is inde-

pendent of the temporary consciousness; because the knowledge
of self, as distinct from the particular feeling, implies the remembrance of former feelings—of feelings which, together with
the present, we ascribe to one thinking principle; recognizing the
principle, the self, the *me*, as the same, amid all its transient
diversities of consciousness.

Let us now, then, instead of supposing life, as in the former
case, to be extinguished immediately after the first sensation,
suppose another sensation to be excited, as, for instance, that
which is produced by the sound of a flute. The mind either will
be completely absorbed in this new sensation, without any
subsequent remembrance—in which case the consciousness of
the sensation, as in the case of the fragrance that preceded it,
will be only another more paraphrastic expression of the simple sensation—or the remembrance of the former feeling will
arise. If the remembrance of the former feeling arises, and the
two different feelings be considered by the mind at once, it
will now, by that irresistible law of our nature, which impresses
us with the conviction of our identity, conceive the two sensations, which it recognizes as different in themselves, to have
yet belonged to the same being—that being, to which, when it
has the use of language, it gives the name of self, and in relation to which it speaks, as often as it uses the pronoun *I*.
The notion of self, as the lasting subject of successive transient
feelings, being now, and not till now, acquired, through the
remembrance of former sensations or temporary diversities of
consciousness, the mind will often again, when other new sensations may have arisen, go through a similar process, being not
merely affected with the particular momentary sensation, but
remembering other prior feelings, and identifying it with them,
in the general designation of self. In these circumstances, the
memory of the past will often mingle with and modify the
present; and, now, indeed, to form the verbal proposition, *I
am conscious of a particular sensation*—since the very word *I*
implies that this remembrance and identification has taken
place—may be allowed to express something more than the mere
existence of the momentary sensation, for it expresses also that

the mind, which now exists in the state of this particular sensation, has formerly existed in a different state. There is a remembrance of former feelings, and a belief that the present and the past have been states of one substance. But this belief, or in other words, this remembrance of former feelings, is so far from being essential to every thought or sensation, that innumerable feelings every moment arise, without any such identification with the past. They are felt, however, for this is necessarily implied in their existence; but they exist, as transient thoughts or sensations only, and the consciousness, which we have of them, in these circumstances, is nothing more than the thoughts or sensations themselves, which could not be thoughts or sensations if they were not felt.

In the greater number of our successions of momentary feelings, then, when no reference is made to former states of the mind, the consciousness is obviously nothing more than the simple momentary feeling itself as it begins and ceases; and when there is a reference to former states of the mind, we discover on analysis only a remembrance, like all our other remembrances, and a feeling of common relation of the past and the present affection of the mind to one permanent subject. It is the belief of our continued identity which involves this particular feeling of relation of past and present feelings: and consciousness, in this sense of the term, is only a word expressive of that belief.

That the fragrance of a rose, the sound of a flute, and in general all the other objects of sense, might have excited precisely the same immediate sensations as at present, Dr. Reid admits, though the belief of our personal identity had not been impressed upon us; for he ascribes this belief to an instinctive principle only, and acknowledges, that there is nothing in our sensations themselves, from which any such inference could be drawn by reason. If, then, this instinctive belief of identity had not been, as at present, a natural law of human thought, operating irresistibly on the remembrance of our different feelings, we should have had no notion of *self*, of *me*, the sentient and thinking being, who exists at the present moment, and who existed before the present moment: and what, then, would have been the consciousness, accompanying, and different from, our sensations, when they merely flashed along the mind and vanished? The most zealous defender of consciousness, as a separate intellectual power, must surely admit, that, in such circumstances, it would have been nothing more than sensation itself. It is the belief of our identity only, which gives us the notion of self, as the subject of various feelings, and it is the notion of self, as the subject of various former feelings, which leads us to regard the consciousness of the moment, as different from the sensation of the moment; because it suggests to us those former feelings, which truly were different from it, or at least that subject *mind*, which unquestionably existed before the present sensation.

If it be said, that the faculty of consciousness is nothing more than this reference to the past, and consequent belief of identity, we may in that case very safely admit its existence; though the classification of it, as a peculiar intellectual power, would in that case be a most singular anomaly in arrangement, and would involve a very absurd, or at least a very awkward use of a term. To assert this signification of it, however, would be to admit every thing for which I have contended. But it certainly is not the sense which has been attached to it by philosophers; and indeed, in this sense, consciousness, instead of having for its objects, as Dr. Reid says, all "our present pains, our pleasures, our hopes, our fears, our desires, our doubts, our thoughts of every kind; in a word, all the passions, and all the actions and operations of our own minds, while they are present," would be limited to the comparatively few, of which the consideration of our personal identity forms a part. In far the greater number of our feelings, as I have already said, the sensation dies away, almost in the moment—not, indeed, without being enjoyed or suffered, but without any reference to self, as the subject of various feelings, or remembrance of any prior state of mind, as distinct from the present. The belief of our identity is surely not the only belief that arises from an instinctive principle; and if its existence entitle us, in our systematic arrangements, to the possession of a new intellectual power, every other belief that arises instinctively from a principle of our constitution, must give us a similar title to enlarge the catalogue of our faculties. The never-failing and instant faith, by which we expect, without the slightest doubt of the similarity of the future, that events will continue to follow each other, in the same order as at present—that bodies will fall to the ground, fire burn, food satisfy the craving of our appetite—that immediate intuitive principles of belief, on which all our foresight depends, and according to which we regulate our whole conduct in providing for the future, should certainly, in that case, be ascribed by us to some peculiar intellectual power, for which it would be easy to invent a name. It is not by any inference of our reason we believe that the sound of a flute which preceded the fragrance of a rose, and the fragrance of a rose which followed the sound of a flute, excited sensations that were states of the same identical mind; for there is nothing, in either of the separate sensations, or in both together, from which such an inference can be drawn; and yet, notwithstanding the impossibility of inferring it, we believe this at least as strongly as we believe any of the conclusions of our reasoning. In like manner, it is not by any inference of reason we believe, that fire will warm us tomorrow, as it has warmed us today; for there is nothing, in the fire of today, or in the sensation of warmth, considered as a mere sequence of it, from which the succession of a similar sensation to the fire of tomorrow can be inferred; yet we also rely on this future sequence, at least as strongly, as we believe any of the conclusions of our reasoning. In both cases the parallel is complete; and, in both, the evidence of a particular intellectual faculty must consequently be alike—or in neither is there sufficient evidence of such a power.

There is, indeed, one other sense, in which we often talk of our consciousness of a feeling, and a sense in which it must be allowed that the consciousness is not precisely the same as the feeling itself. This is, when we speak of a feeling, not actually existing at present, but past—as when we say, that we are conscious of having seen, or heard, or done something. Such a use of the term, however, is pardonable only in the privileged looseness and inaccuracy of familiar conversation; the consciousness, in this case, being precisely synonymous with remembrance or memory, and not a power different from the remembrance. The remembrance of the feeling, and the vivid feeling itself, indeed, are different. But the remembrance, and the consciousness of the remembrance, are the same—as the consciousness of a sensation, and the sensation, are the same; and to be conscious that we have seen or spoken to any one, is only to remember that we have seen or spoken to him.

Much of this very confusion with respect to memory, however, I have no doubt, has been always involved in the assertion of a consciousness as a peculiar and distinct power of the mind. When we think of feelings long past, it is impossible for us not to be aware that our mind is then truly retrospective; and memory seems to us sufficient to account for the whole. But when the retrospect is of very recent feelings—of feelings, perhaps, that existed as distinct states of the mind, the very moment before our retrospect began, the short interval is forgotten, and we think that the primary feeling, and our consideration of the feeling, are strictly simultaneous. We have a sensation—we look instantly back on that sensation—such is consciousness as distinguished from the feeling that is said to be its object. When it is any thing more than the sensation, thought, or emotion, of which we are said to be conscious, it is a brief and rapid retrospect. Its object is not a present feeling, but a past feeling, as truly as when we look back, not on the moment immediately preceding, but on some distant event or emotion of our boyhood. . . .

Consciousness, then, I conclude, in its simplest acceptation, when it is understood as regarding the present only, is no distinct power of the mind, or name of a distinct class of feelings, but is only a general term for all our feelings, of whatever species these may be—sensations, thoughts, desires; in short, all those states or affections of mind, in which the phenomena of mind consist; and when it expresses more than this, it is only the remembrance of some former state of the mind, and a feeling of the relation of the past and the present as states of one sentient substance. The term is very conveniently used for the purpose of abbreviation, when we speak of the whole variety of our feelings, in the same manner as any other general term is used, to express briefly the multitude of individuals that agree in possessing some common property of which we speak; when the enumeration of these, by description and name, would be as wearisome to the patience, as is would be oppressive to the memory. But still, when we speak of the evidence of consciousness, we mean nothing more than the evidence implied in the mere existence of our sensations, thoughts, desires—which it is utterly impossible for us to believe to be and not to be; or, in other words, impossible for us to feel and not to feel at the same moment.

CHAPTER VII

Sir William Hamilton
(1788–1856)

The Man and His Work

By NOAH PORTER

SIR WILLIAM HAMILTON, BART., born at Glasgow, 1788. Ed. at Glasgow and Oxford. Called to the Bar 1813. Professor of Universal History in Edinburgh, 1821—of Logic and Metaphysics, 1836. Died in 1856. Published Essays in *Edinburgh Review* on Philosophy, viz.: "On the Philosophy of the Unconditioned," October, 1829, vol. 50. "On the Philosophy of Perception," October, 1830, vol. 53. "On Logic," recent English Treatises, October, 1832, vol. 56. "On the Deaf and Dumb," July, 1835, vol. 61; "On Idealism," Arthur Collier, April, 1839, vol. 68. These were published as *Articles on Literature and Education,* collected with notes and appendices, 1852, 2d ed. 1853. Many of these essays have been translated into French, with biographical and critical introduction by W. Peisse; also into Italian by S. Lo Gatto. A selection from these discussions was republished in America, with introduction by Robert Turnbull, D.D., New York, 1855. From the discussions and the notes, etc., attached to the works of Reid, O. W. Wight edited a volume, *The Philosophy of Sir William Hamilton;* New York, 1853, 3d ed. 1855. In 1846—London and Edinburgh—Hamilton published the *Works of Thomas Reid, D.D.,* fully collected, with abundant notes and supplementary dissertations—edition not finished till after his death—and in part from his papers, 1853. Also, in 1854, he began to edit the *Works of Dugald Stewart* in eleven volumes (edition not complete at his death). Hamilton's *Lectures on Metaphysics and Logic* were edited after his death by Rev. H. L. Mansel, of Oxford, since Dean of St. Paul's, and John Veitch, since Professor in Glasgow, London, and Edinburgh, 1859–60, also Boston, 1859–60.

These works have been abridged and edited for schools, viz.: *The Metaphysics*, by Prof. Francis Bowen, Cambridge, 1861. *The Logic*, by Prof. Henry N. Day, Cincinnati, 1863. *An Outline of Sir William Hamilton's Philosophy:* a textbook for students, was prepared by Prof. J. Clark Murray, Boston, 1870.

Cf. *Memoir of Sir William Hamilton, Bart., Professor of Logic and Metaphysics in the University of Edinburgh,* by John Veitch, M. A., Professor of Logic and Rhetoric in the University of Glasgow, William Blackwood & Sons, 1869.

Sir William Hamilton is the most conspicuous figure in the history of English Philosophy within the present century. His influence has been more efficient than that of any other person in arousing the attention of his countrymen to a fresh interest in the profoundest problems of philosophy, and in the careful study of its erudition and history. He was confessedly the most learned student of his time. No writer had so completely mastered the works of the Aristotelian commentators, of the schoolmen and their successors. His erudition was more than a dry accumulation of the principles and doctrines of past thinkers. He uniformly studied the philosophies of the past in the light of the discussions of the present, and saw with clear and comprehensive insight the relations of the one to the other. The dissertations appended to his edition of the collected works of Reid are eminent examples of his comprehensive and sagacious learning. He was also an acute critic. The critical reviews, published as discussions, etc., as well as the footnotes upon Reid, are examples of his critical sagacity. But he was pre-eminently a logician, delighting in the forms of the syllogism and in the history of all logical doctrines. He was also interested in psychological observations and in metaphysical analysis, and pre-eminently able in both.

In Logic, Hamilton introduced what he called the Quantification of the Predicate, the design of which was to dispense altogether with the necessity of the conversion of propositions. This change involved an entirely new scheme of logical notation, which was perfected by Hamilton, and has been introduced or noticed in many subsequent treatises on Formal Logic. . . .

In Psychology, Hamilton follows in general the method and the terminology of Reid. He was, however, in respect to some points, very largely influenced by Kant. Kant's influence over him, however, varied in different periods of his life, and occasioned some apparent inconsistencies of opinion in his works.

The phenomena of the soul were divided by him into the phenomena of Knowledge, the phenomena of Feeling, and the phenomena of Conation, which included those of will and desire. The cognitive Faculties he divided into the Presentative, the Conservative, the Reproductive, the Representative, the Elaborative, and the Regulative. Consciousness is defined as the recognition by the thinking subject of its own acts and affections. As such, it is actual and not potential knowledge, it is immediate and not mediate, it implies contrast, judgment and memory. But Hamilton agrees with Brown, and differs from Reid and Stewart, in holding that there is no faculty of consciousness coordinate with the other intellectual powers. He however divides the Presentative Faculty into External Perception and Internal Perception or Self-consciousness. The office of self-consciousness is limited to the apprehension of the phenomena of spirit. These phenomena it apprehends under the forms of Time and of Self.

Although Hamilton uses the term self-consciousness, he denies in the most explicit terms that we have any direct consciousness of the ego or self. Our knowledge of mind, as of matter, is limited to its phenomena. The reality—a being to which these pertain—would be "suggested," in the language of Reid, Stewart, and Brown, by these phenomena, and Hamilton would seem to agree with them in thought, if not in terminology.

By External Perception we apprehend the phenomena of the external world, or of the Non-ego under the form of Space. External Perception consists of two elements, viz. Sensation and

Perception proper, which are contrasted with one another respectively as feeling and knowledge, and which coexist and energize in an inverse ratio to each other. By the first, we are aware of certain special affections of the soul as an animated organism—by the second, of general relations under which this organism exists as material. The direct objects of perception proper are the phenomena and relations of the material organism. These are subdivided into the three classes of qualities or attributes of matter, viz., the primary, the secundo-primary, and the secondary; the first being percepts proper, the second being percepts proper and sensations proper, the third being sensations proper. By the first, we apprehend matter as occupying space and contained in space, involving divisibility, size and shape, mobility and place. The second class are contained under the category of resistance or pressure, and include gravity, cohesion, the compressible elastic, and relatively movable or immovable. The third are the powers to produce sensations in us.

Of this Non-ego we have a direct, and not a representative knowledge. The doctrine of Representative Perception is the special subject of criticism and refutation by Hamilton. The various forms in which this theory has been held were collected by him with exhaustive erudition and arranged in a subtle and comprehensive classification. . . . As to what this Non-ego is, whether it consists of phenomena with their relations, giving the so-called Qualities of matter only, or whether it also includes matter as a Being, there is a difference of opinion among the followers, interpreters, and critics of Hamilton. His most friendly interpreters must confess that his language has been more or less influenced by the principles of Kant, and usually teaches that matter is in itself unknown, and that, so far as it is perceived, it is perceived only in its relations to the sentient and percipient mind. . . .

The Conservative faculty, or the faculty of retention, is treated by Hamilton as a special faculty, for the reason that it, as he asserts, is governed by laws of its own, and is exerted by different individuals with differing energy. Its activity is out of consciousness, and may be analogous to other latent modifications of the soul's energy, such as must be assumed to explain the sense-perceptions. These modifications do not, however, pertain to any physical or physiological organ of memory. The reproductive or resuscitative faculty is the power by which one thought suggests another under what are called the laws of association. These laws are subjected by Hamilton to special historical research and scientific criticism. *Works of Reid,* Note D** and D*** *Met. Lecs.* 31–32. All these laws are reduced to a single law or principle, viz., the law of redintegration, according to which parts of the same mental state tend to recall one another. To this law Hamilton, in the Dissertations, adds certain relations of similarity and contrast as not covered by the law of redintegration. The Representative power is not clearly defined as a third generic faculty, but is treated under that special modification usually recognized as the Imagination, the creative function of which is limited to the capacity of selection and combination, and the dignity of which is made dependent on the presence and interfusion of the thought-power, or the faculty of relations. Of the representative power, pure and simple, he treats only in hazarding the remark that to every representation of a sense-percept the activity of the appropriate sense organ is required as a condition.

The Elaborative Faculty is called by Hamilton the Faculty of Relations, the Faculty of Comparison, the Discursive Faculty, and the Faculty of Thought. It begins with comparison, involving a judgment of existence, of discrimination, of similarity, and a collection of several like attributes; upon this, classification is superinduced, giving two kinds of notions, the collective and the abstract, the last involving two relations, viz., of extension and comprehension. The product is the Concept. In respect to the nature of this product Hamilton ranks himself against the Realists and the extreme Conceptualists and with the moderate Nominalists, such as Berkeley. Judgment enters into all the cognitive faculties, but, as proper to the Elaborative faculty, it involves the comparison of a partial with a total conception and may be in the line of extension or comprehension. Reasoning is a double comparison, in which two parts and wholes mutually

related are compared. It is either from the whole to the parts
or from the parts to the whole, and is respectively Deduction
and Induction. It may be in the line of either comprehension or
extension. The only Induction which Hamilton recognizes is
what he calls purely logical. That which is ordinarily so called
he rejects as illogical.

The Regulative Faculty is the faculty of *a priori* principles
or relations. It is called a faculty by courtesy, not as "a proximate
cause of a definite energy, but as the source of necessary cognitions." It is designated by various names, among others by
the appellation *common sense*. To the justification of the use
of this term and to the vindication of common sense as an
authority in Philosophy, Hamilton devotes one of the ablest and
the most learned of his dissertations in the Appendix to the
works of Reid—A. The essential characters of the original cognitions are Incomprehensibility, Simplicity, Necessity, and absolute Universality and comparative Evidence and Certainty.
The characteristics of all positive knowledge moreover are
two—Non-contradiction and Relativity. By this last it appears
that the mind can conceive only the limited and the conditionally limited. We cannot therefore conceive an absolute whole
nor an absolute part: neither an infinite whole nor an infinite
part. The conditioned is the mean between two extremes, both
unconditioned, neither of which can be conceived as possible,
and yet one must be assumed as necessary. Relativity is not a
law of things but a law of thought. So far as the relations of
existence are concerned they are intrinsic or extrinsic. The intrinsic relations are those of substance and quality involving one
another, but neither thinkable apart. The Extrinsic are the relations of time, space, and degree. These three are absolutely inconceivable and but relatively conceivable. Things in time and
space and degree are likewise conceivable relatively to one
another.

Causation is subjected by Hamilton to a special analysis.
Eight theories in respect to the origin of this relation and of
our belief in it are proposed and criticized—4 *a posteriori* and
4 *a priori*. *Met. Lec.* 39, 40. Subsequently causation is explained

as a special application of the law of the conditioned as follows: The mind is unable to conceive of anything except under the forms of existence and of time. Whenever a phenomenon is apprehended as a fact, it cannot be conceived as non-existent, but it can be conceived as existing at another time under another form. The same being necessarily conceived as existing in two forms at different times is reciprocally cause or causes and effect. We believe this relation not in the exercise of a power or positive capacity of our nature, but under the constraint of a powerlessness of our nature to think otherwise. The same is true of our belief in God and Free-Will. We cannot conceive of an uncaused or self-existent Being, but we can believe that such a Being exists. Similarly, we cannot conceive of a free act, i.e., an absolute commencement, but we are compelled to believe it. We rise above the antinomies that must necessarily attend the effort to conceive Time, Space, Freedom, and God, and affirm that all these in some sense are. In a letter to Mr. H. Calderwood, *Met.* App. No. V., Hamilton asserts: "When I deny that the Infinite can by us be known, I am far from denying that by us it is, must, and ought to be believed. . . ." Hamilton's influence has been more efficient in exciting an interest in, and a taste for, Philosophical researches than in founding a school or giving currency to a system. His vast erudition, acute criticism, catholic spirit, and his devotion to truth, have brought blessings to the English-speaking people which they will be slow to forget.

The Scottish Philosophy

By Sir William Hamilton

This selection is a portion of an introductory lecture dated 1836. It gives Sir William's appraisal of David Hume, and of the Scottish School of Philosophy, of which he was himself perhaps the most gifted and distinguished member. Note his discussion of "a strong general analogy between the philosophies of Reid and Kant" in contrast with Stewart's unappreciative appraisal of Kant's philosophy. This selection is from Appendix B of Volume I of Sir William Hamilton's *Lectures on Metaphysics,* edited by the Rev. H. L. Mansel and John Veitch (in four volumes; 2d edition; Edinburgh: William Blackwood and Sons, MDCCCLXI), pp. 393–99.

IN FORMER AGES, Scotland presented but few objects for scientific and literary ambition; and Scotsmen of intellectual enterprise usually sought in other countries, that education, patronage, and applause, which were denied them in their own. It is, indeed, an honourable testimony to the natural vigour of Scottish talent, that, while Scotland afforded so little encouragement for its production, a complement so large in amount and of so high a quality should have been, as it were, spontaneously supplied. During the sixteenth and seventeenth centuries, there was hardly to be found a Continental University without a Scottish professor. It was, indeed, a common saying that a Scottish pedlar and a Scottish professor were everywhere to be met with. France, however, was long the great nursery of Scottish talent; and this even after the political and religious estrangement of Scotland from her ancient ally, by the establishment of the Reformation and the accession of the Scottish monarch to the English crown; and the extent of this foreign patronage may be estimated from the fact, that a single prelate—the illustrious Cardinal du Perron—is recorded to have found places in the seminaries of France for a greater number of literary Scotsmen than all the schools and universities of Scotland maintained at home.

But this favour to our countrymen was not without its reasons; and the ground of partiality was not their superior erudition. What principally obtained for them reputation and patronage abroad, was their dialectical and metaphysical acuteness; and this they were found so generally to possess, that philosophical talent became almost a proverbial attribute of the nation.

During the ascendant of the Aristotelic philosophy, and so long as dexterity in disputation was considered the highest academical accomplishment, the logical subtlety of our country-men was in high and general demand. But they were remarkable less as writers than as instructors; for were we to consider them only in the former capacity, the works that now remain to us of these expatriated philosophers—these *Scoti extra Scotiam agentes*—though neither few nor unimportant, would still never enable us to account for the high and peculiar reputation which the Scottish dialecticians so long enjoyed throughout Europe.

Such was the literary character of Scotland, before the estab-lishment of her intellectual independence, and such has it con-tinued to the present day. In illustration of this, I cannot now attempt a comparative survey of the contributions made by this country and others to the different departments of knowledge, nor is it necessary; for no one, I am assured, will deny that it is only in the Philosophy of Mind that a Scotsman has established an epoch, or that Scotland, by the consent of Europe, has bestowed her name upon a School.

The man who gave the whole philosophy of Europe a new impulse and direction, and to whom, mediately or immediately, must be referred every subsequent advance in philosophical speculation, was our countryman—David Hume. In speaking of this illustrious thinker, I feel anxious to be distinctly under-stood. I would, therefore, earnestly request of you to bear in mind, that religious disbelief and philosophical skepticism are not merely not the same, but have no natural connection; and that while the one must ever be a matter of reprobation and regret, the other is in itself deserving of applause. Both were united in Hume; and this union has unfortunately contributed to associate them together in popular opinion, and to involve them equally in one vague condemnation. They must, therefore, I repeat, be accurately distinguished; and thus, though decid-edly opposed to one and all of Hume's theological conclusions, I have no hesitation in asserting of his philosophical skepticism, that this was not only beneficial in its results, but, in the circum-stances of the period, even a necessary step in the progress of Philosophy towards truth. In the first place, it was requisite in order to arouse thought from its lethargy. Men had fallen asleep over their dogmatic systems. In Germany, the Rationalism of Leibnitz and Wolf; in England, the Sensualism of Locke, with all its melancholy results, had subsided almost into established faiths. The Skepticism of Hume, like an electric spark, sent life through the paralyzed opinions; philosophy awoke to renovated vigour, and its problems were again to be considered in other aspects, and subjected to a more searching analysis.

In the second place, it was necessary in order to manifest the inadequacy of the prevailing system. In this respect, skepticism is always highly advantageous; for skepticism is only the carrying out of erroneous philosophy to the absurdity which it always virtually involved. The skeptic, *qua* skeptic, cannot himself lay down his premises; he can only accept them from the dogmatist; if true, they can afford no foundation for the skeptical inference; if false, the sooner they are exposed in their real character the better. Accepting his principles from the dominant philosophies of Locke and Leibnitz, and deducing with irresistible evidence these principles to their legitimate results, Hume showed, by the extreme absurdity of these results themselves, either that Philosophy altogether was a delusion, or that the individual systems which afforded the premises, were erroneous or incomplete. He thus constrained philosophers to the alternative, either of surrendering philosophy as null, or of ascending to higher principles, in order to re-establish it against the skeptical reduction. The dilemma of Hume constitutes, perhaps, the most memorable crisis in the history of philosophy; for out of it the whole subsequent Metaphysic of Europe has taken its rise.

To Hume we owe the Philosophy of Kant, and, therefore, also, in general, the later philosophy of Germany. Kant explicitly acknowledges that it was by Hume's *reductio ad absurdum* of the previous doctrine of Causality, he was first roused from his dogmatic slumber. He saw the necessity that had arisen, of placing philosophy on a foundation beyond the reach of skepticism, or of surrendering it altogether; and this it was that led him to those researches into the conditions of thought, which, considered whether in themselves or in their consequences, whether in what they established or in what they subverted, are, perhaps, the most remarkable in the annals of speculation.

To Hume, in like manner, we owe the Philosophy of Reid, and, consequently, what is now distinctively known in Europe as the Philosophy of the Scottish School.

Unable to controvert the reasoning of Berkeley, as founded on the philosophy of Descartes and Locke, Reid had quietly resigned himself to Idealism; and he confesses that he would never have been led to question the legitimacy of the common doctrine of Perception, involving though it did the negation of an external world, had Hume not startled him into hesitation and inquiry, by showing that the same reasoning which disproved the Existence of Matter, disproved, when fairly carried out, also the Substantiality of Mind. Such was the origin of the philosophy founded by Reid—illustrated and adorned by Stewart; and it is to this philosophy, and to the writings of these two illustrious thinkers, that Scotland is mainly indebted for the distinguished reputation which she at present enjoys, in every country where the study of Mind has not, as in England, been neglected for the study of Matter.

The Philosophy of Reid is at once our pride and our reproach. At home mistaken and undervalued; abroad understood and honoured. The assertion may be startling, yet is literally true, that the doctrines of the Scottish School have been nowhere less fairly appreciated than in Scotland itself. To explain how they have been misinterpreted, and consequently, neglected, in the country of their birth, is more than I can now attempt; but as I believe that an equal ignorance prevails in regard to the high favour accorded to these speculations by those nations who are now in advance, as the most enlightened cultivators of philosophy, I shall endeavour, as briefly as possible, to show that it may be for our credit not rashly to disparage what other countries view as our chief national claim to scientific celebrity. In illustration of this, I shall only allude to the account in which our Scottish Philosophy is held in Germany and in France.

There is a strong general analogy between the philosophies

of Reid and Kant; and Kant, I may observe by the way, was a Scotsman by proximate descent. Both originate in a recoil against the skepticism of Hume; both are equally opposed to the Sensualism of Locke; both vindicate with equal zeal the moral dignity of man; and both attempt to mete out and to define the legitimate sphere of our intellectual activity. There are, however, important differences between the doctrines, as might be anticipated from the very different characters of the men; and while Kant surpassed Reid in systematic power and comprehension, Reid excelled Kant in the caution and security of his procedure. There is, however, one point of difference in which it is now acknowledged, even by the representatives of the Kantian philosophy, that Kant was wrong. I allude to the doctrine of Perception—the doctrine which constitutes the very corner-stone of the philosophy of Reid. Though both philosophies were, in their origin, reactions against the skepticism of Hume, this reaction was not equally determined in each by the same obnoxious conclusion. For, as it was primarily to reconnect Effect and Cause that Kant was roused to speculation, so it was primarily to regain the worlds of Mind and Matter that Reid was awakened to activity. Accordingly Kant, admitting, without question, the previous doctrine of philosophers, that the mind has no immediate knowledge of any existence external to itself, adopted it without hesitation as a principle—that the mind is cognizant of nothing beyond its own modifications, and that what our natural consciousness mistakes for an external world, is only an internal phenomenon, only a mental representation of the unknown and inconceivable. Reid, on the contrary, was fortunately led to question the grounds on which philosophers had given the lie to the natural beliefs of mankind; and his inquiry terminated in the conclusion, that there exists no valid ground for the hypothesis, universally admitted by the learned, that an immediate knowledge of material objects is impossible. The attempt of Kant, if the attempt were serious, to demonstrate the existence of an external and unknown world was, as is universally admitted, a signal failure; and his Hypothetical Realism was soon analyzed by an illustrious disciple—

Fichte—into an Absolute Idealism, with a logical rigour that did not admit of refutation. In the meanwhile, Reid's doctrine of Perception had attracted the attention of an acute opponent of the Critical Philosophy in Germany; and that doctrine, divested of those superficial errors which have led some ingenious reasoners in this country to view and represent Reid as holding an opinion on this point identical with Kant's, was, in Kant's own country, placed in opposition against his opinion, fortified as that was by the authority of all modern philosophers. And with what result? Simply this—that the most distinguished representatives of the Kantian school now acknowledge Kant's doctrine of Perception to be erroneous, and one analogous to that of Reid they have adopted in its stead. Thus, while, in Scotland, the fundamental position of Reid's philosophy has been misunderstood, his criticism of the ideal theory treated as a blunder, and his peculiar doctrine of perception represented as essentially the same with that of the philosophers whom he assailed; in Germany, and by his own disciples, Kant's theory of perception is admitted to be false, and the doctrine of Reid, on this point, appreciated at its just value, and recognized as one of the most important and original contributions ever made to philosophy.

But in France, I may add Italy, the triumph of the Scottish School has been even more signal than in Germany. The philosophy of Locke, first recommended to his countrymen by the brilliant fancy of Voltaire, was, by the lucid subtlety of Condillac, reduced to a simplicity which not only obtained an ascendant over the philosophy of Descartes, but rendered it in France the object of all but universal admiration. Locke had deduced all knowledge from Experience, but Condillac analyzed every faculty into Sense. Though its author was no materialist, the system of transformed sensation is only a disguised materialism; and the import of the doctrine soon became but too apparent in its effects. Melancholy, however, as it was, this theory obtained an authority in France unparalleled for its universality and continuance. For seventy years, not a single work of an opposite tendency made the smallest impression on the public mind; all discussion of principles had ceased; it remained only to develop the remoter consequences of the system; philosophy seemed accomplished.

Such was the state of opinion in France until the downfall of the Empire. In the period of tranquillity that followed the Restoration, the minds of men were again turned with interest towards metaphysical speculation; and it was then that the doctrines of the Scottish Philosophy were, for the first time, heard in the public schools of France. Recommended by the powerful talent and high authority of Royer-Collard, these doctrines made converts of some of the loftiest intellects of France. A vigorous assault, in which the prowess of Cousin was remarkable, was made against the prevalent opinions, and with a success so decisive, that, after a controversy of twenty years, the school of Condillac is now, in its own country, considered as extinct; while our Scottish Philosophy not only obtained an ascendant in public opinion, but, through the influence of my illustrious friend M. Cousin, forms the basis of philosophical instruction in the various Colleges connected with the University of France. It must not, however, be supposed, that the French have servilely adopted the opinions of our countrymen. On the contrary, what they have borrowed they have so ably amplified, strengthened, simplified, and improved, that the common doctrines of Reid and Stewart, of Royer-Collard and Jouffroy (for Cousin falls under another category), ought in justice to be denominated the *Scoto-Gallican Philosophy*—a name, indeed, already bestowed upon them by recent historians of philosophy in Germany. . . .

The Nature of Consciousness

By Sir William Hamilton

This selection, which should be compared with the one by the same title from Thomas Brown, is taken from Lecture XI of Sir William Hamilton's *Lectures on Metaphysics,* edited by the Rev. H. L. Mansel and John Veitch (in four volumes; 2d edition; Edinburgh: William Blackwood and Sons, MDCCCLXI), Vol. I, pp. 182–83 and 186–95. The title is abbreviated.

IN TAKING a comprehensive survey of the mental phenomena, these are all seen to comprise one essential element, or to be possible only under one necessary condition. This element or condition is Consciousness, or the knowledge that I, that the Ego exists, in some determinate state. In this knowledge they appear, or are realized as phenomena, and with this knowledge they likewise disappear, or have no longer a phenomenal existence; so that consciousness may be compared to an internal light, by means of which, and which alone, what passes in the mind is rendered visible. Consciousness is simple—is not composed of parts, either similar or dissimilar. It always resembles itself, differing only in the degrees of its intensity; thus, there are not various kinds of consciousness, although there are various kinds of mental modes, or states, of which we are conscious. Whatever division, therefore, of the mental phenomena may be adopted, all its members must be within consciousness; that is, we must not attempt to divide consciousness itself, which must be viewed as comprehensive of the whole phenomena to be divided; far less should we reduce it, as a special phenomenon, to a particular class. Let consciousness, therefore, remain one and indivisible, comprehending all the modifications—all the phenomena, of the thinking subject.

But taking, again, a survey of the mental modifications, or phenomena, of which we are conscious—these are seen to divide themselves into THREE great classes. In the first place, there are the phenomena of Knowledge; in the second place, there are the phenomena of Feeling, or the phenomena of Pleasure and Pain; and, in the third place, there are the phenomena of Will and Desire.

Let me illustrate this by an example. I see a picture. Now, first of all, I am conscious of perceiving a certain complement of colours and figures—I recognize what the object is. This is the phenomenon of Cognition or Knowledge. But this is not the only phenomenon of which I may be here conscious. I may ex perience certain affections in the contemplation of this object. If the picture be a masterpiece, the gratification will be un-alloyed; but if it be an unequal production, I shall be conscious, perhaps, of enjoyment, but of enjoyment alloyed with dissatis-faction. This is the phenomenon of Feeling—or of Pleasure and Pain. But these two phenomena do not yet exhaust all of which I may be conscious on the occasion. I may desire to see the picture long—to see it often—to make it my own; and, perhaps, I may will, resolve, or determine so to do. This is the complex phenomenon of Will and Desire. . . .

This division of the phenomena of mind into the three great classes of the Cognitive faculties—the Feelings, or capacities of Pleasure and Pain—and the Exertive or Conative Powers—I do not propose as original. It was first promulgated by Kant (*Kritik der Urtheilskraft,* Einleitung); and the felicity of the distribution was so apparent, that it has now been long all but universally adopted in Germany by the philosophers of every school. . . . To the psychologists of this country it is apparently wholly un-known. They still adhere to the old scholastic division into powers of the Understanding and powers of the Will; or, as it is otherwise expressed, into Intellectual and Active powers.

By its author the Kantian classification has received no illus-tration; and by other German philosophers, it has apparently been viewed as too manifest to require any. Nor do I think it needs much; though a few words in explanation may not be inexpedient. An objection to the arrangement may, perhaps, be taken on the ground that the three classes are not co-ordinate. It is evident that every mental phenomenon is either an act of knowledge, or only possible through an act of knowledge, for consciousness is a knowledge—a phenomenon of cognition; and, on this principle, many philosophers—as Descartes, Leibnitz, Spinoza, Wolf, Platner, and others—have been led to regard the knowing, or representative faculty, as they called it, the faculty of cognition, as the fundamental power of mind, from which all others are derivative. To this the answer is easy. These philosophers did not observe that, although pleasure and pain—although desire and volition, are only as they are known to be; yet, in these modifications, a quality, a phenomenon of mind, absolutely new, has been superadded, which was never involved in, and could, therefore, never have been evolved out of, the mere faculty of knowledge. The faculty of knowledge is certainly the first in order, inasmuch as it is the *conditio sine qua non* of the others; and we are able to conceive a being possessed of the power of recognizing existence, and yet wholly void of all feeling of pain and pleasure, and of all powers of desire and volition. On the other hand, we are wholly unable to conceive a being possessed of feeling and desire, and, at the same time, without a knowledge of any object upon which his affections may be employed, and without a consciousness of these affections themselves.

We can further conceive a being possessed of knowledge and feeling alone—a being endowed with a power of recognizing objects, of enjoying the exercise, and of grieving at the restraint, of his activity—and yet devoid of that faculty of voluntary agency—of that conation, which is possessed by man. To such a being would belong feelings of pain and pleasure, but neither desire nor will, properly so called. On the other hand, however, we cannot possibly conceive the existence of a voluntary activity independently of all feeling; for voluntary conation is a faculty which can only be determined to energy through a pain or pleasure—through an estimate of the relative worth of objects.

In distinguishing the cognitions, feelings, and conations, it is not, therefore, to be supposed that these phenomena are possible independently of each other. In our philosophical systems, they may stand separated from each other in books and chapters;

in nature, they are ever interwoven. In every, even the simplest, modification of mind, knowledge, feeling, and desire or will, go to constitute the mental state; and it is only by a scientific abstraction that we are able to analyze the state into elements, which are never really existent but in mutual combination. These elements are found, indeed, in very various proportions in different states—sometimes one preponderates, sometimes another; but there is no state in which they are not all co-existent.

Let the mental phenomena, therefore, be distributed under the three heads of phenomena of Cognition, or the faculties of Knowledge; phenomena of Feeling, or the capacities of Pleasure and Pain; and phenomena of Desiring or Willing, or the powers of Conation.

The order of these is determined by their relative consecution. Feeling and appetency suppose knowledge. The cognitive faculties, therefore, stand first. But as will, and desire, and aversion, suppose a knowledge of the pleasurable and painful, the feelings will stand second as intermediate between the other two.

Such is the highest or most general classification of the mental phenomena, or of the phenomena of which we are conscious. But as these primary classes are, as we have shown, all included under one universal phenomenon—the phenomenon of consciousness—it follows that Consciousness must form the first object of our consideration.

I shall not attempt to give you any preliminary detail of the opinions of philosophers in relation to consciousness. The only effect of this would be to confuse you. It is necessary, in the first place, to obtain correct and definite notions on the subject, and having obtained these, it will be easy for you to understand in what respects the opinions that have been hazarded on the cardinal point of all philosophy, are inadequate or erroneous. I may notice that Dr. Reid and Mr. Stewart have favoured us with no special or articulate account of consciousness. The former, indeed, intended and promised this. In the seventh chapter of the first Essay *On the Intellectual Powers*, which is entitled "Division of the Powers of the Mind," the concluding paragraph is as follows:

I shall not, therefore, attempt a complete enumeration of the powers of the human understanding. I shall only mention those which I propose to explain, and they are the following:

1st, The powers we have by means of our External Senses; 2dly, Memory; 3dly, Conception; 4thly, The powers of Resolving and Analyzing complex objects, and compounding those that are more simple; 5thly, Judging; 6thly, Reasoning; 7thly, Taste; 8thly, Moral Perception; and last of all, Consciousness.

The work, however, contains no essay upon Consciousness; but, in reference to this deficiency, the author, in the last paragraph of the book, states, "As to Consciousness, what I think necessary to be said upon it has been already said; Essay vi., chap. v."—the chapter, to wit, entitled "On the First Principles of Contingent Truths." To that chapter you may, however, add what is spoken of consciousness in the first chapter of the first Essay, entitled, "Explication of Words," Section 7. We are, therefore, left to glean the opinion of both Reid and Stewart on the subject of consciousness, from incidental notices in their writings; but these are fortunately sufficient to supply us with the necessary information in regard to their opinions on this subject.

Nothing has contributed more to spread obscurity over a very transparent matter, than the attempts of philosophers to define consciousness. Consciousness cannot be defined—we may be ourselves fully aware what consciousness is, but we cannot, without confusion, convey to others a definition of what we ourselves clearly apprehend. The reason is plain. Consciousness lies at the root of all knowledge. Consciousness is itself the one highest source of all comprehensibility and illustration—how, then, can we find aught else by which consciousness may be illustrated or comprehended? To accomplish this, it would be necessary to have a second consciousness, through which we might be conscious of the mode in which the first consciousness was possible. Many philosophers—and among others Dr. Brown—have defined consciousness as *feeling*. But how do they define a feeling? They define, and must define it, as something of which we are conscious; for a feeling of which we are not conscious, is no feeling at all. Here, therefore, they are guilty of a logical see-saw, or circle. They define consciousness by feeling, and feeling by consciousness—that is, they explain the same by the same, and thus leave us in the end no wiser than we were in the beginning. Other philosophers say that consciousness is a knowledge—and others, again, that it is a belief or conviction of a knowledge. Here, again, we have the same violation of logical law. Is there any knowledge of which we are not conscious? Is there any belief of which we are not conscious? There is not, there cannot be; therefore, consciousness is not contained under either knowledge or belief, but, on the contrary, knowledge and belief are both contained under consciousness. In short, the notion of consciousness is so elementary, that it cannot possibly be resolved into others more simple. It cannot therefore, be brought under any genus, any more general conception; and, consequently, it cannot be defined.

But though consciousness cannot be logically defined, it may, however, be philosophically analyzed. This analysis is effected by observing and holding fast the phenomena or facts of consciousness, comparing these, and, from this comparison, evolving the universal conditions under which alone an act of consciousness is possible.

It is only in following this method that we can attain to precise and accurate knowledge of the contents of consciousness; and it need not afflict us if the result of our investigation be very different from the conclusions that have been previously held.

But, before proceeding to show you in detail what the act of consciousness comprises, it may be proper, in the first place, to recall to you, in general, what kind of act the word is employed to denote. I know, I feel, I desire &c. What is it that is necessarily involved in all these? It requires only to be stated to be admitted, that when I know, I must know that I know—when I feel, I must know that I feel—when I desire, I must know that I desire. The knowledge, the feeling, the desire, are possible only under the condition of being known, and being known by me. For if I did not know that I knew, I would not know—if I did not know that I felt, I would not feel—if I did not know that I desired, I would not desire. Now, this knowledge, which I, the subject, have of these modifications of my being, and through which knowledge alone these modifications are possible, is what we call *consciousness*. The expressions *I know that I know, I know that I feel, I know that I desire*, are thus translated by *I am conscious that I know, I am conscious that I feel, I am conscious that I desire*. Consciousness is thus, on the one hand, the recognition by the mind or ego of its acts and affections—in other words, the self-affirmation, that certain modifications are known by me, and that these modifications are mine. But, on the other hand, consciousness is not to be viewed as anything different from these modifications themselves, but is, in fact, the general condition of their existence, or of their existence within the sphere of intelligence. Though the simplest act of mind, consciousness thus expresses a relation subsisting between two terms. These terms are, on the one hand, an I or Self, as the subject of a certain modification—and, on the other, some modification, state, quality, affection, or operation belonging to the subject. Consciousness, thus, in its simplicity, necessarily involves three things—(1) A recognizing or knowing subject; (2) A recognized or known modification; and (3) A recognition or knowledge by the subject of the modification.

From this it is apparent, that consciousness and knowledge each involve the other. An act of knowledge may be expressed by the formula, *I know;* an act of consciousness by the formula, *I know that I know:* but it is impossible for us to know without at the same time knowing that we know; so it is impossible to know that we know without our actually knowing. The one merely explicitly expresses what the other implicitly contains. Consciousness and knowledge are thus not opposed as really different. Why, then, it may be asked, employ two terms to express notions, which, as they severally infer each other, are really identical? To this the answer is easy. Realities may be in themselves inseparable, while, as objects of our knowledge, it may be necessary to consider them apart. Notions, likewise, may severally imply each other, and be inseparable even in thought; yet for the purpose of science, it may be requisite to distinguish them by different terms, and to consider them in their relations or correlations to each other. Take a geometrical example—a triangle. This is a whole composed of certain parts. Here the whole cannot be conceived as separate from its parts, and the parts cannot be conceived as separate from their whole. Yet it is scientifically necessary to have different names for each, and it is necessary now to consider the whole in relation to the parts, and now the parts in correlation to the whole. Again, the constituent parts of a triangle are sides and angles. Here the sides suppose the angles, the angles suppose the sides, and, in fact, the sides and angles are in themselves in reality, one and indivisible. But they are not the same to us, to our knowledge. For though we cannot abstract in thought, the sides from the angle, the angle from the sides, we may make one or other the principal object of attention. We may either consider the angles in relation to each other, and to the sides; or the sides in relation to each other, and to the angles. And to express all this, it is necessary to distinguish, in thought and in expression, what, in nature, is one and indivisible.

As it is in geometry, so it is in the philosophy of mind. We require different words, not only to express objects and relations different in themselves, but to express the same objects and relations under the different points of view in which they are placed by the mind, when scientifically considering them. Thus, in the present instance, consciousness and knowledge are not distinguished by different words as different aspects. The verbal distinction is taken for the sake of brevity and precision, and its convenience warrants its establishment. Knowledge is a relation, and every relation supposes two terms. Thus, in the relation in question, there is, on the one hand, a subject of knowledge— that is, the knowing mind—and on the other, there is an object of knowledge—that is, the thing known; and the knowledge itself is the relation between these two terms. Now, though each term of a relation necessarily supposes the other, nevertheless one of these terms may be to us the more interesting, and we may consider that term as the principal, and view the other only as subordinate and correlative. Now, this is the case in the present instance. In an act of knowledge, my attention may be principally attracted either to the object known, or to myself as the subject knowing; and, in the latter case, although no new element be added to the act, the condition involved in it—*I know that I know*—becomes the primary and prominent matter of consideration.

The Unconditioned

By SIR WILLIAM HAMILTON

This selection is from Sir William Hamilton's *Discussions.* It was originally published as an article in the *Edinburgh Review,* for October, 1829, under the title "Refutation of the Various Doctrines of the Unconditioned, Especially of Cousin's Doctrine of the Infinite-Absolute." Reprinted here from O. W. Wight, *Sir William Hamilton's Philosophy* (New York: D. Appleton & Co., 1860), pp. 454–57. Some footnotes are here omitted, and one (p. 457) is transferred to the text.

IN OUR OPINION the mind can conceive, and consequently can know, only the *limited, and the conditionally limited.* The unconditionally unlimited, or the *Infinite,* the unconditionally limited, or the *Absolute,* cannot positively be construed to the mind; they can be conceived, only by a thinking away from, or abstraction of, those very conditions under which thought itself is realized; consequently the notion of the Unconditioned is only negative—negative of the conceivable itself. For example, on the one hand we can positively conceive, neither an absolute whole, that is, a whole so great, that we cannot also conceive it as a relative part of a still greater whole; nor an absolute part, that is, a part so small, that we cannot also conceive it as a relative whole, divisible into smaller parts. On the other hand, we cannot positively represent, or realize, or construe to the mind (as here understanding and imagination coincide), an infinite whole, for this could only be done by the infinite synthesis in thought of finite wholes, which would require an infinite time for its accomplishment; nor, for the same reason, can we follow out in thought an infinite divisibility of parts. The result is the same, whether we apply the process to limitation in *space*, in *time*, or in *degree*. The unconditional negation, and the unconditional affirmation of limitation; in other words, the *infinite* and the *absolute, properly so called*, are thus equally inconceivable to us.

As the conditionally limited (which we may briefly call the *conditioned*) is thus the only possible object of knowledge and of positive thought—thought necessarily supposes conditions. *To think is to condition* and conditional limitation is the fundamental law of the possibility of thought. For, as the greyhound cannot outstrip his shadow, nor (by a more appropriate simile) the eagle out-soar the atmosphere in which he floats, and by which alone he may be supported; so the mind cannot transcend that sphere of limitation, within and through which exclusively the possibility of thought is realized. Thought is only of the conditioned; because, as we have said, to think is simply to condition. The *absolute* is conceived merely by a negation of conceivability; and all that we know, is only known as

—"won from the void and formless *infinite*."

How, indeed, it could ever be doubted that thought is only of the conditioned, may well be deemed a matter of the profoundest admiration. Thought cannot transcend consciousness; consciousness is only possible under the antithesis of a subject and object of thought, known only in correlation, and mutually limiting each other; while independently of this, all that we know either of subject or object, either of mind or matter, is only a knowledge in each of the particular, of the plural, of the different, of the modified, of the phenomenal. We admit that the consequence of this doctrine is, that philosophy, if viewed as more than a science of the conditioned, is impossible. Departing from the particular, we admit that we can never, in our highest generalizations, rise above the finite; that our knowledge, whether of mind or matter, can be nothing more than a knowledge of the relative manifestations of an existence, which in itself it is our highest wisdom to recognize as beyond the reach of philosophy, in the language of St. Austin—"*cognoscendo ignorari, et ignorando cognosci.*"

The conditioned is the mean between two extremes—two inconditionates, exclusive of each other, neither of which *can be conceived as possible,* but of which, on the principles of contradiction and excluded middle, one *must be admitted as necessary.* On this opinion, therefore reason is shown to be weak, but not deceitful. The mind is not represented as conceiving two propositions subversive of each other, as equally possible; but only, as unable to understand as possible, either of two extremes; one of which, however, on the ground of their mutual repugnance, it is compelled to recognize as true. We are thus taught the salutary lesson, that the capacity of thought is not to be constituted into the measure of existence; and are warned from recognizing the domain of our knowledge as necessarily coextensive with the horizon of our faith. And by a wonderful revelation, we are thus, in the very consciousness of our inability to conceive aught above the relative and finite, inspired with a belief in the existence of something unconditioned beyond the sphere of all comprehensible reality.

True, therefore, are the declarations of a pious philosophy: "A God understood would be no God at all . . ."—"To think that God is, as we can think him to be, is blasphemy." The Divinity, in a certain sense, is revealed; in a certain sense is concealed: He is at once known and unknown. But the last and highest consecration of all true religion, must be an altar—"*To the unknown and unknowable God.*" In this consummation, nature and revelation, paganism and Christianity, are at one; and from either source the testimonies are so numerous that I must refrain from quoting any.

CHAPTER VIII

James Frederick Ferrier

(1808–1864)

The Man and His Work

By Noah Porter

James Frederick Ferrier, 1808–1864; born in Edinburgh; University of Edinburgh and Baliol Coll., Oxford, 1825–1831; Professor of Civil History, Edin., 1842; Prof. of Moral Philosophy and Political Economy, St. Andrews, 1845, contributed various articles in *Blackwood's Magazine:* e.g., in 1838–9 a series under the title of "An Introduction to the Philosophy of Consciousness"; in 1847, *Reid and the Philosophy of Common Sense.* In 1854, he published *Institutes of Metaphysics: The Theory of Knowing and Being,* 2d ed. 1856, which provoked sharp replies, viz.: "An Examination of Professor Ferrier's Theory of Knowing and Being," by Rev. John Cairns. "An Examination of Cairns' Examination of Professor Ferrier's Theory of Knowledge and Being," by Rev. J. Smith. "The Scottish Philosophy, a Vindication and Reply," by Rev. J. Cairns. "Scottish Philosophy, the Old and New," by Prof. Ferrier.

After the author's death his *Remains* were published, viz., *Lectures on Greek Philosophy and other Philosophical Remains of James Frederick Ferrier,* etc. Edited by Sir Alexander Grant, Bart., LL.D., and E. L. Lushington, M.A. 2 vols., 1866. New edition in 3 vols., 1888. These *Remains* consist of the "Introduction to the Philosophy of Consciousness," and other philosophical articles from *Blackwood's Magazine,* and some other controversial and explanatory papers.

Ferrier took from the first a critical and polemic attitude with respect to the current philosophy of Reid and the school of common sense, not merely in many points of detail, but in respect of its fundamental peculiarity, as he viewed it, of absorbing philosophy into psychology. It would seem, indeed, from his starting point in the analysis of the phenomena and fact of consciousness, that he was only an expounder of psychology. But he insisted that he was unfolding a "theory of knowing and being"; that he did not confine himself to the observation of facts, but provided for a statement of the fundamental conceptions of philosophy and the deduction of authorized conclusions, or what he calls "a reasoned philosophy." The distinctive peculiarity of his system is that he begins with the fact of consciousness as involving the Ego which is conscious of itself and its acts, and which recognizes itself as present and necessarily entering into all its products, so that we can neither conceive of matter, or the *not me*, except as made up also of the *me* as perpetually present, and a necessary constituent of the conception of matter, both as a whole and in its separate portions. In Ferrier's own language:

The only material world which truly exists is one which either actually is or may possibly be known. But the only material world which either actually is or may possibly be known, is one along with which intelligence is and must be also known. Therefore, the only material world which truly exists, is one along with which intelligence also exists. Therefore the *mere* material world has no real and absolute existence. But neither is it a nonentity (I am no idealist), for there is no nonentity any more than there is entity out of relation to intelligence. (*Remains,* Vol. I., p. 397.)

The speculation is threefold. *First,* the theory of knowing (epistemology); *secondly,* the theory of ignorance (agnoiology); *thirdly,* the theory of being (ontology). The theory of ignorance is that which merits most attention, if not on its own account, at any rate on account of its consequences. It seems to me to be an entire *novelty* in philosophy.

There are two kinds of ignorance, but only one of them is

ignorance properly so called. There is, *first,* an ignorance which is incident to some minds as compared with others, but not necessarily incident to all minds.

Secondly, there is an ignorance or nescience which is of necessity incident to *all* intelligence by *its very nature,* and which is no defect or imperfection or limitation, but rather a perfection. . . . No man can be ignorant that two and two *make five;* for this is a thing not to be known on any terms or by any mind. This fixes the law of ignorance, which is, that we can be ignorant only of what can (possibly) be known [or in barbarous locution] the knowable alone is the ignorable.

What then is the knowable alone, the only possibly knowable * * * The Epistemology answers this question, and fixes *thing mecum, object plus subject, matter plus mind,* as the only knowable.

But what becomes of "Thing *minus me,*" "Object *by itself,*" "Matter *per se,*" Kant's *"Ding an sich"?* "It is," says Kant, "that of which we are ignorant."

It is not that of which we are ignorant, because it is not that which can possibly be known by any intelligence on any terms. To know thing *per se* or *sine me,* is as impossible and contradictory as it is to know two straight lines enclosing a space; because mind by its very law and nature must know the thing *cum alio,* i.e., along with *itself* knowing it. Therefore it is just as impossible for us to be ignorant of matter *per se,* thing *minus me,* *"Ding an sich,"* as it is impossible for us to know this.

Now for a glimpse of Ontology. . . . In answer to the question What is real and absolute Being? we must either reply, It is that which we know, in which case it will be *object plus subject,* because this is the only knowable; or we must reply, It is that which we are ignorant of, in which case, also, it will be *object plus subject.* (*Remains,* I., pp. 483, 484, 485.)

Ferrier reminds us of the earlier philosophy of J. G. Fichte, in his method of reasoning. Among all English writers he has a rare pre-eminence for the clearness and liveliness, the elegance and force of his style. He has called attention to many single principles which are often overlooked; but his system has found few if any disciples.[1]

What a System of Philosophy Is

By James Frederick Ferrier

This selection is from the Introduction to James F. Ferrier's *Institutes of Metaphysics* (Edinburgh: William Blackwood and Sons, MDCCCLVI), pp. 1–7. The title has been supplied.

A SYSTEM OF PHILOSOPHY is bound by two main requisitions—it ought to be true, and it ought to be reasoned. If a system of philosophy is not true, it will scarcely be convincing; and if it is not reasoned, a man will be as little satisfied with it as a hungry person would be by having his meat served up to him raw. Truth is the ultimate end of philosophy; hence a system of philosophy ought to be true. The formation of reason (as effected by the discharge of its proper function, which is the ascertainment and concatenation of necessary principles and conclusions) is the proximate end of philosophy; hence a system of philosophy ought to be reasoned. Philosophy, therefore, in its ideal perfection, is a body of reasoned truth.

Of these obligations, the latter is the more stringent: it is more proper that philosophy should be reasoned, than that it should be true; because, while truth may perhaps be unattainable by man, to reason is certainly his province, and within his power. In a case where two objects have to be overtaken, it is more incumbent on us to secure the one to which our faculties are certainly competent, than the other, to which they are perhaps inadequate. Besides, no end can be so important for man as the cultivation of his own reason.

---

[1] For a discussion of Ferrier as a precursor of absolute idealism see the end of my Introduction. (Editor's note.)

This consideration determines the value of a system of philosophy. A system is of the highest value only when it embraces both of these requisitions—that is, when it is both true and reasoned. But a system which is reasoned without being true, is always of higher value than a system which is true without being reasoned.

The latter kind of system is of no value; because philosophy is "the attainment of truth *by the way of reason*." That is its definition. A system, therefore, which reaches the truth, but *not* by the way of reason, is not philosophy at all; it has no scientific worth. No man can be called upon to take truth *upon trust* at the hands of his brother man. But truth not reasoned is truth proposed upon trust. The best that could be said of such a system would be, that it was better than one which was neither true nor reasoned.

Again—an unreasoned philosophy, even though true, carries no guarantee of its truth. It may be true, but it cannot be certain; because all certainty depends on rigorous evidence—on strict demonstrative proof. Therefore no certainty can attach to the conclusions of an unreasoned philosophy.

Further—the truths of science, in so far as science is a means of intellectual culture, are of no importance in themselves, or considered apart from each other. It is only the study and apprehension of their vital and organic connection which is valuable in an educational point of view. But an unreasoned body of philosophy, however true and formal it may be, has no living and essential interdependency of parts on parts; and is, therefore, useless as a discipline of the mind, and valueless for purposes of tuition.

On the other hand, a system which is reasoned, but not true, has always some value. It creates reason by exercising it. It is employing the proper means to reach truth, although it may fail to reach it. Even though its parts may not be true, yet if each of them be a step leading to the final catastrophe—a link in an unbroken chain on which the ultimate disclosure hinges—and if each of the parts be introduced merely because it is such a step or link—in that case it is conceived that the system is not without its use, as affording an invigorating employment to the reasoning powers, and that general satisfaction to the mind which the successful extrication of a plot, whether in science or in romance, never fails to communicate.

Such a system, although it falls short of the definition of philosophy just given, comes nearer to it than the other; because to reach truth, but not by the way of reason, is to violate the definition in its very essence; whereas to miss truth, but by the way of reason, is to comply with the fundamental circumstance which it prescribes. •If there are other ways of reaching truth than the road of reason, a system which enters on any of these other paths, whatever else it may be, is not a system of philosophy in the proper sense of the word.

But, as has been said, a system of philosophy ought to be both true in all its positions, and also thoroughly reasoned out in a series of strict demonstrations, which, while each is complete and impregnable in itself, shall present, in their combinations, only one large demonstration from the beginning to the end of the work. This, indeed, is the only kind of system to which much value can be assigned, or from which any large intellectual profit can be expected. Philosophical books may be read; philosophical lectures may be listened to; but nothing except a strictly reasoned system can be either *taught* or *learned*.

Without offering any opinion as to how far the systems of philosophers may be true, we may affirm with certainty of the whole of them, that they are not reasoned—meaning by "reasoned," an unbroken chain of clear demonstration carried through from their first word to their last. To whatever extent preceding inquirers may have fulfilled one of the requirements of philosophy, they have neglected the more essential and obligatory of the two. And the consequence makes itself heard in a murmur, over the whole world, of deep dissatisfaction, to which the words of the following paragraph may give a faithful, though perhaps feeble, expression.

It is a matter of general complaint that, although we have plenty of disputations and dissertations on philosophy, we have no philosophy itself. This is perfectly true. People write about it, and about it; but no one has grasped with an unflinching hand the very thing itself. The whole philosophical literature of the world is more like an unwieldy commentary on some text which has perished, or rather has never existed, than like what a philosophy itself should be. Our philosophical treatises are no more philosophy than Eustathius is Homer, or than Malone is Shakespeare. They are mere partial and desultory annotations on some text, on which, unfortunately, no man can lay his hands, because it nowhere exists. Hence the embroilment of speculation; hence the dissatisfaction, even the despair, of every inquiring mind which turns its attention to metaphysics. There is not now in existence even the shadow of a tribunal to which any point in litigation can be referred. There is not now in existence a single book which lays down with precision and impartiality the Institutes of all metaphysical opinion, and shows the seeds of all speculative controversies. Hence philosophy is not only a war, but it is a war in which none of the combatants understands the grounds either of his own opinion or that of his adversary; or sees the roots of the side of the question, which he is either attacking or defending. The springs by which these disputatious puppets are worked, lie deep out of their own sight. Every doctrine which is either embraced or rejected, is embraced or rejected blindly, and without any insight into its merits; and every blow which is struck, whether for truth or error, is struck ignorantly, and at haphazard.

The Primary Law or Condition of All Knowledge

By JAMES FREDERICK FERRIER

This selection is Proposition I, and the Observations and Explanations accompanying it, from the *Institutes of Metaphysics*, Section I, "The Epistemology, or Theory of Knowing," pp. 79–89. Note how it is based upon Sir William Hamilton's conception of consciousness as the fundamental principle of all knowledge. According to the *Century Dictionary,* Ferrier was probably the first writer to use the word *epistemology.* Paragraph numbers have been omitted.

PROPOSITION I

ALONG WITH whatever any intelligence knows, it must, as the ground or condition of its knowledge, have some cognizance of *itself.*

OBSERVATIONS AND EXPLANATIONS

Self or the "me" is the common centre, the continually known rallying-point, in which all our cognitions meet and agree. It is the *ens unum, et semper cognitum, in omnibus notitiis.* Its apprehension is essential to the existence of our, and of all, knowledge. . . . What is the one feature present in all our knowledge—the common point in which all our cognition[s] unite and agree—the element in which they are identical? The *ego* is this feature, point, or element; it is the common centre which is at all times known, and in which all our cognitions, however diverse they may be in other respects, are known as uniting and agreeing; and besides the *ego,* or oneself, there is no other identical quality in our cognitions—as any one may convince himself upon reflection. He will find that he cannot lay his finger upon anything except *himself,* and say—This article of cognition I *must* know along with whatever I know.

The apprehension of oneself by oneself is the most general and essential circumstance on which knowledge depends, because, unless this law be complied with, no intellectual apprehension of any kind is possible; and wherever it is complied with, some kind of knowledge is necessary. Each of the subsequent propositions (with the exception of the last of the epistemology) gives expression to a necessary law of knowledge; but this first proposition lays down the fundamental necessity to which all intelligence is subject in the acquisition of knowledge. It states the primary canon in the code of reason from which all the other necessary laws are derivations.

The condition of knowledge here set forth is not an operation which is performed once for all, and then dispensed with, while we proceed to the cognition of other things. Neither is it an operation which is ever entirely intermitted, even when our attention appears to be exclusively occupied with matters quite distinct from ourselves. The knowledge of self is the running accompaniment to all our knowledge. It is through and along with *this* knowledge that all *other* knowledge is taken in.

An objection may be raised to this proposition on the ground that it is contradicted by experience. It may be said that when we are plunged in the active pursuits of life, or engaged in the contemplation of natural objects, we frequently pass hours, it may be days, without ever thinking of ourselves. This objection seems to militate against the truth of our first proposition. How is it to be obviated?

If the proposition maintained, that our attention was at all times clearly and forcibly directed upon ourselves, or that the *me* was constantly a prominent object of our regard, the objection would be fatal to its pretensions. The proposition would be at once disproved by an appeal to experience; for it is certain that during the greater part of our time we take but little heed of ourselves. But a man may take very little note, without taking absolutely no note of himself. The proposition merely asserts that a man (or any other intelligence) is never altogether incognisant, is never totally oblivious, of himself, even when his attention is most engaged with other matters. However far it may be carried, the forgetfulness of self is only partial and apparent; it is never real and total. There is always a latent reference of one's perceptions and thoughts to oneself as the person who experiences them, which proves that, however deeply we may be engrossed with the objects before us, we are never stripped entirely of the consciousness of ourselves. And this is all that our proposition contends for. There is a calm unobtrusive current of self-consciousness flowing on in company with all our knowledge, and during every moment of our waking existence; and this self-consciousness is the ground or condition of all our other consciousness. Nine hundred and

ninety-nine parts of our attention may be always devoted to the
thing or business we have in hand: it is sufficient for our argument if it be admitted that the thousandth part, or even a
smaller fraction, of it is perpetually directed upon ourselves.

But how is our apparent self-oblivion to be explained? If
it is not to be accounted for on the supposition that we ever
drop entirely out of our own observation, we must be prepared
to explain it on some other principle. And so we are. This oversight, which in many cases is all but complete, may be accounted
for in the most satisfactory manner by means of a principle of
our nature which may be termed the law of familiarity, the
effect of which law is well expressed in the old adage "Familiarity breeds neglect." Whatever we are extremely intimate with,
we are very apt to overlook; and precisely in proportion to the
novelty or triteness of any event are the degrees of our attention called forth and exercised. We are enchained by the
comparatively rare, we are indifferent towards the comparatively
frequent. That which is strange rivets our intellectual gaze, that
to which we are accustomed passes by almost unheeded. No
influence has a greater effect than use and wont in dimming the
eye of attention, and in blunting the edge of curiosity. This
truth might be illustrated to an unlimited extent. It is sufficient
for the present purpose to remark, that each of us is *more* familiar, and is therefore *less* occupied, with himself than he is with
any other object that can be brought under his consideration.
We are constantly present to ourselves, hence we scarcely
notice ourselves. We scarcely remark the condition of our knowledge, so unremittingly do we obey it. Indeed, in our ordinary
moods we seem to slip entirely out of our own thoughts. This
is the inevitable consequence of our close familiarity, our continued intimacy, our unbroken acquaintance with ourselves. But
we never do slip entirely out of our own thoughts. However
slender the threads may be which hold a man before his own
consciousness, they are never completely broken through.

There is this consideration, also, to be taken into account,
that the part of our knowledge which consists of things of sense
always naturally attracts our attention much more forcibly than

that part of it which is apprehended by intellect merely. But that which we call "I" is the object of intellect alone. We are never objects of sense to ourselves. A man can see and touch his body, but he cannot see and touch himself. This is not the place to offer any observations on the nature of the thinking principle. The assertion that it either is, or is not, immaterial, must at present be avoided, as dogmatic, hypothetical, and premature—indeed, as altogether inconsistent with the purpose and business of the epistemology. But this much may be affirmed, that, when the cognizance of self is laid down as the condition of all knowledge, this of course does not mean that certain objects of sense (external things, to wit) are apprehended through certain *other* objects of sense (our own bodies, namely), for such a statement would be altogether futile. It would leave the question precisely where it found it; for we should still have to ask, On what condition are these other objects of sense apprehended? To say that the things of sense are made known to us by means of the things of sense, does not advance us one step on the highroad to truth. The *me*, therefore, whether it be material or not—a point on which, at present, we offer no opinion—is certainly not our own bodies, in so far as these are, or may be made, objects of sense; and not being an object of sensible, but only of intellectual experience, and our attention being naturally held captive by the things of sense, it is not surprising that these latter should cause us to attend but slightly to ourselves in our ordinary moods, and in the common transactions of life. Thus the slight degree of notice which we usually take of ourselves is sufficiently explained—without its being necessary to resort to the hypothesis that the oversight is ever total—by means of these two circumstances—the operation of the law of familiarity, and the fact that the *ego* is no object of sensible experience.

A theory of self-consciousness, opposed to the doctrine advanced in our first proposition, has been sometimes advocated. It reduces this operation to a species of reminiscence: it affirms that we are *first* cognizant of various sensible impressions, and are not conscious of ourselves until we reflect upon them *after-*

wards. But this doctrine involves a contradiction; for it supposes us to recollect certain impressions to have been ours, *after* they have been experienced, which we did not know to be ours *when* they were experienced. A man cannot remember what never happened. If the impressions were not known to be ours at the time, they could not subsequently be remembered to have been ours, because their recollection would imply that we remembered an antecedent connection between ourselves and them; which connection, however, had no place in our former experience, inasmuch as this theory declares that no self was in the first instance apprehended; therefore, if the impressions are recognized on reflection to have been ours, they must originally have been known to be ours. In other words, we must have been conscious of self at the time when the impressions were made.

Looked at in itself, or as an isolated truth, our first proposition is of no importance; but viewed as the foundation of the whole system, and as the single staple on which all the truths subsequently to be advanced depend, it cannot be too strongly insisted on, or too fully elucidated. Everything hinges on the stability which can be given to this proposition—on the acceptance it may meet with. If it falls, the system entirely fails; if it stands, the system entirely succeeds. It is to be hoped that the reader will not be stopped or discouraged by the apparent truism which it involves. He may think that, if the main truth which this philosophy has to tell him is, that all his cognitions and perceptions are known by him to be his own, he will have very little to thank it for. Let him go on, and see what follows. Meanwhile, considering the great weight which this proposition has to bear, we may be excused for bestowing a few more words on its enforcement.

If this first proposition is not very clearly confirmed by experience, it is at any rate not refuted by that authority. No one, by any effort of the mind, can ever apprehend a thing to the entire exclusion of himself. A man cannot wittingly leave himself altogether out of his account, and proceed to the consideration of the objects by which he is surrounded. On the contrary, he will find that, *nolens volens,* he carries himself consciously along with him, faint though the consciousness may be, in all the scenes through which he passes, and in all the operations in which he is engaged. He will find that, when he is cognizant of perceptions, he is always cognizant of them *as his.* But this cognizance is equivalent to self-consciousness, and therefore it is reasonable to conclude that our proposition is not only not overthrown, but, moreover, that it is corroborated by experience.

But it is Reason alone which can give to this proposition the certainty and extension which are required to render it a sure foundation for all that is to follow. Experience can only establish it as a limited matter of fact; and this is not sufficient for the purposes of our subsequent demonstrations. It must be established as a necessary truth of reason—as a law binding on intelligence universally—as a conception, the opposite of which is a contradiction and an absurdity. Strictly speaking, the proposition cannot be demonstrated, because, being itself the absolute starting-point, it cannot be deduced from any antecedent data; but it may be explained in such a way as to leave no doubt as to its axiomatic character. It claims all the stringency of a geometrical axiom, and its claims, it is conceived, are irresistible. If it were possible for an intelligence to receive knowledge at *any one* time without knowing that it was *his* knowledge, it would be possible for him to do this at *all* times. So that an intelligent being might be endowed with knowledge without once, during the whole term of his existence, knowing that he possessed it. Is there not a contradiction involved in that supposition? But if that supposition be a contradiction, it is equally contradictory to suppose that an intelligence can be conscious of his knowledge, at any single moment, without being conscious of it as his. A man has knowledge, and is cognizant of perceptions only when he brings them home to himself. If he were not aware that they were his, he could not be aware of them at all. Can *I* know without knowing that it is *I* who know? No, truly, But if a man, in knowing anything, must always know that he knows it, he must always be self-conscious. And therefore reason establishes our first proposition as a necessary truth—as an axiom, the denial of which involves a contradiction, or is, in plain words, nonsense.

Ignorance and The Law of All Ignorance

By James Frederick Ferrier

This selection contains Propositions I: "What Ignorance Is," II: "Ignorance Remediable," and III: "The Law of All Ignorance," from the *Institutes of Metaphysics*, Section II, "The Agnoiology, or Theory of Ignorance," pp. 405–16. It also contains the demonstrations and the observations and explanations following the statement of each of these three propositions. Paragraph numbers have been omitted.

PROPOSITION I
WHAT IGNORANCE IS

IGNORANCE is an intellectual defect, imperfection, privation, or shortcoming.

DEMONSTRATION

The deprivation of anything whose possession is consistent with the nature of the Being which wants it, is a defect. But ignorance is a deprivation of something which is consistent with the nature of intelligence: it is a deprivation of knowledge. Therefore ignorance is an intellectual defect, imperfection, privation, or shortcoming.

OBSERVATIONS AND EXPLANATIONS

The demonstration, and even the enunciation, of so obvious a truism may appear superfluous. It is introduced, however, in order that the doctrine of ignorance may be cleared from the very beginning and to obviate any complaint to which the subsequent propositions might be exposed on the ground that their data of proof had been left doubtful or unexpressed.

There have been many inquiries into the nature of knowledge: there has been no inquiry into the nature of ignorance. This section of the science has positively no forerunner; it is an entire novelty in philosophy—a circumstance which is mentioned merely to account for the fewness and brevity of the accompanying annotations. The agnoiology makes its way through a comparatively unencumbered field. There is something to pull down and something to build up; but the work both of demolition and of construction is much simpler than it was in the epistemology.

This research, however, is indispensable. It is impossible to pass to the third section of the science except through the portals of this inquiry. For, suppose we were at once to carry forward the result of the epistemology into the ontology, and in answer to the question, What truly and absolutely is? were to reply, Objects *plus* a subject, the ego with some thing or thought present to it—this, and this alone, is what truly and absolutely is—we should be instantly stopped by the rejoinder that this synthesis is, at best, merely the *known* absolute, merely the substantial *in cognition*. It does not follow, the objector would say, that this synthesis alone is true and absolute Being— that it is the only true substantial *in existence*. He would argue that what truly and absolutely exists may be something very different from this—may be matter *per se* or mind *per se,* or something else of which we can form no sort of conception, and to which we can attach no predicate; in short, that it may be, and is, that of which we are profoundly ignorant.

This plea has hitherto operated as an insurmountable barrier to the advance of metaphysics into the region of ontology. The fact of our extreme ignorance being undeniable, and the science of absolute existence being apparently inaccessible except on the postulation of a universal and unlimited knowledge, the difficulty of reconciling these two apparent incompatibilities seems to have disconcerted every system hitherto propounded. Any

reasoned ontological conclusion establishing what alone absolutely exists, is obviously impossible in a system which admits
our ignorance without entering into any critical inquiry as to its
nature; while, on the other hand, the ontology of a system which
denies our ignorance, or passes it over *sub silentio,* must either
rest upon a false ground, or upon no ground at all—on a false
ground if our ignorance is denied—on no ground at all if it is
not taken into account. In one or other of these predicaments
all previous systems appear to be placed in reference to the
problem of absolute existence; and hence a reasoned and systematic ontology has remained until this day a desideratum in
speculative science, because a reasoned and systematic agnoiology has never yet been projected.

The only way in which a deliverance from this dilemma can
be effected is, by admitting our ignorance to the full, and then
by instituting a searching inquiry into its nature and character.
Conceding, then, that the conclusion of the epistemology cannot
at present, with any logical propriety, be given out as valid for
the ontology, the system proceeds to this investigation, and dealing not with the abstract, but only, or chiefly, with the concrete,
it goes on to consider and to point out *what* we are, and can
be, and *what* we are not, and cannot be, ignorant of. It is
conceived that the research, thus conducted, will result in an
effectual clearance of the ground for the establishment of a
demonstrated ontology. . . .

PROPOSITION II
IGNORANCE REMEDIABLE

All ignorance is *possibly* remediable.

DEMONSTRATION

No kind of knowledge is absolutely inconsistent with the
nature of all intelligence. But unless all ignorance were *possibly*
remediable, some kind of knowledge would be inconsistent with
the nature of all intelligence, to wit, the knowledge by which

the ignorance in question might be remedied. Therefore all ignorance is *possibly* remediable.

Or again, All defects are possibly remediable, otherwise they would not be defects. But ignorance is a defect (Prop. I). Therefore all ignorance is possibly remediable.

OBSERVATIONS AND EXPLANATIONS

This proposition does not prove that all ignorance is *actually* remedied: in other words, that omniscience pervades the universe; but only that every form of ignorance is of such a character that it may *possibly* be removed; and that if certain kinds of ignorance are incident to certain orders of the intelligence, they are not, *of necessity*, incident to other orders of intelligence. The subsequent movements of the system do not require that more than this should be proved. Neither does this proposition prove that all *human* ignorance is possibly remediable. It only proves that what man or any other intelligence may happen to be ignorant of, need not, of necessity, be unknown to all other intelligences (supposing that other intelligences exist). In other words, it merely proves that whatever any intelligence is ignorant of, may nevertheless be known—known *actually* if an intelligence exists competent to know it—and known *potentially* even although no such intelligence should exist. Unless this were true, all ignorance would not be possibly remediable; and if all ignorance were not possibly remediable, some kind of knowledge would be inconsistent with the nature of all intelligence—in which case, ignorance would be no defect, because a defect is always the privation of some quality or attribute which is consistent with the nature of the being who is deprived of it. . . .

PROPOSITION III
THE LAW OF ALL IGNORANCE

We can be ignorant only of what can possibly be known; in other words, there can be an ignorance only of that of which there can be knowledge.

DEMONSTRATION

If we could be ignorant of what could not possibly be known by any intelligence, all ignorance would not be possibly remediable. The knowledge in which we were deficient could not be possessed by any intelligence. But all ignorance is possibly remediable (by Prop. II). Therefore, we can be ignorant only of what can possibly be known; in other words, there can be an ignorance only of that of which there can be a knowledge.

OBSERVATIONS AND EXPLANATIONS

This is the most important proposition in the agnoiology: indeed, with the exception of the first of the epistemology, it is the most fruitful and penetrating proposition in the whole system. It announces—for the first time, it is believed—the primary law of all ignorance, just as the first of the epistemology expresses the primary law of all knowledge. It is mainly by the aid of these two propositions that this system of Institutes is worked out. All the other propositions have an essential part to play in contributing to the final result; but these two are the most efficient performers in the work. If the reader has got well in hand these two truths—*first,* that there can be a knowledge of things only with the addition of a self or subject; and, *secondly,* that there can be an ignorance only of that of which there can be a knowledge—he will find himself in possession of a lever powerful enough to break open the innermost secresies of nature. These two instruments cut deep and far—they lay open the universe from stem to stern.

Ignorance, properly so called—that is, the ignorance which is a defect—must not be confounded with a nescience of the opposites of the necessary truths of reason; in other words, with a nescience of that which it would contradict the nature of all intelligence to know. Such nescience is no defect or imperfection—it is, on the contrary, the very strength or perfection of reason; and therefore such nescience is not to be regarded as ignorance. This simple but very important distinction must be explained and illustrated, for it is one which is very apt to be lost sight of, or confounded; indeed, it has been altogether overlooked until now.

When boys at school are taught Euclid, they learn that "the enclosure of space by two straight lines" is what cannot be known—that "if equals be added to equals the wholes are *un-equal*" is what cannot be known—that "a part is greater than the whole" is what cannot be known, and so forth; but they do not learn that they are equally incapable of being ignorant of such matters. It is not necessary to apprise them of this in order to carry them forward in the study of mathematics. Nothing in geometry depends on the circumstance that we cannot be ignorant of what is deponed to in the opposites of the axioms. Hence this study merely shows us that there can be no knowledge of these opposites; it does not open our eyes to the fact that there can be no ignorance of them. It is obvious, however, that it is just as impossible for us to be ignorant of them as it is impossible for us to know them. No man can know that two and two make five—but just as little can any man be ignorant of this; for suppose him ignorant of it, in that case his ignorance could be removed only by teaching him that two and two *do* make five; but such instruction, instead of removing his ignorance, would remove his knowledge, and instead of giving him knowledge, would give him ignorance, or rather absurdity. The cure in this case would be itself the disease.

An attention to the fact, that it is impossible for us (or for any intelligence) to be ignorant of the contradictory, that is, of the opposites of the necessary truths of reason, or, in other words, of that which cannot be known on any terms by any intelligence, though of no importance in mathematics, is of the utmost importance in metaphysics. Speculation can obtain a footing in ontology only by attending carefully to this circumstance, and by working it out through all its consequences. This truth is the key to the whole philosophy of ignorance. When we consider it well, we discover that the supposition that we can be ignorant of that which is absolutely and necessarily unknowable to all intelligence, is as extreme a violation of the law of contradiction as it is possible to conceive. We perceive that a nescience of the contradictory is not ignorance, but is the very essence of intelligence; and that there can be an ignorance only of that which can be known, or, otherwise expressed, of that which is non-contradictory. With this discovery, light breaks into every cranny and recess of our science: the "holy jungle" of metaphysic is laid open to the searching day, and now no obstacle can stop the onward course of speculation. . . .

What Absolute Existence Is

By James Frederick Ferrier

This selection contains Proposition X, and some of the observations accompanying it, from Section III, "The Ontology, or Theory of Being," pp. 511–20. Paragraph symbols and numbers and some cross references to various propositions contained in the *Institutes of Metaphysics* have been omitted.

PROPOSITION X
WHAT ABSOLUTE EXISTENCE IS

Absolute Existence is the synthesis of the subject and object— the union of the universal and the particular—the concretion of the ego and non-ego; in other words, the only true, and real, and independent Existences are minds-together-with-that-which-they-apprehend.

DEMONSTRATION

Absolute Existence is either that which we know or that which we are ignorant of. If Absolute Existence is that which we know, it must be the synthesis of subject and object—the union of the universal and the particular, the concretion of the ego and the non-ego, because this, and this alone, is knowable. This synthesis alone is the conceivable. This, and this alone, is the substantial and absolute in cognition. Again, if Absolute Existence is that which we are ignorant of, it must equally be the synthesis of subject and object, the union of the universal and the particular, the concretion of the ego and the non-ego, because this, and this alone, is what we can be ignorant of. Therefore, whichever alternative be adopted, the result is the same. Whether we claim a knowledge, or profess an ignorance, of the Absolutely Existent, the conclusion is inevitably forced upon us that the Absolutely Existent is the synthesis of the subject and object—the union of the universal and the particular—the concretion of the ego and non-ego; in other words, that the only existence to which true, and real, and independent Being can be ascribed are minds-together-with-that-which-they-apprehend.

OBSERVATIONS AND EXPLANATIONS

This proposition solves the problem of ontology. It demonstrates what is—what alone absolutely exists: and thus the end or aim which it was the business and duty of this section of the science to accomplish, has been overtaken. A predicate declaratory of its character has been affixed to Absolute Existence, and this predicate applies to it equally whether we are cognizant of it, or are ignorant of it. If we are cognizant of Absolute Existence, it must be object *plus* subject, because this, and this alone, is what any intelligence can know. If we are ignorant of Absolute Existence, it must be still object *plus* subject, because we can be ignorant only of what can be known— and object *plus* subject is what alone can be known. Thus the concluding truth of the ontology is demonstratively established, and comes out all the same whether we claim a knowledge, or avow an ignorance, of that which truly exists. Thus the ultimate end of the system is compassed—compassed by legitimate means, and its crowning pledge triumphantly redeemed.

The solution of the ontological problem affords moreover, an answer to the ultimate question of philosophy—What is truth? Whatever absolutely is, is true. The question, therefore, is—But what absolutely is? And the answer, as now declared, is, that object *plus* subject is what absolutely is—that this, and this alone, truly and really exists. This synthesis, accordingly, is THE TRUTH: the Ground—below which there is neither anything nor nothing.

The reader who has followed the system up to this point, should now be at no loss to understand how the synthesis of the particular and the universal is alone entitled to the name of "the Existent." This doctrine, or at least an approximation to it, was the burden of the philosophy of antiquity—the truth mainly insisted on by the early Greek speculators. But the doctrine at that time, and as *they* expounded it, was of necessity unintelligible. None of them knew, or at any rate none of them *said,* what the universal was which entered into the synthesis of Existence. None of them named it. Hence their statement made no impression on the popular mind, and it has remained an enigma to all succeeding generations. No one could understand why the particular (that is, material things by themselves) was denied to be truly existent. But these Institutes have now distinctly shown *what* this universal is, and the darkness is dissipated—the ancient doctrine becomes luminous. The Institutes have shown that this universal is *oneself:* oneself, first, inasmuch as this element must form a part of everything which any intelligence can know; oneself, secondly, inasmuch as this element must form a part of everything which any intelligence can conceive; oneself, thirdly, inasmuch as this element must form a part of everything which any intelligence can be ignorant of. These points having been demonstratively established, it is conceived that people should have now no difficulty to understanding how oneself or the ego must also form a part of everything which really and truly *exists,* and consequently how the Absolutely Existent should in all cases be the union of the universal and the particular; and further, how Absolute Existence cannot be accorded to the particular—that is, to mere material things— inasmuch as these, by themselves, are the contradictory to all knowledge, and likewise the contradictory to all ignorance; and, therefore, cannot have true Being ascribed to them, unless we are prepared to maintain that the nonsensical, or that which is neither nothing nor anything, is the truly and absolutely existent.

It was formerly remarked that the equation or coincidence of the known and the existent is the ultimate conclusion which philosophy has to demonstrate. This demonstration has been supplied, and the conclusion has been reasoned out from the bottom. The universal and the particular (ego and non-ego) *in cognition* are also in all essential respects the universal and the particular *in existence;* or, expressed more popularly, the conclusion is that every true and absolute existence is a consciousness-together-with-its-contents, whatever these contents may be. Thus Knowing and Being are shown to be built up out of the same elements; and thus the laws of cognition are demonstrated to be in harmony with the laws of existence; and thus psychology, the whole spirit of whose teaching is to inculcate the frightful doctrine that there is no parallelism between them, is overthrown.

It has now, moreover, been shown, by means of strict demonstration, that the substantial and absolute in existence equates, *in essentialibus,* with the substantial and absolute in cognition. The substantial and absolute in cognition was found to be the synthesis of the ego and non-ego—of the subject and object—of the universal and the particular. This same synthesis was found to be the substantial and absolute in ignorance, and hence it follows that this same synthesis is the substantial and Absolute in Existence; because the substantial and absolute in existence must be either that which we know or that which we are ignorant of. And thus we obtain further proof and corroboration of the coincidence of the Known and the Existent. The ego is the *summum genus* of existence, no less than of cognition.

To remove any ground of misapprehension, it is necessary, at this place, to direct attention to the words *"in essentialibus"* in the preceding paragraph. The Absolute, as known *by us,* has been proved to be identical with the existing Absolute, not in all respects *accidental* as well as essential, but only in all *essential* respects: in other words, the Absolute in existence cannot be declared to coincide exactly with the Absolute in *our* cogni-

tion, but only with the absolute in *all* cognition: or to express
the restriction differently—the ontology gives out as the existing Absolute the result which is obtained from the study of
the necessary laws of knowledge *only,* and not the result which
is obtained from the study of *both* the necessary and the contingent laws of knowledge. An illustration, or concrete example,
will enable the reader to understand clearly this somewhat abstract statement.

The absolutely Existent which each of us is individually cognizant of, is—himself-apprehending-things-*by-the-senses.* A man
cannot be cognizant of himself merely, or of things merely, or
of senses merely. He, therefore, cannot be cognizant of these
three as existences, but only as factors or elements of existence;
and the only true and absolute existence which he can know is,
as has been said, their synthesis—to wit, himself-apprehending-
things-*by-the-senses.* Now the circumstance to be particularly
attended to is, that the part of the synthesis here printed in
italics is contingent in its character. Our five senses are the accidental part of the absolute in *our* cognition: they are not a
necessary part of the Absolute in *all* cognition, and therefore
they are not a necessary part of every absolute existence. Other
intelligences may be cognizant of them-selves-apprehending-
things-*in-other-ways-than-we-do.* In which case *their* Absolute,
both in cognition and existence, would be different from ours,
in its *accidentals,* but not in its *essentials.* So that all that the
ontology professes to have proved in regard to absolute existence is, that every Absolute Existence must consist of the two
terms—ego and non-ego—subject and object—universal and particular; in other words, of a self, and something or other (be it
what it may) in union with a self.

It was formerly remarked that it would be necessary in the
ontology to qualify the assertion that "Plato's intelligible world
was our sensible world." The foregoing observation may enable
the reader to understand to what extent that assertion has to be
qualified. Plato's intelligible world is our sensible world, in so
far as all the essential elements both of cognition and of existence are concerned; but not in so far as the contingent elements,

either of cognition or of existence, are concerned: in other words, Plato's intelligible world is our sensible world to this extent, that it is that which *must* embrace a subjective and an objective factor—an ego and a non-ego—but not to this extent that it is that into whose constitution (whether considered as known or as existent) such senses as ours must of necessity enter. Hence what we term the sensible world is the only intelligible or truly existing world in so far as it consists of ourselves and things, but it is not the only intelligible and truly existing world in so far as the senses are embraced in this synthesis, for these are the contingent and (possibly) variable conditions of the known; and are consequently the contingent and (possibly) variable condition of the existent. The other terms (ego and non-ego) *must* co-exist wherever there is either knowledge or existence. Hence it may be truly said that every existence is a *co*-existence; and that to attempt, as all psychology does, to cut down this co-existence into two separate existences (mind and its objects), is to aim at the establishment of contradiction in the place of knowledge, and of nonsense in the place of existence.

A word must here be added to explain in what sense, and to what extent, we are cognizant of absolute existence, and in what sense, and to what extent, we are ignorant of the same. Every man is cognizant of absolute existence when he knows—himself and the objects by which he is surrounded, or the thoughts or feelings by which he is visited; every man is ignorant (in the strict sense of having no experience) of all absolute existence except this—his own individual case. But a man is not ignorant of all absolute existences except himself and his own presentations, in the sense of having no conception of them. He can conceive them as conceivable, that is to say, as non-contradictory. He has given to him, in his own case, the type or pattern by means of which he can conceive other cases of absolute existence. Hence he can affirm, with the fullest assurance, that he is surrounded by Absolute Existences constituted like himself, although it is impossible that he can ever know them as they know themselves, or as he knows himself. He will find, however, that every attempt to construe to his mind an absolute and real existence which is *not* a synthesis of subject and object, resolves itself into a contradiction, and precipitates him into the utterly inconceivable. But although absolute exist-ences are innumerable—although every example of objects *plus* a subject is a case of Absolute Existence—there is, nevertheless, only *one* Absolute Existence which is strictly *necessary,* as the next and concluding proposition of the ontology will show.

CHAPTER IX

James McCosh
(1811–1894)

The Man and His Work

By HARVEY GATES TOWNSEND

JAMES McCOSH has been neglected in the study of American philosophy. This may be accounted for in part by the fact that he did not come to America until he was fifty-seven years old. By that time, he had already identified himself with the Scottish School of Thomas Reid and Sir William Hamilton. He was born in Ayrshire, Scotland, in 1811, and studied philosophy at the universities of Glasgow and Edinburgh. . . . McCosh attracted attention, while at Edinburgh, for a paper on the Stoics, as a result of which he was recommended for a Master's degree by Sir William Hamilton. He became a minister in the Scottish church, but kept in the academic eye through publication. In 1850 there appeared his *Method of Divine Government, Physical and Moral.* This was followed ten years later by *The Intuitions of the Mind, Inductively Investigated,* and in 1862 by *The Supernatural in Relation to the Natural.* Meanwhile, in 1852, he had become a professor of philosophy in Queen's College, Belfast. McCosh came to America as the president of the College of New Jersey in 1868.

An additional reason for the neglect of McCosh may be that he came to America at a time when the philosophy which he taught, already outmoded, had a slightly antique flavor. Scottish realism did not find in him so much a source as a culmination and crystallization. This fact, however, makes him all the more

worthy of study, for we find in him perhaps the most articulate
summary of American academic philosophy in the first three-
quarters of the century. He remained at Princeton nearly twenty
years and exerted during that time a very great influence as a
teacher and a preacher. There was a blunt dogmatism about
McCosh which suited well the temper of the time. He had the
courage of unwavering conviction combined with a ready pen
and great expository power.

In 1875 he published *The Scottish Philosophy, Biographical,
Expository, Critical, from Hutcheson to Hamilton.* He declared
that in bringing Scottish philosophy to America he was engaged
in a "labor of love." "The English-speaking public, British and
American, has of late been listening to diverse forms of philosophy—to Coleridge, to Kant, to Cousin, to Hegel, to Comte, to
Berkeley—and is now inclined to a materialistic psychology. Not
finding permanent satisfaction in any of these, it is surely possible that it may grant a hearing to the sober philosophy of
Scotland." (Preface.)

Halfway through the book (p. 183), he recognized John
Witherspoon as the man who "introduced Scottish thought into
the new world." It is in this connection that he declared that
"idealism has never struck deep into the American soil." He
meant Berkeley's idealism, of which he was contemptuous. Returning to the point many years later in the introduction to his
Realistic Philosophy (1887), he said, "America has arrived at
a stage at which there is a body of men and women who have
leisure and taste to cultivate the liberal arts and advance the
higher forms of civilization. . . . The time has come, I believe,
for America to declare her independence in philosophy. She will
not be disposed to set up a new monarch, but she may establish
a republic confederated like the United States. . . . But what
is to be the nature of the new philosophic republic formed of
united states? . . . If a genuine American philosophy arises, it
must reflect the genius of the people. Now, Yankees are distinguished from most others by their practical observation and
invention. They have a pretty clear notion of what a thing is,

and, if it is of value, they take steps to secure it. It follows that, if there is to be an American philosophy, it must be Realistic. I suspect that they will never produce an Idealistic philosophy like that of Plato in ancient times, or speculative systems like those of Spinoza, Leibnitz, and Hegel in modern times. The circumstance that Emerson is an American may seem to contradict this, but then Emerson, while he opens interesting glimpses of truth, is not a philosopher; his thoughts are like strung pearls, without system and without connection. On the other hand, the Americans believe that there are things to be known, to be prized and secured, and will never therefore look approvingly on an agnosticism which declares that knowledge is unattainable. The American philosophy will therefore be a Realism, opposed to Idealism on the one hand and to Agnosticism on the other" (pp. 1-4).

The work which most secured for McCosh the attention of the academic world was *The Intuitions of the Mind, Inductively Investigated.* In it we find his systematic philosophy. Though he lived and wrote for half an ordinary lifetime after the publication of his chief work, he spent his energies in support and defense of the dogma announced in it. He was the kind of man who does not modify his position very much once it is taken. His style is clear, cogent, direct, simple. The effect upon the reader is to establish conviction rather than awaken doubt. Subtle dialectic is absent; in its stead we find blunt, explicit, straightforward discourse, neatly arranged under heads and subheads.

He held that the intuitions of the mind are direct, immediate perceptions of a real objective order. However complex the object may be, the intuition as such is simple. It seizes its object directly, whether the object be sensory, relational, or abstract. There is no error possible at this primitive level of knowledge. Error arises out of false association and inference, and therefore it can be corrected by additional and more careful observation.

The laws of intuition are revealed in its exercise. The exercise of intuition exhibits native human aptitudes for dealing with a real world; these are "regulative" in character and widely distributed among men. The healthy or normal mind is equipped to know in much the same sense that any other natural entity is equipped to function according to inherent characteristics or attributes. McCosh warned his readers that intuitions are not to be confused with vague and cloudy feelings, premonitions, and the like. While they are in some sense ultimate and inexplicable, there is no mystery about them. It is the nature of a mind to know, much as it is the nature of a body to gravitate. In his statement that the intuitions are "regulative," he does not mean that they regulate conduct but knowledge; i.e., they are basic points of reference in knowledge. He does not follow Kant and Hamilton in the supposition that the mind is shut off from its objects. (3rd edition, p. 36, n. 1.) He holds rather that it is joined to its object in the operation of knowing.

In following McCosh it is important to remember that he was seeking to avoid Hume's skepticism on the one hand and Kant's "idealism" on the other. Space, time, cause, and the other categories are not mere forms of the isolated mind, but principles of union between thought and things intuitively present in the act of knowing. Though the primitive intuitions of the mind are particular, they are not confined to objects of sense impression, but include apprehensions of simple and complex relations and systematic wholes. He would have agreed with William James that we apprehend relations as such.

His treatment of the problems of induction is significant, though far from profound. "We have truth," he declares, "when our ideas are conformed to things." (*Realistic Philosophy*, I, 30.) It follows that there is no high *a priori* road to such a truth, but only the way of patient observation of facts one by one. Among these facts, however, he believes that we find direct intuitions of causation and the uniformity of nature. The way to remedy the faults of knowledge is not to leap to conclusions but to study cases. What we call chance is a name for our ignorance, but "there is another sense in which it may be said that there is such a thing as chance. There cannot be an occurrence without a purpose on the part of God, who has ordered the causes producing it. *But there may be a concurrence without a design.*" (*Ibid.*, I, 79. Italics mine.)

His treatment of induction is significant because it clearly enunciates some of the basic contentions of realistic logics. Speaking of metaphysics, he wrote, "Like every other science which has to do with facts, it must be conducted in the Inductive method, in which observation is the first process, and the last process, and the main process throughout; the process with which we start, and the process by which we advance all along, and at the close test all that is done; but in which, at the same time, analysis and generalization are employed as instruments, always working, however, on facts observed." (*The Intuitions of the Mind,* 3rd edition, pp. 282, 283.)

Causation, he contended, is multiple and admits of the distinction made by Aristotle. Each of the "four causes"—material, efficient, formal, and final—plays an indispensable part in the order of things. The mistake of mechanism is in supposing that because efficient causes can be shown to be always present, final causes are excluded as redundant. As a matter of fact, the two may be co-extensive and, to this degree, independent.

The outline of McCosh's metaphysics follows, almost point by point, the outline of his epistemology. Things are what they appear to be, although they are very much more than they appear in any intuition or series of intuitions. There are bodies in space and time related to each other in various ways; there are minds related to each other and to bodies; and there are classes, mathematical forms, and moral obligations very much as the plain man supposes. McCosh side-stepped the subtle net of antinomies. He found no serious difficulty in the union of induction and deduction, the understanding and reason, faith and knowledge, thought and things, because he made the initial assumption that our knowledge is a knowledge of objects.

His ethical doctrine was likewise beautifully simple. The intuitions of moral obligation are direct and unambiguous. He shared the orthodox moral-sense hedonism, and theocratic optimism of his Scottish colleagues. Certitude in morals is at bottom immediate, self-evident knowledge, as it is in all other realms of man's inquiry. If he keeps his eyes open and looks sharply, man need not go astray. With his confidence in the reality of final causes, McCosh could assert with entire conviction, "As the ages roll on there is a greater fullness of sentient life, and a larger capacity of happiness." (*Realistic Philosophy,* I, 162.)

Notwithstanding the somewhat archaic simplicity of McCosh's realism, there are features of it which have special interest for the student of the subsequent history of ideas in America. For example, his declaration that advance in philosophy is to be made by following the method and spirit of the natural sciences is an early expression of what has come to be almost a ritual with later realists. He also argued that the problems of philosophy must be clearly and precisely defined in order to limit the scope of the inquiry, and thus make the application of scientific method possible. His treatment of chance, though brief and unsatisfactory, reminds the reader that this problem was taking root in American philosophy. McCosh had a strong metaphysical bias and in numerous ways displayed the growing concern with chance as a metaphysical rather than as a merely logical problem. There are distinct "pragmatisms" to be found in the pages of McCosh. Thus we read, "The two, knowledge and faith, differ psychologically, and there are important psychological ends to be served by distinguishing them; but after all it is more important to fix our attention on their points of agreement and coincidence. The belief has a basis of cognition, the cognition has a superstructure of beliefs." (*Intuitions of the Mind,* p. 172.) Throughout his writing, there is revealed a deep suspicion of the shadow-boxing of epistemological dialectic. He cuts straight through verbal antinomies with a distinction between methodology and result in science. He sees that hypothesis is an instrument for the discovery of evidence, but that evidence is more than verbal—that in the activity of knowing we grapple directly with a recalcitrant objectivity.[1]

---

[1] For the source of this biographical sketch and a discussion of McCosh's criticism of John Stuart Mill see my Introduction. (Editor's note.)

Characteristics of the Scottish School and Comparison of It With the Critical Philosophy of Kant

By JAMES McCOSH

This selection is taken from James McCosh's *Realistic Philosophy*, Vol. II, *Historical and Critical* (New York: Macmillan and Company, 1887), pp. 181–86 and 239–44. Compare this with the selection from Sir William Hamilton, pp. 220 ff.

I. IT PROCEEDS *throughout by observation.* It has all along professed a profound reverence for Bacon, and in its earliest works it attempted to do for metaphysics what Newton had done for physics. It begins with facts and ends with facts. Between, it has analyses, generalizations, and reasonings; but all upon the actual operations of the mind. Its laws are suggested by facts and are verified by facts. It sets out, as Bacon recommends, with the necessary "rejections and exclusions," with what Whewell calls the "decomposition of facts," but all to get at the exact facts it means to examine. Its generalizations are formed by observing the points in which the operations of the mind agree, and it proceeds gradually—*gradatim,* as Bacon expresses it—rising from particulars to generals, and from lower to higher laws. It is afraid of rapid and high speculation, lest it carry us like a balloon, not into the heavens, but into a cloud, where it will explode sooner or later. It is suspicious of long and complicated ratiocinations like those of Spinoza and Hegel, for it is sure—such is human fallibility—that there will lurk in them some error or defect in the premise, or some oversight or weak link in the process, weakening the whole chain. Thomas Reid was not sure whether Samuel Clarke's demonstration of the existence of God was more distinguished for ingenuity than sublimity.

II. *It observes the operations of the mind by the inner sense—that is, consciousness.* In this philosophy consciousness, the perception of self in its various states, comes into greater prominence than it had ever done before. Bacon did not appreciate its importance; he recommended in the study of the human mind the gathering of instances, to be arranged in tables, of memory, judgment, and the like. Descartes appealed to consciousness, but only to get a principle such as *cogito,* to be used in deduction, *ergo sum;* in which *sum* there is an idea of an infinite, a perfect. Locke was ever appealing to internal observation, but it was to support a preconceived theory that all our ideas are derived from sensation and reflection. Turnbull and Hutcheson and Reid were the first to avow and declare that the laws of the human mind were to be discovered only by internal observation, and that mental philosophy consisted solely in the construction of these. They held that consciousness, the internal sense, was as much to be trusted as the external senses; and that as we can form a natural philosophy out of the facts furnished by the one, we can construct a mental philosophy by the facts furnished by the other. They held resolutely that the eye cannot see our thoughts and feelings even when aided by the microscope or telescope. They were sure that no man ever grasped an idea by his muscular power, tasted the beauty of a rose or lily, smelt an emotion, or heard the writhings of the conviction of conscience. But they thought that the mind could observe the world within by consciousness more directly and quite as accurately as it could observe the world without by sight, touch, and the other senses, and could in the one case as in the other make a scientific arrangement of its observations and construct a science.

III. *By observation principles are discovered which are above observation, universal and eternal.* All the genuine masters and followers proceed on this principle, and apply it more or less successfully. I am not sure that they have expressly avowed it and explicitly stated it. I am responsible for the form which is given it at the head of this paragraph. No man can understand or appreciate or do justice to the philosophy of Scotland who does not notice it as running through and through their whole investigations and conclusions. It was in this way that Reid opposed Hume. It was in this way that Dugald Stewart, and indeed the whole school, sought to lay a foundation on which all truth might be built. They were fond of representing the principles as fundamental, and they guarded against all erroneous, against all extravagant and defective statements and applications of them, by insisting that they be shown to be in the constitution of the mind, and that their nature be ascertained before they are employed in speculation of any kind. By insisting on this restriction, their mode of procedure has been described as timid, and their results as mean and poor, by those speculators who assume a principle without a previous induction, and mount up with it, wishing to reach the sky, but stayed in the clouds. By thus holding that there are truths above and prior to our observation of them, they claim and have a place in the brotherhood of our higher philosophers, such as Plato and Aristotle in ancient times, Descartes, Leibnitz, and Kant in modern times.

They present these principles in the mind under various aspects and in different names. Reid called them principles of common sense in the mind itself, and common to all men. Hamilton defended the use of the phrase common sense. I am not sure it is the best one, as it includes two meanings: one, good sense, of mighty use in the practical affairs of life; and the other, first principles in the minds of all men, in which latter sense alone it can be legitimately employed in philosophy. He also calls them, happily, reason in the first degree, which discerns truth at once, as distinguished from reason in the second degree, which discovers truth by arguing. Stewart represented them as "fundamental laws of human thought and belief," and is commended for this by Sir James Mackintosh, who is so far a member of the school. Thomas Brown represented them as intuitions, a phase I am fond of, as it presents the mind as looking into the nature of things. Perhaps the phrase "intuitive reason," used by Milton when he talks of "reason intuitive and discursive," might be as good a phrase as any by which to designate these primary principles. Hamilton, who sought to add the philosophy of Kant to that of Reid, often without his being able to make them cohere, sometimes uses the Scotch phrases, and at other times the favorite Kantian designation, *a priori.* I remember how Dr. Chalmers, who was truly of the Scottish school, was delighted in his advanced years, on becoming acquainted with the German philosophy through Morell's *History of Philosophy,* to find that there was a wonderful correspondence between the *a priori* principles of Kant and the fundamental laws of Stewart.

I may be allowed to add, that having before me the views and the nomenclature of all who hold by these primary principles, I have ventured to specify their characteristics, and this in the proper order:

First, they look at things external and internal. They are not forms or laws in the mind apart from things. They are intuitions of things. Under this view they are SELF-EVIDENT, which is their first mark. The truth is perceived at once by looking at things. I perceive self within and body without by barely looking at them. I discover that two straight lines cannot enclose a space, that benevolence is good, that cruelty is evil, by simply contemplating the things. *Secondly,* they are NECESSARY. This I hold with Aristotle, Leibnitz, Kant, and most profound thinkers. Being self-evident, we must hold them, and cannot be made to think or believe otherwise. *Thirdly,* they are UNIVERSAL, being entertained by all men.

But it is asked, How do you reconcile your one element with the other—your observation with your truth anterior to observation? I do hold with the whole genuine Scottish school, that there are principles in the mind called common sense, primary reason, intuition, prior to and independent of our observation of them. But I also hold, and this in perfect consistency, that it is by observation we discover them, that they exist, and what they are. I have found it difficult to make some people understand and fall in with this distinction. Historians and critics of philosophy are apt to divide all philosophies into two grand schools, the *a priori* and *a posteriori,* or in other words, the rational and the experiential. They are utterly averse to call in a third school, which would disturb all their classifications, and thus trouble them, and require the authors among them, especially the followers of Kant or Cousin, to rewrite all they have written. They do not know very well what to make of the Scottish school, and I may add of the great body of American thinkers, who will not just fall into either one or other of their grand trunk-divisions. In particular, when they condescend to notice the author of this paper they feel as if they do not know what to make of him. "Are you," they ask, "of the *a posteriori* or empirical school? You seem as if you are so, you are constantly appealing to facts and experience. If so, you have no right to appeal to or call in *a priori* principles, which can never be established by a limited observation. But you are inconsistently ever bringing in necessary and universal principles, such as those of cause and effect, and moral good." Or they attack me at the other horn of the dilemma. "You hold rather by *a priori* principles; you are ever falling back on principles, self-evident, necessary, and universal, on personality, on identity, on substance and quality, causation, on the good and the infinite." I have sometimes felt as if I were placed between two contending armies, exposed to the fire of both. Yet I believe I am able to keep and defend my position. Now I direct a shot at the one side, say at John S. Mill, and at other times a shot at the other side, say at Kant—not venturing to attack Hegel, who is in a region which my weapons can never reach. They pay little attention to me, being so engrossed with fighting each other. But I do cherish the hope that when each of the sides finds it impossible to extinguish the other they may become weary of the fight, look for the *juste milieu,* and turn a favorable look toward the independent place which the Scotch and the great body of the Americans who think on these subjects are occupying. We invite you to throw down your arms, and come up to the peaceful height which we occupy. Hither you may bring all the wealth you have laid up in your separate positions, and here it will be safe. You have here primitive rocks strong and deep as the granite on which to rest it, and here you may add to it riches gathered from as wide regions as your ken can reach, and establish a city which can never be moved or shaken. . . .

Sir James Mackintosh and Dr. Chalmers, who were trained in the Scottish school, upon becoming somewhat acquainted in mature life with the German system, were greatly interested to notice the points of resemblance between the two philosophies. The two—the Scotch and the German—agree, and they differ. Each has a fitting representative: the one in Thomas Reid and the other in Immanuel Kant. The one was a careful observer, guided by common sense—with the meaning of good sense—suspicious of high speculations as sure to have error lurking in them, and shrinking from extreme positions; the other was a powerful logician, a great organizer and systematizer, following his principles to their consequences, which he was ever ready to accept, avow, and proclaim. The two have very important points of agreement. Reid and Kant both lived to oppose Hume, the great sceptic, or, as he would be called in the present day, agnostic. Both met him by calling in great mental principles, which reveal and guarantee truth, which can never be set aside, and which have foundations deep as the universe. Both appeal to reason, which Reid called reason in the first degree, and the other pure reason. The one presents this reason to us under the name of common sense—that is, the powers of intelligence common to all men; the other, as principles necessary and universal. The one pointed to laws, native and fundamental; the other, to forms in the mind. The one carefully observed these by consciousness and sought to unfold their nature; the other determined their existence by a criticism, and professes to give an inventory of them. All students should note these agreements as confirmatory of the truth of both.

The Scotch and German people do so far agree, while they also differ. Both have a considerable amount of broad sense, and, I may add, of humor; but the Scotch have greater clearness of thinking, and the Germans of attractive idealism. Scotland and Germany, in the opinion of foreigners, are not very far distant from each other. But between them there roars an ocean which is often very stormy. I proceed to specify the differences of the two philosophies.

First, they differ in their Method. The Scotch follows the Inductive Method as I have endeavored to explain it. The German has created and carried out the Critical Method, which has never been very clearly explained and examined. It maintains that things are not to be accepted as they appear; they are to be searched and sifted. Pure reason, according to Kant, can criticize itself. But every criticism ought to have some principles on which it proceeds. Kant, a professor of Logic, fortunately adopted the forms of Logic which I can show had been carefully inducted by Aristotle, and hence has reached much truth. Others have adopted other principles, and have reached very different conclusions. The philosophies that have followed that of Kant in Germany have been a series of criticisms, each speculator setting out with his own favorite principle—say with the universal *ego,* or intuition, or identity, or the absolute—and, carrying it out to its consequences, it has become so inextricably entangled, that the cry among young men is, "Out of this forest, and back to the clearer ground occupied by Kant." The Scottish philosophy has not been able to form such lofty speculations as the Germans, but the soberer inductions it has made may contain quite as much truth.

Secondly, the one starts with facts, internal and external, revealed by the senses, inner and outer. It does not profess to prove these by mediate reasoning: it assumes them, and shows that it is entitled to assume them; it declares them as self-evident. The other, the German school, starts with phenomena—not meaning facts to be explained (as physicists understand the phrase), but *appearances.* The phrase was subtilely introduced by Hume, and was unfortunately accepted by Kant. Let us, he said, or at least thought, accept, what Hume grants, phenomena, and guard the truth by mental forms—forms of sense, understanding, and reason. Our knowledge of bodies and their actions, our knowledge even of our minds and their operations, is phenomenal. Having assumed only phenomena, he never could rise to anything else. Having only phenomena in his premises he never could reach realities in his conclusions except by a palpable paralogism, which he himself saw and acknowledged. We human beings are phenomena in the unknown and unknowable of Herbert Spencer, implying no doubt a known, but which never can be known by us. We all know that Locke, though himself a most determined realist, laid down principles which led logically to the idealism of Berkeley. In like manner, Kant, though certainly no agnostic, has laid down a principle in his phenomenal theory which has terminated logically in agnosticism. We meet all this by showing that appearances properly understood are things appearing, and not appearances without things.

Thirdly, the two differ in that the one supposes that our perceptive powers reveal to us things as they are, whereas the other supposes that they add to things. According to Reid and the Scottish school, our consciousness and our senses look at once on real things; not discovering all that is in them, but perceiving them under the aspect in which they are presented—say this table as a colored surface perceived by a perceiving mind. According to Kant and the German school, the mind adds to the things by its own forms. Kant said we perceive appearances under the forms of space and time superimposed by the mind, and judge by categories, and reach higher truth by ideas of pure reason, all of them subjective. Fichte gave consistency to the whole by making these same forms create things.

Our thinking youth in the English and French speaking countries having no very influential philosophy at this present time, and no names to rule them, are taking longing looks towards Germany. When circumstances admit, they go a year or two to a German university—to Berlin or to Leipsic. There they get into a labyrinth of showy and binding forms, and have to go on in the paths opened to them. They return with an imposing nomenclature, and clothed with an armor formidable as the panoply of the middle ages. They write papers and deliver lectures which are read and listened to with the profoundest reverence—some, however, doubting whether all these distinctions are as correct as they are subtle, whether these speculations are as sound as they are imposing. All students may get immeasurable good from the study of the German philosophy. I encourage my students to go to Germany for a time to study. But let them meanwhile maintain their independence. They may be the better for a clew to help them out of the labyrinth when they are wandering. The children of Israel got vast good in the wilderness as they wandered: saw wonders in the pillar of cloud and fire, in the waters issuing from the rock, and the manna on the ground; but they longed all the while to get into a land of rest, with green fields and living rivers. We may all get incalculable good from German speculation, but let us bring it all to the standard of consciousness and of fact, which alone can give us security and rest.

I am quite aware that a large body of speculators will look down with contempt on the sober views I have been expounding, and not think it worth their while to examine them. Metaphysical youths from Britain and America, who have passed a year or two at a German university, and have there been listening to lectures in which the speaker passed along so easily, and without allowing a word of cross-examination, such phrases as subject and object, form and matter, *a priori* and *a posteriori,* real and phenomenon and noumenon, will wonder that any one should be satisfied to stay on such low ground as I have done, while they themselves are on such elevated heights. But I can bear their superciliousness without losing my temper, and I make no other retort than that of Kant on one occasion, "that their master is milking the he-goat while they are holding the sieve." [1] I am sure that the agnostics, whether of the philosophical or physiological schools, will resent my attempt to give knowledge so firm a foundation. I may not have influence myself to stop the crowd which is moving on so exultingly; I may be thrown down by the advancing calvacade; but I am sure I see the right road to which men will have to return sooner or later;

---

[1] President McCosh did not know that this saying, made famous by Kant, was borrowed by him from the cynic philosopher Demonax. See my essay: "Kant and Demonax—A Footnote to the History of Philosophy," in *Philosophy and Phenomenological Research,* Vol. X, pp. 374–79. Reprinted in my *Crucial Issues in Philosophy* (Boston: Christopher Publishing House), Chap. XXVII. (Editor's note.)

and I am satisfied if only I have opened a gate ready for those who come to discover that the end of their present broad path is darkness and nihilism.

First and Fundamental Truths

By James McCosh

This selection is taken from James McCosh's *Realistic Philosophy*, Vol. I, *Expository* (New York: Macmillan and Company, 1887), pp. 33–41. Compare this with the selection from Dugald Stewart, pp. 173 ff.

THE MIND must start with something. There are things which it knows at once. I know pleasure and pain. I do more: I know myself as feeling pleasure and pain. I know that I am surrounded with material objects extended and exercising properties. I know by barely contemplating them that these two straight lines cannot contain a space. These are called first truths. There must be first truths before there can be secondary ones; original before there can be derivative ones. Can we discover and enunciate these? I believe we can.

We are not at liberty, indeed, to appeal to a first principle when we please, or because it suits our purpose. When we are left without evidence, we are not therefore allowed to allege that we need no evidence. When we are defeated in argument, we are not to be permitted to escape by falling back on what is unproved and unprovable. It is true that we cannot prove everything, for this would imply an infinite chain of proofs every link of which would hang on another, while the whole would hang on nothing—that is, be incapable of proof. We cannot prove everything by mediate evidence, but we can show that we are justified in assuming certain things. We cannot prove that two straight lines cannot enclose a space, but we can show that

we are justified in saying so. We can do so by the application
of certain tests.

SELF-EVIDENCE is the primary test of that kind of truth which
we are entitled to assume without mediate proof. We perceive
the object to exist by simply looking at it. The truth shines in
its own light, and in order to see we do not require light to
shine upon it from any other quarter. We are conscious directly
of self as understanding, as thinking, or as feeling, and we need
no indirect evidence. Thus, too, we perceive by the eye a colored surface, and by the muscular touch a resisting object, and
by the moral sense the evil of hypocrisy. The proof is seen by
the contemplative mind in the things themselves. We are convinced that we need no other proof. A proffered probation from
any other quarter would not add to the strength of our conviction. We do not seek any external proof, and if any were pressed
upon us we would feel it to be unnecessary—nay, to be an en-
cumbrance, and almost an insult to our understanding.

But let us properly understand the nature of this self-evidence. It has constantly been misunderstood and misrepresented.
It is not a mere feeling or an emotion belonging to the sensitive
part of our nature. It is not a blind instinct or a belief in what
we cannot see. It is not above reason or below reason; it is an
exercise of primary reason prior, in the nature of things, to
any derivative exercises. It is not, as Kant represents it, of
the nature of a form in the mind imposed on objects contemplated and giving them a shape and color. It is a perception, it
is an intuition of the object. We inspect these two straight lines,
and perceive them to be such in their nature that they cannot
enclose a space. If two straight lines go on for an inch without coming nearer each other, we are sure they will be no
nearer if lengthened millions of miles as straight lines. On contemplating deceit we perceive the act to be wrong in its very
nature. It is not a mere sentiment, such as we feel on the contemplation of pleasure and pain; it is a knowledge of an object.
It is not the mind imposing or superinducing on the thing what
is not in the thing; it is simply the mind perceiving what is in
the thing. It is not merely subjective, it is also objective—to use

phrases very liable to be misunderstood; or, to speak clearly, the perceiving mind (subject) perceives the thing (object). This is the most satisfactory of all evidence; and this because in it we are immediately cognizant of the thing. There is no evidence so ready to carry conviction. We cannot so much as conceive or imagine any evidence stronger.

NECESSITY is a secondary criterion. It has been represented by Leibnitz and many metaphysicians as the first and the essential test. This I regard as a mistake. Self-evidence comes first, and the other follows and is derived from it. We perceive an object before us and we know so much of its nature; and we cannot be made to believe that there is no such object, or that it is not what we know it to be. I demur to the idea so often pressed upon us that we are to believe a certain proposition because we are necessitated to believe in it. This sounds too much like fatality to be agreeable to the free spirit of man. It is because we are conscious of self that we cannot be made to believe that we do not exist. The account given of the principle by Herbert Spencer is a perverted and a vague one: all propositions are to be accepted as unquestionable whose negative is inconceivable. This does not give us a direct criterion, as self-evidence does, and the word inconceivable is very ambiguous. But necessity, while it is not the primary, is a potent secondary test. The self-evidence convinces us; the necessity prevents us from holding any different conviction.

UNIVERSALITY is the tertiary test. By this is meant that it is believed by all men. It is the argument from catholicity, or common consent—the *sensus communis*. All men are found to assent to the particular truth when it is fairly laid before them, as, for instance, that the shortest distance between two points is a straight line. It would not be wise nor safe to make this the primary test, as some of the ancients did. For, in the complexity of thought, in the constant actual mixing up of experiential with immediate evidence, it is difficult to determine what all men believe. It is even conceivable that all men might be deceived by reason of the deceitfulness of the faculties and the illusive nature of things. But this tertiary comes in to corrobo-

rate the primary test, or rather to show that the proposition can
stand the primary test which proceeds on the observation of
the very thing, in which it is satisfactory to find that all men are
agreed.

Combine these and we have a perfect means of determining
what are first truths. The first gives us a personal assurance of
which we can never be deprived; the second secures that we
cannot conquer it; the third that we can appeal to all men as
having the same conviction. The first makes known realities;
the second restrains us from breaking off from them; the third
shows that we are surrounded with a community of beings to
whom we can address ourselves in the assurance of meeting with
a response.

But in order to be able to apply these criteria properly we
must carry along with us certain explanations and limitations.

1. It should be noticed of intuitive truths that they are, in
the first instance, *individual* or *singular,* and that we need to
generalize the single perceptions in order to reach general maxims. In them we begin with contemplating a single object, say
an external object, and know it to be extended and solid, or
an act of benevolence and know it to be good, or an act of
cruelty and proclaim it to be evil. But we can generalize the
individual perceptions, and then we have general maxims or
axioms, which we can apply to an infinite number of cases. We
perceive that these two parallel lines will never meet; and we
are sure that we should affirm the same of every other set of
parallel lines, and hence we reach the general maxim that parallel lines will never meet. We perceive, on the bare contemplation of this deed of deceit, that it is base, but we would feel
the same of every other deed of deceit, and hence the maxim
deceit is evil. But it should be observed that in the formation
of these general principles there is a discursive act, in the shape
of a generalizing process, involved. It is here that there may
creep in error, which is not in the intuitive but in the discursive process; for we may form a partial, a one-sided, or
exaggerated generalization. Thus, on discovering a particular
effect we at once judge or decide that it has a cause. But when

we would make the principle universal we may fall into a mistake, and declare that "everything has a cause," which would require an infinite series of causes and make it necessary to hold that God himself has a cause. In such a case our generalization is wrong. But let the maxim take the form that "everything which begins to be has a cause," and we perceive that on a thing presenting itself to us as beginning we should proclaim it to have had a producing power. We thus see that there may be both truth and error in our metaphysical or moral maxims: truth in the primitive perception at the basis of the whole, while there may be hastiness leading to mutilation in the expression. Hence the wrangling in metaphysics. Thus, everybody acknowledges that two parallel lines can never meet, but there may be disputes as to the fit form in which to put the axiom. So, in regard to the generalized principles that every effect has a cause, that every quality implies a substance, that virtue is commendable, there may be a difficulty in expressing exactly what is meant by cause and effect, what by substance and quality, and what by virtue and moral good; and we may find that when we would make the expressions definite we fall into grievous mistakes, and this while we are certain that there is a self-evident, necessary, and universal truth if only we can seize it.

2. First truths are of various kinds, which we shall endeavor to classify. Some of them are

Primitive Cognitions. In these the object is now before us, and is perceived by us. We perceive that this body has three dimensions in space, and cannot be made to believe otherwise. We decide that this thing, material or mental, cannot be and not be at the same time; that these two things, being each equal to the same thing, are equal to one another. In these cases the object is perceived at once and immediately. But there are others in which the object is not present, and the convictions may be regarded as

Primitive Beliefs. Here there is still an object. It is not present, but still it is contemplated. We have known the object somehow, and on conceiving it beliefs become attached to it. Thus, we know time in the concrete, and in regarding it we believe that time is continuous, that time past has run into

time present, and that time present will run into time to come.
A number of such faiths gather round our primitive cognitions
and widen them indefinitely. We see two points in space; we
are sure there is space between, and that the shortest line
between the two is a straight line. We can rise to still higher
faiths. We believe of certain objects, say space and time, and
God—when we come to know him—that they are infinite, that
is, that they are always beyond our widest image or concept
and such that nothing can be added to or taken from them. The
senses cannot give us these beliefs, nor can the understanding
construct them out of the materials supplied by the senses. Some
of them, such as the idea of the infinite, the perfect, lift us
above our immediate experience into a higher sphere. We begin
in all such cases with realities perceived or apprehended; and
we are sure, if we proceed legitimately, that we end with realities. It should be remarked that in order to our having these
cognitions and beliefs it is not necessary to express them or even
put them in the shape of propositions. It is necessary first to
have cognitions or beliefs regarding them before we form com-
parisons of them or affirm that they exist or possess certain
properties. But out of these we can form

Primitive Judgments, in which we predicate—that is, make
affirmations or denials—or discover certain properties or relations, as when we say space and time are without bounds and
exist independent of the contemplative mind. In order that these
judgments may be primitive they must be pronounced as to
objects which have been perceived by intuition.

I ought here to add that the mind is capable of perceiving
at once certain moral qualities, and we have

Moral Cognitions, Beliefs, and Judgments. On contemplating
an act as self-sacrifice done for a friend or a good cause we know
it at once to be good, or an act of selfishness we perceive it
to be evil. When these acts are done by our neighbors we cannot
notice them directly, but we are sure that they are good or
evil; and these may be regarded as beliefs. When we put them
in propositions we exercise judgment, as when we declare that
sin deserves punishment.

But it will be asked, do we perceive the good and evil to

be a reality, to be in the very thing. It might be allowed, it is urged, that intuitively we perceive matter to be extended and that two straight lines cannot enclose a space; for the matter, and the straight lines are before us. But moral excellence and depravity have no such reality, they exist only in our conceptions. To all this I reply that we have the acts before us in the one case as in the other; we have before us every day a deed and an implied affection of benevolence or of cruelty, and in it we perceive the morally good or the morally evil. The benevolence in this act of charity has a reality quite as much as the hand that bestows the alms or the alms bestowed. The malevolence in this calumny is a reality, quite as much as the tongue that uttered it or the newspaper that published it. The reality is of a different kind, no doubt, but it is of a kind which all acknowledge when they approve of the charity and disapprove of the scandal, and perhaps impose a penalty upon the person who has been guilty of it.

It is of vast moment, to ourselves and to the community, that we and all others should acknowledge, theoretically and practically, that there are other realities besides those of sense, and these higher and more enduring. It is the worst influence of the prevailing agnosticism that while it can have little power to keep us from believing in the things that are seen, it may have a mighty influence in keeping us from believing in and realizing the things that are spiritual, and therefore unseen, but eternal. The idealist errs when he denies the reality of a material world which, though temporal, is real. But the sensualist errs far more egregiously when he denies the existence of a spiritual world, which is real and eternal. It should be the aim of the highest philosophy to carry us up, as Plato endeavored to do, to this high and pure region which has as high an existence as the heavens, which are its special dwelling-place. We should train ourselves, and especially train the young, to retreat from time to time into the higher world, that they may there hold communion with all that is great and good and elevating.

INDEX